MAKING MODEL AIRCRAFT

MAKING
MODEL
AIRCRAFT

Bryan Philpott

Charles Scribner's Sons
NEW YORK

Contents

This book is dedicated
to my children
Corrine, Claire and Andrew

Foreword

Model making is one of the oldest hobbies known to man as is evidenced by the models of soldiers, ships, animals, birds and other similar items recovered by archaeologists from burial tombs and excavation sites that date many centuries before the birth of Christ.

Since aircraft became a part of everyday life making models of them has added another subject to the ever growing list of items that people have wanted to capture in miniature.

The advent of the plastic kit brought the hobby within the reach of those with limited skills, who can now produce acceptable models of practically any subject they choose.

Model aircraft have always been popular and a complete industry has mushroomed to provide the needs of those who practise the art, however seriously they might take it. One of the attractions of the hobby is that it relieves the strain of everyday life, for however demanding one's normal occupation is, it can only be followed successfully if some time is spent away from it in a world that is completely divorced from reality. Modelling provides such therapy; for even an hour spent recreating a model of a subject that one has a personal interest in, or that will recapture some aspect of a past event, is time well spent, and should leave the participant completely relaxed.

Most people are born with a certain amount of inherent skill and only they can develop this from its dormant state to a level that they are prepared to accept as their own ultimate. Such skills can be cultivated by reading and watching others, but the acid test comes when they are applied in a practical way. In this book I have attempted to lay the foundations, but not complete the house. Some of the methods I have found useful might not appeal to everyone, but if they sow the seeds from which alternative ways of achieving a common end result, they will have fulfilled my intentions.

Modelling is a very personal thing, a fact that I make no apologies for continually repeating in the text, so whatever you attempt or complete, is done solely for your own benefit and if the results please you then that is all that matters.

Acknowledgements

In writing this book I have had to call on the generosity of many to obtain help in areas where my own interests and skills have not matched theirs. The fact that they all co-operated, and in some cases went to considerable lengths in doing so, is sufficient evidence that modellers are a friendly crowd and always ready to pass the benefits of their accumulated knowledge to others.

I am particularly grateful to Tony Woollett, who contributed the basis of the chapter on scratch-building and the Comper Swift; Gordon Stevens of Rareplanes, and John Tarvin of Airframe, who helped in relation to vac-form kits; Mike Ingham and Dave Howley, who answered many questions with considerable patience; and the following modellers, manufacturers, historians, companies and museums who all contributed something.

Geoff Prentice, John Carpenter, Mike Gething, Alan W. Hall, Mike Silk, Charles King, Mike McEvoy, Les Vowles, Carl Wiegand, Larry Buettner, Joe Daileda, Jim Maas, Richard Leask Ward; members of various branches of the International Plastic Modellers' Society; *Flight International, Airfix Magazine, Aviation News;* The Royal Air Force Museum; Hawker Siddeley Aviation, North American Aviation, McDonnell-Douglas, The Imperial War Museum; Krasel Industries Inc, Morris & Ingram (London) Ltd, Airfix Products Ltd, Lesney Ltd, Revell (GB) Ltd, Monogram Models Inc; Al Trendle of Minicraft; and other manufacturers whose products have been used; Martin Holbrook who has provided all the drawings; and John Carter who did a great deal to help with photography.

Finally to my wife Susan, whose constant encouragement has only been matched by her output of coffee and uncomplaining wielding of household equipment to keep my study clear of the debris of modelmaking.

one

Methods and motivation

It is practically impossible to say exactly when the first model aircraft was constructed. Since it is not yet 75 years since the Wright brothers made what is regarded as the first flight by man, this may seem an odd statement, as it could be argued that until aeroplanes existed, models of them could not be made. This is indeed true as far as actual scale replicas of full-size machines are concerned, but one must not overlook the fact that for centuries the human race has been fascinated by flying and many models were made — some of which still exist — of the creations that various pioneers felt would unlock the secrets of aviation for them.

At Le Mans in France there is a painting of the Virgin Mary holding the Christ child on her lap, clutched in his hands is what appears to be some form of flying model which bears a remarkable resemblance to a similar toy featured in paintings by Flemish artists in the early 14th century. The painting in France is dated about 1460 at which time the famous scientist and painter, Leonardo da Vinci, who it is known studied aeronautics and made many experiments with flying models, was eight years old. So this single piece of evidence points quite conclusively to the existence of even earlier pioneers.

Da Vinci and the other early experimenters based most of their designs on the principle of obtaining flight by emulating the birds; the power being derived by some form of flapping wing or mechanism, hence the name ornithopter. In the late 18th and early 19th Century Sir George Cayley, a gifted Englishman, took the studies started by his predecessors a stage further when he produced the first model that followed the now accepted configuration of a fuselage, wings and tailplane. He also realised that a cambered surface produced lift and that control could be exercised by moving various parts of such surfaces. The biggest problem that confronted all of these early aeronauts was the provision of a suitable power unit. Manpower was considered in some detail but even today this still eludes us and there is considerable monetary reward awaiting the first aircraft to fly over a mile powered by this means.

Once the problems had been ironed out of the internal combustion engine, it was soon realised that here was the perfect answer, and it then became just a matter of time before a unit which was light enough, and developed adequate power, was made and fitted into a suitable airframe.

The Wright brothers made this early breakthrough and from their tentative steps the conquest of the air accelerated to such a degree that within 15 years of their flight at Killdevil Hill the aeroplane was being used in a major war. During the following years the design of the aeroplane became more and more sophisticated, passenger-carrying craft were produced and put into operation, more effective methods of waging war with the aeroplane were perfected, the jet engine was invented, and the whole cycle was reproduced using this form of motive power. The result is that today it is possible for passengers to fly in supersonic airliners at speeds that were not even dreamed about by the Wright brothers and were barely figments of the imagination only 25 years ago.

Alongside the evolution of the aeroplane has grown the hobby of making model aircraft which now stands as one of the most skilful and absorbing interests open to both young and old alike.

Flying models have developed at a pace akin to that of their full-size counterparts, with present day multi-channel radio-controlled models being as complex, in their own way, as modern jet fighters and airliners.

Apart from the hobby aspect of model

9

aircraft, they also feature very prominently in the design and development of real aircraft. Most of these proceed from the drawing board to three-dimensional models used in wind tunnels to ascertain their aerodynamic qualities, and then to perfect scale replicas either as a sales aid or a method by which future developments can be planned. In some cases such models are in fact full-size replicas in which instrument layouts, seating and the installation of control systems is planned to a very fine degree. So it is a natural step for those who are in some way or another motivated by aeroplanes and aviation, to make their own models of subjects that appeal to them. The reasons behind such motivation are often very personal, varying from individual to individual, and similarly the materials and methods used. But whatever the guiding force, or the way the end result is achieved, there is a common bond uniting all such enthusiasts whatever their occupation, colour, creed or age.

In addition to being used by aircraft manufacturers, models are also used extensively by the armed forces, as training aids in aircraft recognition, theory of flight, logistics, and 101 other diverse subjects. A whole industry geared to

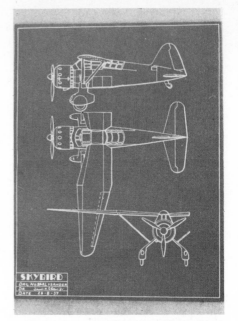

The instruction sheet for Skybird kit 24A, Westland Lysander. This double-sided sheet and the 'blueprint' drawing are all the instructions included with this 1937 kit.

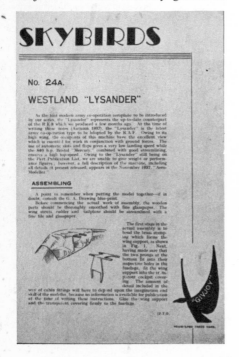

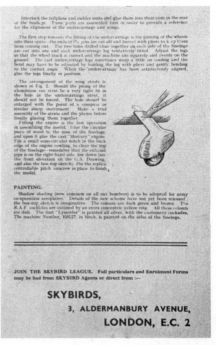

produce models for these, and other purposes, has evolved over the years, but even so the numbers employed in the capacity of professional model makers is minute when compared to those who simply make models for a hobby.

Until the 1930s wood was the commonest material used in the construction of full-size aeroplanes, and being readily available, easy to work with and comparatively inexpensive, was also the medium chosen by modellers from which to create their replicas. Long after this material was abandoned by aircraft manufacturers it was still the most popular medium for modellers, and indeed is still used today either to produce complete models, to complement more modern materials, or as a basis from which to make master moulds from which component parts can be formed.

In the early days of the hobby, modellers drew their own plans from photographs, line drawings that appeared in contemporary magazines, or by studying the actual subjects at air pageants. As the popularity of the hobby increased it was natural that a need would arise, from those who perhaps lacked the skills to carry out the necessary groundwork, for commercially available kits. This demand was met by several companies, who up until the end of the Second World War blossomed into an industry devoted solely to meeting the needs of model aircraft enthusiasts. One of the most famous of these commercially available ranges was marketed under the name of Skybirds, the design of all of their models being in the hands of that well-known aviation exponent, the late James Hay Stevens. The component parts of the kit were neatly presented in a flat cardboard box which contained a line drawing of the model and a flat piece of cardboard to which all the various parts were attached. The major parts, such as the fuselage, wings and tailplanes, were cut roughly to shape in hardwood, whilst smaller components were of celluloid, brass and metal pressings. The first kit released was the DH80 Puss Moth which retailed at 1/6d (7½p). Although lacking in certain detail and in some respects being suspect in accuracy, the range proved popular and was soon extended to include military as well as civil types, two notable examples being the Handley Page Heyford bomber and the Armstrong-Whitworth

Atalanta airliner. Although cabin windows had to be painted on to the wooden fuselages, cockpit canopies were provided for aircraft that had them, and over the years standards improved in much the same way as they have with the present day injection-moulded plastic kit.

During World War 2 construction kits of most of the aircraft used in that conflict became available, advertisements and catalogues of the period listing such gems as the Chingford Model Aerodrome Ltd range of 1:48 scale kits including the Blackburn Skua and Boulton Paul Defiant at 6/9d; the Lockheed Lightning and Douglas Boston at 8/9d, and the Caproni Re 2000 or Fw 190 at 6/-. Model Aircraft Stores (Bournemouth) Ltd, in their 'Truscale' series of 1:72 scale models, listed the inevitable Spitfire and Bf 109 at 1/10d, with the Anson and Hampden at 2/6d and 3/1d being popular multi-engined kits. The same company also listed a series of optional extras such as bombs, two and three bladed propellers, wheels and transfer sheets, thus following the tradition started by Skybirds who also had a range of extras including hangars, ground equipment and personnel.

These wartime kits introduced balsa wood as the medium for their main components although retaining hardwood and metal pressings for cowlings, wheels, engines and propellers.

Enthusiasts of the period tended to eye the commercial kit with some scorn, preferring to stick by their totally scratch-built models, but most of them eventually made the change using the kit as a basis from which to build and improvise to the high standards they had set themselves.

James Hay Stevens chose a scale of one inch = six feet, or 1:72, for his range of Skybird models, and this became the accepted scale by serious collectors, as it allowed both small and large aircraft to be modelled in a size that did not present too many difficulties as far as display and storage was concerned, but at the same time was big enough to allow detail to be included. The wisdom of his choice is echoed by the fact that today this scale is still the most popular and there are far more 1:72 aircraft kits produced than any other.

In the United States of America, modelling was just as popular following similar development as in England.

The original Frog Penguin 1:72 scale catalogue. This was printed in full colour and some of the subjects shown would be welcomed in present day ranges by most modellers. The prices are also of interest, since 15/- (75p) in 1937 would have represented a much higher percentage of a weekly wage in those days than a similarly priced kit does today.

However, the American modeller favoured the larger quarter inch = one foot or 1:48 scale and the two most prolific producers of kits in that country, Aircraft and Hawk — who are still, incidentally, in business producing plastic kits — chose this scale for their kits. These were produced in the same way as their British counterparts using pre-shaped balsa and hardwood parts with metal pressings and acetate canopies. The American kits were sought after in England and several companies obtained agencies and imported them, although prices were higher than their home-built competitors.

Hardwoods such as Obechi, Pine, and Spruce were favoured by serious modellers for, although it was more difficult to work with, the end result was much better. But balsa also had its advantages, being easy to obtain and carve but needing considerably more attention to final finishing if an acceptable paint job was to result. Magazines frequently published

plans to 1:72 and 1:48 scales, whilst in England the Aeromodeller Plans Service could provide scale drawings of a wide range of contemporary aircraft at reasonable prices. Their opposite number in the USA was *Model Aeroplane News*, which, although, like its English equivalent, was slanted primarily at flying models, also provided a plans service for non-flying scale models.

Just prior to the outbreak of World War 2 the British company Frog produced what can really be considered as the forerunner of the modern plastic kit when they launched the Penguin range. These kits were moulded in a type of acetate plastic which could be glued together with balsa cement, and the kits included all the major components moulded in the correct shapes together with transparent canopies, and nicely detailed wheels and engines. The range included most of the well-known aircraft of World War 2 as well as some other interesting subjects such as the Short Empire flying boat, the Short Singapore III and the Monospar ST25 Universal Ambulance.

Many thought that this type of kit would spell the death knell of the wooden kit but this was not the case, for although they were popular and in fact are still sought after as collectors' items, they only had a short life after the war and went out of production long before the last surviving wooden kit manufacturer put up his shutters. Penguin kits were easy to construct but the early type plastic was very prone to warping which proved to be a major disadvantage and one that was not solved until the advent of the polystyrene kit. Modellers, who a few years earlier had deprecated the use of any form of kit, but then gradually changed to it, soon condemned the Penguin range as being too easy and taking the pleasure out of modelling. This attitude manifested itself again during the early days of the polystyrene plastic kit during the 1950s, but the latter became much more established than the Penguin series, and today it is realised by all but the very few, that there is a vast difference between simply assembl-

ing a plastic kit and constructing an accurate model from it. The plastic kit, as did its wooden forerunner, simply provides the basic raw material which in the right hands can be made into an exhibition showpiece. The only difference is that the groundwork required in the wooden kit, carving the basic parts to shape before detailing them, has already been done to a much higher standard than 99 per cent of modellers making wooden kits could hope to achieve.

The first of the new-style plastic kits appeared in late 1949/early 1950, at which time Veron in England were still producing kits in the then conventional solid style with pre-formed balsa parts. The Veron range was probably the last in a long line of such kits and when they eventually ceased production in the face of growing competition from the plastic model manufacturers, their range included aircraft of the World War 2 period as well as the Canberra, Javelin, Wyvern and F-86 Sabre, to mention just a few post-war examples.

Compared with modern plastic kits the offerings of 25 years ago are extremely crude, but such is the mark of progress that in a further quarter century the same

An example of one of the first types of plastic kit, in this case the components of the Penguin Short Singapore flying boat. Kits of this type have become collectors' items and fetch very high prices when offered for sale.

This pair of photographs shows the complexity of the moulds used to produce a modern injection-moulded kit. The moulds require precision machining and cost many thousands of pounds. This particular set is for the Matchbox F-14 Tomcat (photos courtesy Lesney Products Ltd).

words might equally apply to the models we enjoy today which will form the major content of this book.

Although generally speaking most manufacturers now strive for accuracy and produce kits that, when assembled straight from the box, will result in acceptable models, it is as well to remember that to these manufacturers the end product is not aimed at the specialist modeller. Their kits are designed for the youngster who has an interest in aviation and making a model that to him is perhaps no more than a plaything. It is therefore invidious for the small percentage of those who take the hobby seriously to comment about minor errors that they consider should have been put right during the origination of the mould. It is possible to read criticism of such-and-such a kit in which the under-wing camber or some other part is not as it should be, but such critics should remember that, while it is possible for any manufacturer to produce a model that is 100 per cent accurate in every detail, the moulding and tooling costs necessary would result in a model that would be well above the price range for which it is aimed. In any case, if a model that met the pernickety demands of the purists was produced, there would be nothing left for them to practise their skills on, so it is perhaps

best to get the plastic kit into perspective right at the start and view it simply as a means to an end; that end being the use of the kit as raw material to produce a scale model of which the builder can be proud.

The choice that now faces anyone about to start making model aircraft as a hobby is considerable, so from the beginning it is best to decide how far the hobby is to extend, the purpose of the resulting collection, and the standards to be aimed for.

One of the most important factors that governs the hobby and is a natural question which follows the answers to the points raised, is the scale in which the modeller decides to work. If the object of making models is to produce a series of aeroplanes that tell a story, or depict a particular stage in the development of aviation, it is desirable to use the same scale throughout so that comparisons can be made. On the other hand if it is intended to build only the occasional model which has no relationship to its predecessor or successor, then scale is not so important. But the scale finally chosen must be arrived at with some thought. There would be little point in starting out to produce a collection of 1:24 scale models of aircraft used by the Royal Air Force, for apart from the fact that one would soon run out of available kits, there would also be considerable storage or display problems. On the other hand if one wants to spend several months making, for example, a model of a Hellcat that is complete in every minor and major detail, it would be better to select a 1:32 scale kit than a 1:72 scale one.

As with any type of hobby the final path that is pursued is very much a matter of personal choice, so whatever scale you eventually come down in favour of must remain yours and nobody else's decision.

If you are one of those people who are confused by even elementary mathematics a simple rule of thumb when considering the variety of scales from which to choose is, that the larger the model the smaller the fraction used to express it. In the case of a 1:72 scale model the proportions of the model are 72 times smaller than those of the actual aircraft, so an aircraft with a wingspan of 72 feet would be represented by a model with a wingspan of one foot, or expressed in a different way, every one inch on the

model is equal to six feet on the real machine. So it will be appreciated that a model with a scale of 1:100 will be considerably smaller than a model to a scale of 1:24 and so on. Although, as already stated, 1:72 scale is generally regarded as the most popular, especially if a large collection is envisaged, both 1:48 and 1:100 are increasing in popularity, the former enabling the art of adding detail to be practised in a collection that will not present unsurmountable storage problems, whilst the latter is still large enough to add refinements while at the same time keeping even very big aircraft in manageable proportions.

Although it might sound somewhat contradictory to what has been written so far, it sometimes pays to build the occasional model outside the scale chosen as this not only broadens the outlook but can also provide useful information. If, for example, a collection of 1:72 fighters is being produced, it will often be worthwhile building one in 1:32 or 1:24 scale with a view to incorporating the additional detail that is provided by

Scale table showing proportions of scales

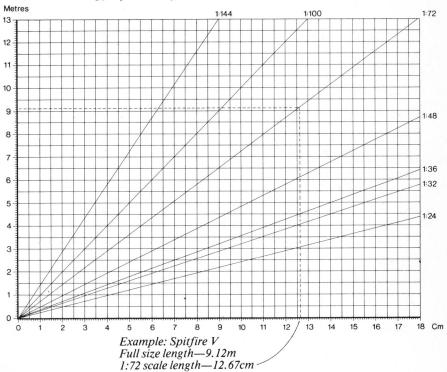

Example: Spitfire V
Full size length—9.12m
1:72 scale length—12.67cm

the manufacturer in the larger kit with scratch-built parts in the smaller one. A very good example of this is the extremely accurate cockpit detail which is included in large scale kits, and can be scaled down and used in a smaller scale equivalent which has rudimentary or no such detail included in the basic kit. One excursion outside the chosen scale is usually enough to get the general idea and it goes without saying that it would be quite wrong to display the completed large scale model along with its smaller brethren.

Once again it is dangerous to be too dogmatic about this for in some cases, to show a truly representative collection of a chosen theme, it may be necessary to use two different scales. A good example of this would be, shall we say, a collection depicting aircraft used by the Royal Air Force in post-war years. Most of the kits required are available in 1:72 scale, but at the time of writing there are no kits in this scale of the Comet, VC 10 or the three V bombers. Unless you want to scratch-build these and maybe other examples in the common scale, the only alternative is to use kits that are available in 1:144 or 1:96 scales, and providing these are displayed quite separately from the main 1:72 scale collection they will not cause any offence. But it cannot be repeated enough that matters such as this and many others in modelling are entirely the decision of the person concerned and should not be influenced in any way by outside agencies.

Having selected a scale and theme it is a good idea to plan the collection by noting the models that are to be included and whether or not they are available in kit form, or indeed likely to be. It is not really too difficult to make an inspired guess at the latter because those models which are likely to have that elusive quality of sales appeal, and will therefore probably appear in some manufacturer's range, become rather obvious with practice. Those rarities which were used in small quantities or are derivatives of existing airframes are not likely to become available in injection-moulded kits and reliance will therefore have to be place on some of the specialist vac-form kit makers, or conversions of existing kits. Such a list will help in several ways, and if you are a complete newcomer to the hobby it is best to start with straight-forward kits and gradually progress to conversions and vac-form kits as your skills develop. If, after a while, it becomes apparent to you that you have neither the expertise nor time to proceed to specialist conversions and models, then you can still derive pleasure from staying with standard kits and adjusting your collection accordingly. Many new-comers have been lost to the hobby by, to use a hackneyed expression, 'trying to run before they can walk', in tackling difficult conversions from the very beginning, getting very frustrated and ending up abandoning model aircraft making completely.

The important thing to keep in the front of your mind is that making models is a hobby and if the end result satisfies you it has achieved its aim. Naturally it is desirable to aim for as high a standard as possible, but if you feel that what you produce is the best you can manage, and it has given you pleasure, then you have succeeded, whatever comments might be made by the many self-appointed experts whom all hobbies attract.

two

Tools and techniques

The type, quality, and quantity of tools necessary to make model aircraft depends on many factors ranging from the depth of the individual's pocket to the extent one wishes to pursue the hobby, and the chosen medium in which the models are to be produced. It is possible to reach a very high standard with a bare minimum but most modellers find that over a period of time they collect a variety of implements that make their chosen task easier. Some of these are tools designed to perform specific functions whilst others are adapted from household objects to perform jobs that are far removed from their originally designed tasks.

Whatever the material chosen, be it plastic, wood or paper, a good quality modelling knife is essential. Such knives are readily obtainable from model shops or those specialising in artists' materials. The type with interchangeable blades is popular but in many cases these can be large and unwieldy so it is better to select

a lightweight style handle and buy two, one for use with large blades for heavy cutting work and the other for finer blades for more detailed work. Knives of the type manufactured by Humbrol and X-Acto are ideal as they will accept all types of blade but the advantage of having two far outweighs the chore of having to constantly change blades. The two types mentioned have round handles with a knurled chuck which makes blade-changing simplicity in itself. Flat handled scalpels, examples of which are produced by Swan Morton, also accept blades of different shapes and sizes but in these the blade clips over a fixing lug. This type of knife is usually found in art shops or medical supply stores, it is a very fine piece of equipment with blades that are extremely sharp, and great care is needed when changing them. A scalpel of this type is worth its weight in gold to the modeller and purchase of, say, the number 3 handle and a variety of blades is strongly recommended.

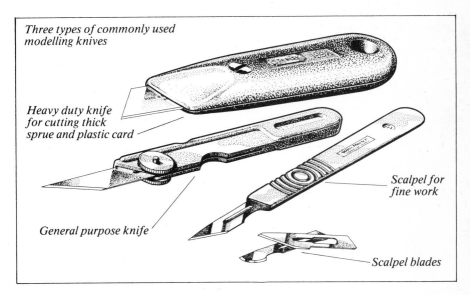

Three types of commonly used modelling knives

Heavy duty knife for cutting thick sprue and plastic card

General purpose knife

Scalpel for fine work

Scalpel blades

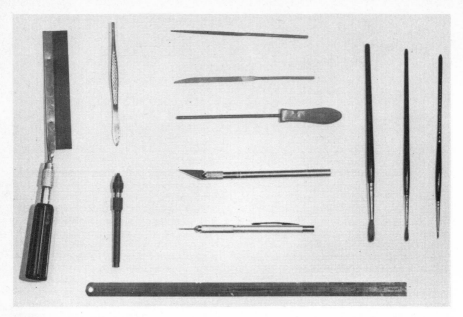

The basic tools which will prove adequate for almost every type of modelling need. On the left is a razor saw, tweezers and pin vise. The centre contains three types of file, a modelling knife and a scriber, while the three most commonly used paintbrushes are on the right. Forming the base is a steel rule which is vital, especially in scratch-building and assembling vac-form kits.

Whatever type of knife is selected it should be looked after with care and the blades changed frequently if sharp, accurate cuts are to be made. Such knives should always be stored carefully away after use, preferably with some form of protection over their blades and in a sealed box. This is especially important if small children have access to the place where modelling equipment is kept when it is not in use. It must be remembered that the sole purpose of any knife is to cut, it is not choosy as to what material it cuts, so fingers poked into boxes in which knives might have been haphazardly thrown are as vulnerable as the material from which your models are being constructed. Blades are not expensive and it is always wise to keep a selection available. Those that become too blunt for their main purpose should also be stored somewhere safe as they can be used for a variety of other tasks, such as scraping, marking control surfaces, or even as a form of spatula for applying filler.

The versatility of a good quality modelling knife will quickly become apparent whatever material is chosen for use. As with any type of tool it is false economy to try and make do with an inexpensive item, as it will be found that it has to be replaced fairly frequently so the outlay over a period of time exceeds the cost of a well-produced item during the initial stages.

There are many occasions when a knife, however good it might be, is just not man enough to tackle some jobs, so thought should be given to purchasing a saw or saws. A razor saw which has a wooden handle with a blade backed by a stiff strengthener will pay for itself over and over again in any sort of modelling, and if you can afford them a small coping saw as well as a fretsaw will provide the answer to some of the more intricate cutting problems that might arise.

Having acquired the basic cutting implements, thought must be given to some form of drill, There are one or two miniature power drills designed specifically for modellers and one of these such as that marketed by Petite Precision or the British company, Expo Drills Ltd, will be the ultimate. These drills can be used with a host of attachments for grinding, cutting and polishing as well as their prime purpose of drilling holes. They are a luxury which one can live without but an ideal piece of equipment for the modeller who is going to spend a lot of time on his hobby and wants the very best. For the average modeller — if indeed there is such a person — a small pin vice and a set of fine drills will prove adequate. Drills and burrs can be expensive but those used in the dental profession are ideal for model making, and a friendly dentist will often be pleased to pass some of his discarded ones to you. Although such discards might be useless as far as drilling molars is concerned, they will still be sharp enough and have plenty of life left when it comes to using them in modelling. A standard pin vice can be obtained at most hardware stores and will accept dental drills as well as the normal small engineering drill. On many occasions, especially if plastic is being used, it will be sufficient to use the drill between the fingers, but on thicker plastic and other materials, the pin vice will give a much better grip and be easier on the fingers.

A steel rule being used in conjunction with a Swann Morton scalpel to cut plastic card. This type of modelling knife is very sharp and when being used in this way must be held firmly but not pressed too hard otherwise the blade will break. The steel rule must also be held rigidly in position to prevent accidents and ensure a straight cutting edge.

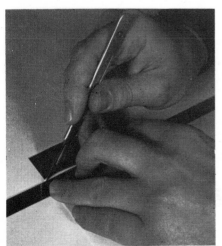

A scriber is a tool that is not expensive to buy but has 101 uses ranging from its designed use of marking lines, to holding and picking up small pieces. Hand-in-glove with the scriber goes a steel rule which, in my opinion, is the only suitable implement to use when marking out on any material either with a scriber or pencil. It can also be used as a straight edge for cutting against since there is no danger of the knife taking out a piece of the rule as there is with the wooden or plastic variety.

There are many occasions during the construction of a model when a third hand helps to retain sanity and stem frustration, at such times a small vice will provide the ideal answer and the type that clamps to the working area is a useful investment.

The handling of small parts can also present problems but these will shrink to insignificance if the help of a pair of tweezers is enlisted. The type that the lady members of the household use for plucking eyebrows is ideal and can be obtained for a modest outlay at most chemist or chain stores. If you want to spend a little more, industrial style tweezers can be bought at hardware shops and one type that is particularly useful has a reverse action to that which is normally accepted. This means that the actual tips that do the gripping are closed until the legs are squeezed whereupon they open, so small components can be held very firmly without having to concentrate on keeping pressure applied with the fingers; once the part is correctly in place, or the work on it completed, slight pressure is applied and the tips release their grip.

A set of files comprising one that is round, a half-round and a flat one just about completes the essentials that need to be purchased. Once again the cost of these depends a great deal on just what you want for your particular modelling, and the use to which they are going to be put. A set of precision Swiss files can cost a great deal of money and in some respects will have a limited use, whereas a fairly good quality set of small files of the shapes mentioned with perhaps a triangular one thrown in, can be bought for a reasonable sum at chain stores or hardware shops. Generally speaking the plastic modeller will be able to manage with less variety than his colleague who chooses wood or those who use a variety of materials in scratch-building.

There are many other items such as soldering irons, magnifying glasses, small power saws or even a miniature engineering lathe, that some modellers will want or have, but one must view the hobby realistically and leave such items to the whim or needs of the person concerned. Many readers will no doubt strongly disagree with my comments in this respect, but the hobby, and what you want from it, and I am looking from the right perspective, and I am looking from the point of view of the person who wants to make models from which he will derive pleasure in moments of leisure rather than the accomplished model engineer, who will probably not need my advice anyway!

Other items that can be classified in the category of tools can be obtained from a multitude of sources. Clamps, to hold parts that are glueing or must be glued together under pressure, can be adapted from nothing more elaborate than the common household spring-peg, while in cases where these do not exert enough pressure, spring clips of the type obtainable in various sizes from stationery shops prove ideal substitutes. Cock-

A Mattell vac-form machine with one half of a Neptune wing tank in position (see chapter seven). The plastic sheet from which the tank will be made is just softening in the heat chamber at the top of the picture.

tail sticks, knitting needles, paperclips, and items that can be found in most domestic tool boxes, such as pliers, wire cutters and even small hammers, can provide the answer to a seemingly difficult problem, so before rushing out to buy a sophisticated tool try to adopt the attitude of looking around the house first then modifying or adapting an apparently useless — as far as modelling is concerned — item. It is surprising just what the human brain will come up with if it is given a free rein now and again.

A good illustration of this philosophy is the use of a cylinder-type vacuum cleaner as the motive power for a home-made vac-form machine. This very useful tool is a boon to all modellers and is an extremely expensive item to acquire from commercial sources, that is unless you are lucky enough to be able to locate one of the small vac-form machines that was marketed in America by the Mattel Toy Company. Readers who are familiar with American modelling magazines will often have read articles on modelling in which the author mentions that he has formed new canopies or components on such a machine, and been left wondering exactly what it is. The Mattel Vac-form was manufactured as a toy and could be bought in the USA as a complete kit with moulds to produce a variety of small toys. It was not long before modellers recognised the use of this item as it pro-

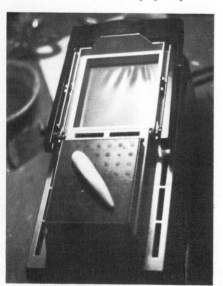

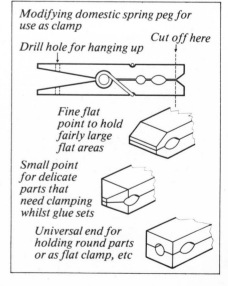

Modifying domestic spring peg for use as clamp

Drill hole for hanging up

Cut off here

Fine flat point to hold fairly large flat areas

Small point for delicate parts that need clamping whilst glue sets

Universal end for holding round parts or as flat clamp, etc

vided a simple foolproof method of moulding without the headaches of having to produce both male and female moulds as is necessary with the method generally in use in this country. The Mattel tool consists of a metal box with a frame at the top in which there is a platform on which the 'master' is placed. Alongside this there is a heating chamber into which fits a clamp for holding the material that is to be formed. When the heating element is switched on the plastic moulding material softens and when it has reached a flexible state it is swung over the original master and the air is extracted from under it by a hand operated pump, which pulls the moulding material over the 'master' and very quickly forms an accurate copy. This vac-form tool was not very expensive and its only limitations were the small moulding area which measures about 7 × 8 cm, adequate for canopies, seats, bombs, wheels and similar small items but not big enough for many major components. Apart from forming pieces carved from wood it could also be used to remould kit canopies where the parts included in the kit were too thick, or were more accurate than parts included in another kit and so could be copied for use with the inferior product. Although the Mattel Vac-U-Form, to give it its full title, appears to be no longer in production, it is worth looking around for one as it will prove a worthwhile investment.

Should you be lucky enough to obtain one you will find that as it is designed for use on the American electrical system it will require a 110 or 115v supply. As the British domestic supply is 240v a step-down transformer is needed, but an auto-transformer with 240v input and several voltage output taps can be obtained for about £4 from specialist radio shops.

However, the fact that this commercially available item may be difficult to obtain should not be too much of a deterent as it is not very difficult to make a vac-form that will perform equally as well.

Basically, the unit consists of a box with an area to accept the master mould, a frame to hold the moulding material (plastic card) and an inlet in which to insert the vacuum cleaner pipe. The accompanying drawings have not been dimensioned as the overall size is related to the size which you will find most convenient for the amount and type of moulding you want to do. It is advisable to avoid too big a box as the area from which the air has to be extracted should not be too large or problems in relation to the amount of suction available from the cleaner will result.

The example I made was approximately 25 × 20 cm which gave a moulding area of 20 × 13 cm, big enough for a complete fuselage for a 1:72 scale Meteor 8 which was one of the main

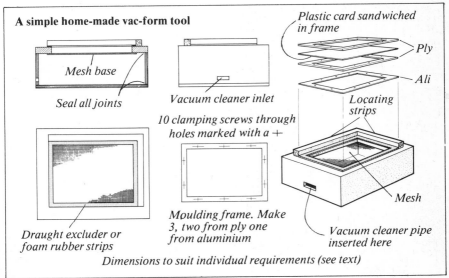

A simple home-made vac-form tool

Mesh base

Seal all joints

Vacuum cleaner inlet

Plastic card sandwiched in frame

Ply

Ali

Locating strips

10 clamping screws through holes marked with a +

Draught excluder or foam rubber strips

Moulding frame. Make 3, two from ply one from aluminium

Mesh

Vacuum cleaner pipe inserted here

Dimensions to suit individual requirements (see text)

reasons why it was produced in the first place.

Start by making a box minus the lid. Use 15 mm thick ply and make sure that all the joints are air-tight, this being achieved by the liberal use of epoxy resin along the seams. One side of the box must have an inlet for the vacuum cleaner pipe and the shape of this depends on the type of cleaner available. The one I used had a very narrow rectangular ended attachment that fitted to the normal extension tube, so a slot was cut into which this was a tight push-fit. It might be necessary to use a tube with a circular cross-section so an inlet can be fabricated from rubber tubing bonded to the hole in the box, the end result will be the same providing adequate care is taken over sealing as this must be absolutely airtight. After making the hole from which the air will be extracted, line the inside around it with foam rubber just to ensure that it is even harder for the air to escape.

Once the basic box is complete make the lid which must have the moulding area cut into it. Use this as a template to mark-out the size of the frames that will hold the moulding material and make sure that this work is carried out accurately. Once the lid has been made, fix a strong piece of wire gauze on the inside completely covering the moulding area, this acts as a base for the master mould and it must be rigid or the vacuum cleaner will suck it down, the result being a curved bottom line to the final mould. Hardware and DIY shops usually have some fine mesh sheet brass which is used to cover ventilation holes in kitchen equipment, and this is ideal for our purpose.

Once the wire gauze has been fitted to the inside of the moulding area, fit the lid to the rest of the assembly, once again ensuring that all joints are air-tight. Around the edges of the hole in the top, fit strips of draught excluder as shown on the drawings, then fit two pieces of wood along one short and one long side — these are the locating points for the moulding frame — and ensure that this always lines-up correctly every time with the moulding area. The frame that holds the plastic card is perhaps the most important part as far as accuracy is concerned, and consists of three components. Two of these are made from ply and the other from asbestos or aluminium. Since the former chips easily and is hard to work with, it will be found that aluminium is ideal. Cut out the three frames then bond one of the ply ones to the aluminium one with a quick-setting epoxy resin such as Devcon, Araldite or Britfix. Drill two holes in each side, a total of eight, making sure that these are of sufficient clearance to allow a bolt to pass through them. Use counter-sunk rather than cheese-head bolts, counter-sinking the aluminium frame to accept the heads. If wing nuts can be obtained they certainly make the task of reloading much easier, but if not, use ordinary hexagonal nuts.

The method of use is to cut a piece of plastic card to fit the frame, drilling the location holes using the frame as a template, then insert this into the frame and tighten the nuts to hold the sandwich rigid. Place the master mould on the moulding bed, holding it in place with two small pegs fixed to its undersurface or a blob of Plasticine. This is not absolutely essential as suction will hold it firm during the moulding process. The vacuum cleaner pipe is pushed into the hole in the base of the box, making sure that it is set to suck not blow! The moulding frame complete with its plastic card insert is held under the cooker grill until the plastic starts to soften, whereupon it is quickly removed and placed over the mould, it is at this point that the importance of the earlier mentioned location strips will be revealed. The vacuum cleaner, which can be switched on just prior to the removal of the frame from the grill, will suck the soft plastic over the shape of the mould and the result should be a perfectly moulded shape. If the tool has been made small enough, or if you have a large grill, the whole assembly can be placed under the grill from the very beginning and the cleaner switched on as soon as the plastic shows signs of softening, this allows heat to be continuously applied while the shape is forming. If this is done do not switch off the cleaner until the heat source has been removed or the shape will quickly disappear. It is also wise to switch off the cleaner as soon as the shape is rigid, for once the air has been removed, providing your joints are airtight, the cleaner motor will start to overheat. The cost of a new motor will lead not only to an expensive model but also a distinct drop in popularity of mod-

It is a good idea to make a modelling table with storage area to keep all parts and equipment easily accessible. This is particularly useful if modelling activities are limited to dining room/kitchen table etc

Lip to keep pieces within work area and stop them being knocked on to floor

Shelves for storing paint, knives, etc

Storage boxes for spare parts, etc

elling in general from the owner of the cleaner!

It is also advisable to wear oven gloves during the moulding process as the heat generated from most domestic cooker grills is very high.

Should you have doubts about your skills in fabricating the original moulding box, a metal conduit box used in electrical installation work, and available in a variety of sizes, will provide a ready-made substitute, but it will still be necessary to make a moulding frame and fit some form of moulding bed to the metal box.

This simple piece of equipment enables parts to be copied from existing kits as well as components carved from balsa or obechi to be produced in quantity. Remember though, that it is illegal to copy components of existing kits and sell them on a commercial basis.

The old method of making a mould from wood then cutting its shape into another piece of wood over which plastic card or acetate sheet is placed and heated for the original to be plunged through, is an effective method of forming parts as will be seen in the chapter on scratch-building, but the vac-form tool does away with the accuracy required in making a female mould, and once its techniques have been mastered will pro-

vide success every time it is used. If you are going to make wooden masters, a hard wood such as Obechi is better than balsa as it will last longer, give a better defined mould, and not leave any grain marks on the inside of the part moulded.

Body-putty or some other form of filler such as the type used in automobile repairs, one of which is popularly known as 'Green Stuff', will need to be used in some quantity during modelling and it is always useful to have some form of spatula with which to apply and smooth it into areas where its presence is required. Such spatulas can be formed from plastic or wood but again if your dentist is a friendly person who can be approached, the type of tool he uses in attending to teeth is very useful. These come with a variety of shaped ends and one particularly useful one has a flat spade-like shape which is ideal for the purpose. The use of all the tools mentioned, and others, will become apparent as further chapters are read, but there will be other occasions when a tool can be successfully used in some job that is far removed from that for which it was originally intended.

Although not strictly coming under the heading of tools, some form of lamp is virtually essential for it is always wise to have adequate light present when modelling. The adjustable type of lamp such as the Anglepoise is ideal as the arm of this can be adjusted at will to give light exactly where and when you need it.

There are very few modellers who have a separate work room or study which is entirely their own to use as and when they want to. Such a room is, of course, an ideal luxury as it can be laid out to suit the individual's needs and parts can be left to set without fear of them being disturbed. However, the majority will have to produce their models in a variety of environments, but this does not mean that they cannot provide themselves with some form of portable work area that can be stored away when not in use and produced during a modelling session without upsetting the domestic harmony of the rest of the household. A simple wooden tray for a modelling board, with tools contained in a separate box, is a neat and simple solution, but for the expenditure of a very small sum of money it is possible to make a custom-built modelling board that is more or less completely self-contained. The drawings illustrate a basic design that can be modified as circumstances dictate, it can be as elaborate as you care to make it and as experience is gained there will be additions to be made as your own interests and techniques develop. The modelling area has a lip similar to the earlier mentioned tea-tray. This is a vital part as it does prevent small pieces being swept on to the floor, but it does have its disadvantages especially when one wants to clean the surface of small offcuts and sanding dust. This is overcome by having a supplementary board that can be placed on the normal working area when a lot of cutting or sanding, as is necessary with wooden or vac-form models, is needed. The shelves at the back enable paintbrushes and other tools to be kept safely and the small drawers, which can be a commercially produced unit of the type available in Woolworths or Halfords, will keep smaller tools and components safe. I have seen a similar work area complete with folding sides and doors that can be closed up and transported with a carrying handle on the top; the final choice is yours but a clean, tidy work area saves time at the start of each session, and will lead to a methodical mind which will produce neater and better models. After all, if at the start of a modelling session you have to hunt around for tools, parts, and other odds and ends, some of which you might not remember where you last put them, a feeling of impatience and frustration will occur and this is quite easily transferred to the model being constructed.

As your modelling develops and the variety of kits purchased grows, there will be an accumulation of spare parts especially as it is now customary for most kit manufacturers to include alternative parts in standard kits. Such parts should NEVER be discarded but consigned to what most modellers call their 'spares box'. It is surprising just how quickly such a box will grow in content and its use cannot be emphasised enough, as it will often produce a part that is ideal for a conversion or scratch-built model. It is well worth considering the purchase of another set of the small boxes mentioned for the work board, as these will enable the accumulation of spare components to be broken down into their classifications thus leading to easy location when they are needed. Should you do this do not throw away all the runners or sprue to which the parts in a kit are attached, as this plastic has a 101 uses and a ready supply of it is always useful. Another source of acquisition for component parts is children's toys, these days a lot of these are produced in plastic, and once junior has broken or discarded them they can yield a treasure chest of pre-shaped curves, plastic windows, wheels and many other bits and bobs. A good example of this is that Tony Woollett, who contributed the chapter on scratch-building, used the seats from a child's double-decker bus as the basis from which he produced the interior for one of his between-the-wars passenger aircraft. This saved Tony endless time in building these components from scratch as the basic seats were there and only needed modifying to meet his particular requirements for the model he was constructing at the time. So try to develop a sort of jackdaw instinct and after a while you will find that many apparently useless pieces of rubbish can be used effectively during your modelling activities.

three

Wooden models

The plastic construction kit is now well established as the most popular method of making scale models as it provides the raw material from which even the most impecunious enthusiast can produce a reasonable replica of an aircraft of his choice. The dedicated modeller uses the plastic kit as a means to an end rather than an end in itself, and considerable skill is required to turn what is basically a mass-produced item into a near-perfect and true to scale model. During the hey-day of the wooden model, or to give it the term it was most commonly known by, the solid model, this in itself was used as the stepping stone from which many splendid collections originated.

The skill of the modeller concerned was an important criteria, as carving the roughly shaped parts provided was not easy and the end result was very depen-

dent on the individual concerned. With practice a model that equalled today's injection moulded kits could be produced, but such a high standard was usually beyond the limits of most who took up the hobby. Nonetheless, solid modelling was a popular hobby that flourished until the more modern style of kit pushed it into the background. In many ways there is little difference between the wooden kit and its modern plastic counterpart, for although the latter, due to its pre-formed shape, removes a great deal of the hit-and-miss of carving, it still leaves considerable scope for the true modeller. There is a vast difference between assembling the components provided then painting them in the colours recommended by the manufacturer, to judging each part on its merits, making alterations to improve

An unusual subject which would make an ideal plastic kit is the Vought F7U-3 Cutlass, seen here in the markings of VF 124 US Navy and modelled in wood by Richard Leask Ward (photo by John Carter).

the fit and appearance, adding extra detail not provided in the kit, then researching the correct colours and markings of the model chosen. So, although the plastic kit does take a lot of the initial hard work out of model making, it still provides a challenge to those who are prepared to treat it as a set of parts that still need a lot of work done to them.

Modellers who take this view will often want to carry out drastic changes to a kit to produce a different variant of the model provided, or even use parts of the plastic kit to produce other aircraft that are unlikely to be featured in manufacturers' ranges. Quite often it is necessary to make new components to make conversions from plastic kits and as wood is one of the most readily available materials it is well-worth spending some time practising working with it. Although you may not intend to combine wooden and plastic parts, if you want to mould your own components from plastic card, a master will be essential, so here again the carving of a wooden shape

will become a prerequisite. In some cases a model that spurs your enthusiasm or is an essential part of a collection, might have to be completely scratch-built and if you do not want to try the methods described in a later chapter, a complete wooden model might provide the answer.

Unless you have some experience of working with the various types of wood that are most suitable for solid scale modelling, it is advisable to obtain several off-cuts and get the feel of the material by carving it to various shapes. Circles, ovals, cones, and triangles are useful cross-sections to attempt at the beginning, and when these have been successfully achieved, take another step by combining one or two different shapes on the same block of wood. These early efforts do not require any prior plan other than one formulated in your mind, they are simply a method to enable you to get the feel of the material and the tools before you try an accurate reproduction of a fuselage or set of wings.

This Saab A-32A Lansen makes an attractive wooden model of a clean Swedish design. Model by Richard Leask Ward (photo by John Carter).

Obechi or close grained pine are ideal woods to use, but balsa, which is more readily available and is much easier to work with — in a modelling sense — will probably be the choice of most modellers whether or not their intention is to produce a complete model, a mould for plastic card, or a component for use with a plastic kit. Balsa can be obtained in a variety of sizes at most of the larger hobby shops especially those which specialise in flying models. It is usually stocked in block as well as sheet form and both types have their uses as far as the solid modeller is concerned. For the initial trial run, a pack of balsa comprising blocks and sheets can be purchased for a nominal sum and this is more than adequate for experimentation purposes. However, when it comes to the actual model it is better to be a little more selective and look for wood with fairly close grain and a good hard texture.

Having decided on the model you wish to construct a set of accurate plans are a must. These must contain drawings showing the cross-sections of the fuselage, wings, tailplanes and other components, as well as outlines of the major assemblies. The Aeromodeller Plans Service have a considerable number from which to choose and these are probably the most accurate to be found anywhere in the world. Other specialist aviation magazines and newspapers publish plans from time to time, but these are not always to a recognised scale, although in the majority of cases cross-sections and the particular scale to which they have been drawn is shown. If a plan of this type is the only one available it need not mean an end to the project, for although your skill in enlarging the drawing to the scale you want might not be sufficient to get you a job as a design draughtsman, it should be possible, with the aid of instruments that can be found in most schoolboys' satchels, to provide a drawing from which you can work.

The easiest way to do this is to place a sheet of tracing paper over the plan and draw a series of squares each side being to the scale shown on the plan. If, for example, the plan scale shows that every ½ inch is equal to 20 feet, draw ½ inch squares on the tracing paper. On a separate piece of paper draw a similar grid but this time use larger squares, say one inch, but draw the same number as you did on the tracing paper, so in this exam-

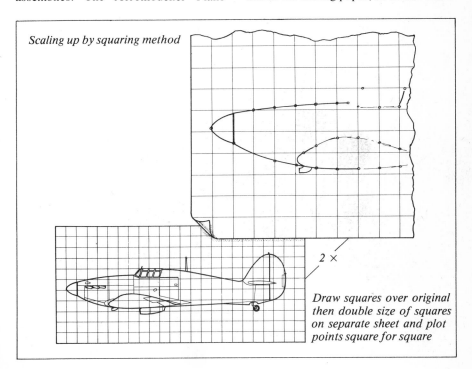

Scaling up by squaring method

2 ×

Draw squares over original then double size of squares on separate sheet and plot points square for square

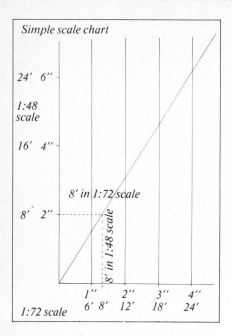

Simple scale chart

24' 6''

1:48 scale

16' 4''

8' in 1:72 scale

8' 2''

8' in 1:48 scale

8' in 1:48 scale

1''   2''   3''   4''
6' 8' 12'   18'   24'

1:72 scale

foot line on the vertical axis and join the zero point where the compass was inserted, through the bisecting point to the top of the last vertical line. The result will be a simple to read table in which the measurements taken off the diagonal bisecting line and projected sideways give the dimensions of the model in 1:72 scale. The drawing illustrates this method very much more clearly than it is described, but it is easy to see that a set of tables such as this can be used to enlarge or reduce any plan to the size you want it. Another method that can be used if you doubt your skills at drawing and have the necessary cash, is to take the original drawing to a printer who has equipment for making printing plates and ask him to enlarge or reduce them to the size you want.

Construction is started by transferring the outline of the fuselage on to the block of wood you have selected for this component. This can be done by either plac-

ple the tracing paper over the drawing has five ½ inch squares, while the separate sheet has five one inch squares. It is now a question of transferring the lines of the aircraft drawing from each ½ inch square to each one inch square, and you will then end up with a drawing that is 1 inch = 20 feet, in other words twice the size of the original. It is not difficult to make simple but working drawings to any scale using this technique if the grid on the drawing you are preparing is drawn to represent the scale you want the finished model to be; if it is 1:72 use a grid in which 1 inch = 6 feet, or in 1:48, 1 inch = 4 feet, but you must remember to relate these squares to the scale shown on the original drawing which determines the size of the grid on your tracing overlay.

Another method that can be used is to draw a scale chart on which the base line is divided into the scale you know, say 1 inch = 6 feet (1:72), therefore the base line can be drawn six inches long giving a scale length of 36 feet. From each of the one inch markings on the base line draw a vertical line making sure that each is exactly parallel to the other. On the first vertical line place the point of a compass which has been set at the scale of the model drawn; if we assume this to be 1:48 scale the compass will be set at two inches for eight feet; now bisect the eight

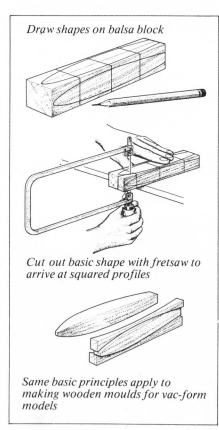

Draw shapes on balsa block

Cut out basic shape with fretsaw to arrive at squared profiles

Same basic principles apply to making wooden moulds for vac-form models

28

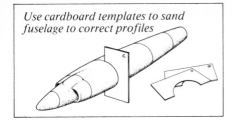

Use cardboard templates to sand fuselage to correct profiles

ing the block under the plan and using carbon paper, or tracing the outline on to a piece of cardboard then cutting out a template which is used to draw the shape on the wood. The block selected for the fuselage can be wide enough to enable the width to be drawn right across it or an alternative, which is better from several points of view, is to use two blocks each half the width required, lightly cemented together. The latter enables the fuselage to be split in half along its vertical axis after carving has been completed thus enabling the cockpit and tail pipe or intake, in the case of a jet, to be hollowed out very much more easily than if one block is used.

Once the side view has been drawn on the block, cut out the shape using a fretsaw, making sure that the blade is kept vertical the whole time, the pieces removed are then pinned or lightly cemented back in place and the top view of the fuselage is marked. By placing the removed wood back in position it is much easier to draw the plan view on to the block since it is being transferred to a perfectly flat surface as was the side view.

Use the fretsaw again to cut out the plan view then remove the pieces of the side view that were pinned or glued back on to the original block. The result will now be a block that has the aircraft's fuselage in both plan and side view ready for shaping. Before starting to carve the fuselage shape, trace the templates that are keyed to datum points on the fuselage plane, on to stiff cardboard and carefully cut these out. Using a sharp modelling knife gradually round-off the sharp corners of the block making several small cuts in preference to a few large ones. Work slowly, constantly checking the area being carved against the templates, and make sure that each side of the point where the template is placed matches. When you are satisfied that the carving has taken you as close to the

final shape as possible, select a medium grade glass-paper and attach it to a sanding block, which is nothing more elaborate than a square block of wood, and carefully continue to shape the fuselage using this. Continue to make frequent checks using the templates, gradually reducing the grade of glass-paper until you are using a very fine one to get a smooth finish. Now mark the cockpit area and attachment points for the wings and tailplanes, then split the block down the centre line so that you have two identical halves. The advantage of using two blocks bonded together in the initial stages will now be evident, but if you have not done this mark the centre line along the length of the fuselage and cut it in half with a fret or razor saw. The type of tools used in the initial carving stages will depend a great deal on the type of wood and size of model. If a hard wood has been used it will be advantageous to use sharp wood chisels or proper woodworking carving tools, but the expenditure on these items is hardly justified unless you intend to do a lot of this type of modelling or have them available anyway.

The extent that the two fuselage halves are hollowed out depends on just how much detail you want to incorporate in the interior. It is well worth hollowing out the cockpit area, for any scale model that does not have at least rudimentary detail in the cockpit immediately loses some of its authenticity. When carrying out this work, start by marking the area to be removed with a ball-point pen then remove it with a modelling knife or gouge, being careful not to 'dig' out the wood too deeply as it is very easy to penetrate the outer shell of the fuselage.

The example shown in this chapter is the Vickers Supermarine Swift, and with this model the cockpit, jet pipe and intakes must be hollowed out. Of these three areas the intakes are likely to prove the most troublesome and it is best to tackle these by drilling a series of small holes in the outside area of the intakes before starting to remove wood from the inside. If this work is done carefully it is not difficult but when it has been completed a bulkhead must be placed inside the fuselage to blank the intakes off otherwise it will be possible to see into an empty shell.

As much attention must be given to obtaining a smooth finish on the inside of

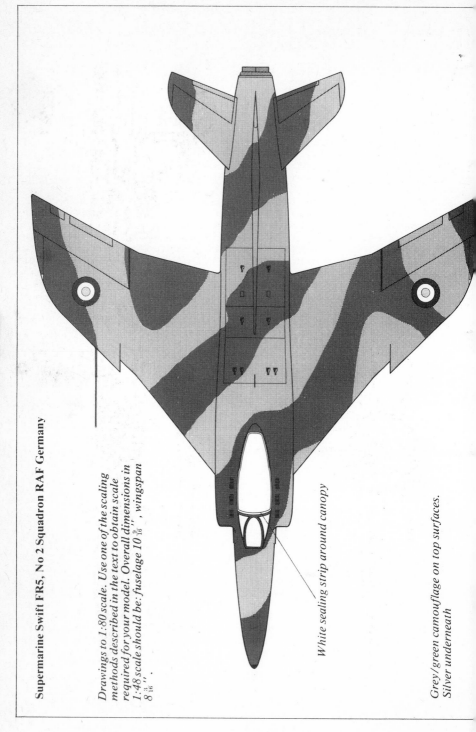

Supermarine Swift FR5, No 2 Squadron RAF Germany

Drawings to 1:80 scale. Use one of the scaling methods described in the text to obtain scale required for your model. Overall dimensions in 1:48 scale should be: fuselage $10\frac{9}{16}''$, wingspan $8\frac{3}{16}''$.

White sealing strip around canopy

Grey/green camouflage on top surfaces. Silver underneath.

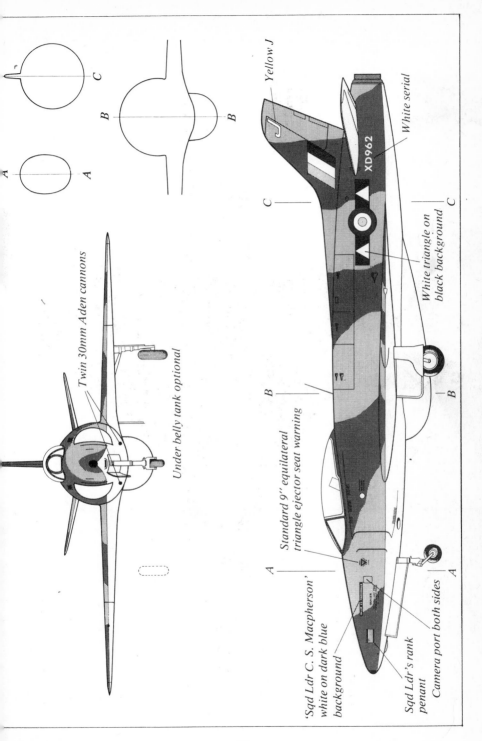

Twin 30mm Aden cannons

Under belly tank optional

Yellow J

White serial

White triangle on
black background

Standard 9" equilateral
triangle ejector seat warning

'Sqd Ldr C. S. Macpherson'
white on dark blue
background

Sqd Ldr's rank
penant

Camera port both sides

XD962

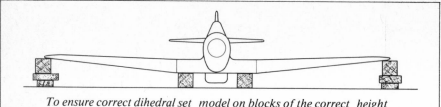

To ensure correct dihedral set model on blocks of the correct height

the model as it is to the outside, this being achieved by the use of varying grades of sandpaper which can be wrapped around dowelling or a pencil to reach inside curves. A tail pipe from hollow dowel or a suitable sized metal or card tube should be added, making sure that it is placed equal about the centre line. A cockpit floor from thin ply or plastic card, as well as side consols and an instrument panel, can also be added before the two halves are joined together again, but it is usually possible to fit the seat after all the work on the fuselage is complete. The techniques described in later chapters on plastic models and scratch-building for adding this type of detail can be applied equally as well in this type of modelling.

Wings, tailplanes and fin/rudders are now marked on to wood of a suitable thickness in the same way as the fuselage shape was transferred to the block used for its construction. When doing this make sure that the grain follows the span of the wings and tailplanes and is vertical on the fin/rudder. Templates are used to obtain the correct aerofoil sections but it is not necessary to use two pieces of wood as was done for the fuselage except in the case of very big models. Wheel wells can be marked out and removed quite easily without the need to split the wings along their lateral axis. In the case of the Swift and most small models, it is usually possible to obtain wood wide enough to make the wings from one piece, but where this is not possible and two widths are needed, make any joins by butt joining along the span and *never* across the wing chord.

When carrying out the final shaping of the wing and tailplane aerofoil sections, leave the leading and trailing edges slightly thicker than they will be on the final model, as it is always wise to give the whole model a final rub down with the finest available glass-paper after it has been assembled, and this is the time

to aim for the standard you want.

Construction of both the wings and tailplanes depends on the model being made, in some cases it is best to make the port and starboard wings as separate items, in others it is best to make them as one complete unit. As far as the Swift is concerned the latter is probably the best line to pursue as it is easier to remove the area where the wings fit from under the fuselage and slot them in, then rebuilding the underline of the fuselage with a piece of wood cemented in place and carved in situ. Where the wings are to fit half way up the fuselage, mark the shape and position of the wing root on the finished fuselage and file a flat area to accept the wings which can be fixed into position with small dowel pins. Once the major components have been made it is advisable to scribe panel lines and control surfaces on them before they are assembled together. Do this by using a scriber and steel rule and to ensure that such items as elevators and ailerons are of equal proportions on each component use a stiff carboard template to make the initial impressions.

If balsa wood has been used for the model the best adhesive to use is balsa cement which is quick drying and gives a tough joint. If Obechi or another hard wood has been used, balsa cement will still work but will not give as good a join as a proprietary wood glue or, better still, epoxy glue. When glueing the components together make sure that the wing dihederal or anhederal is correct by chamfering the wing or tailplane roots to the correct angle or using ply braces inserted into the wings and fuselage. A simple jig to ensure that the components are held firmly in place while they are setting is simply made by using a flat board on which to place the fuselage with blocks of the correct height cemented to it at the point where the wings will rest. In any form of modelling one of the most important virtues the modeller can possess is patience, so once the parts are cemented together leave them alone for at least 24 hours to give the glue a chance to set really hard before further work is carried out. During the time the major components are setting attention can be given to making the various sub-assemblies that will be needed.

Wheels are likely to present the biggest obstacle to the solid modeller as a wood-working lathe is vital if these are to be made accurately from the material the rest of the model is constructed from. The easiest answer is to 'borrow' suitable wheels from a plastic kit or hunt among the odds and ends that have been collected from old models, discarded toys, etc. Wooden dowelling can be obtained from most DIY shops and is available in sizes ranging from 1/16 to one inch or more diameter, this makes an ideal basis for undercarriage legs, wing tanks, bombs, underwing stores or even engine cowlings. Thin gauge piano wire which can be purchased at most model shops is also useful for undercarriage legs as well as aerials, pitot heads, or rigging on large scale biplanes. Ordinary domestic fuse wire has a multitude of uses ranging from recoil springs on cannons to brake pipes and aerials, so there is really no shortage of raw material that can be adapted for use in this and all other types of aircraft modelling.

As every sub-assembly is made it should be stored safely in a small box until it is required, and when the work on making these has been completed attention can once again be turned to the major component which by now should be set really hard. Before carrying out the final work it is wise to check that all the parts have set in the correct positions and carry out any changes if they have not.

Once you are satisfied that all is well, seal all the joins with a thin layer of plastic wood, and during this process use the same material to add wing fairings and blend the fin/rudder assembly into the main fuselage. In cases where the aircraft concerned has very big wing root fairings, such as those on the Spitfire, add these by using suitably shaped blocks or thin plywood curved into the correct shape. This can be achieved by cutting the shape from ply then bending it in steam from a boiling kettle, manipulating it to the shape that is required whilst it is in the steam, then holding it in this position when it is removed from the steam until it sets. This is not as hard as it sounds and experimentation with odd

The F-100C nearest the camera is another of Dick Ward's fine wooden models in the markings of the Thunderbirds aerobatic team. The model in the background is an F-100D made by the author from the Frog/Hasegawa kit and finished with Microscale decals.This is a good example of a solid scale model being made long before the same type of aircraft became available as an injection-moulded kit (photo by John Carter).

pieces will soon give you the feel of the technique.

When all the fairings and filler has been applied and set, the whole model should be sanded with a light grade of glass-paper until a very smooth finish is obtained. Once you are satisfied that the finish is as good as you can possibly make it, the wood grain must be filled. This is vital if balsa has been used as if this is not treated in this way it will absorb any paint which is applied to it. Grain filler can be bought from model shops and is used extensively by the flying model fraternity. However, a suitable alternative which has been used over the years by solid modellers, is a combination of clear dope — again a substance familiar to makers of flying models — and talcum powder. Pour some clear dope into a tin lid or other suitable receptacle, which should not be of the plastic variety, then add talcum powder until you have a fairly stiff but still runny composition. Now paint the whole model with this, allow it to dry hard then sand it down with a light grade glass paper. Apply another coat and repeat the rubbing down process. Repeat this until the model has a finish that is as smooth and hard as glass through which there is no evidence of grain. The model is now ready for painting which can be done with enamel paints as used on plastic kits, or coloured dope. The method of painting wooden models is no different to that for plastic ones and will be dealt

with in a later chapter. The only care that must be taken is with masking, since a very low tack masking tape must be used as it is very easy to remove filler from the wooden surface.

Don't forget to treat all the model's components in the same way as undercarriage doors, weapons, fuel tanks and other parts made from wood, require as much attention before they are painted as does the main structure. All the various sub-assemblies can be added after the main structure has been painted and had markings applied, but these should of course be painted in appropriate colours before they are attached to the model.

In this type of modelling it is almost certain that the cockpit canopy will have to be moulded. This is done by carving the shape in wood then using either a vac-form tool as described in the previous chapter or the male/female moulding technique discussed in the chapter on scratch-building. Once again it might be possible to use a canopy from an existing plastic kit if one of the correct size and shape can be found. In the hey-day of the wooden kit some companies specialised in producing canopies for all types of models from acetate sheet. These are now almost impossible to find, but they are still around as in early 1975 I located a box containing canopies for the Swift, Thunderjet, Cutlass, F-80, Avro 707A, Meteor 8, Javelin, Sabre and Hunter at the back of a shelf in a large

A solid wooden model of a Supermarine Swift FR 5 of No 2 Squadron RAF. The model was made using the principles outlined in the text by Dick Ward (photo by John Carter).

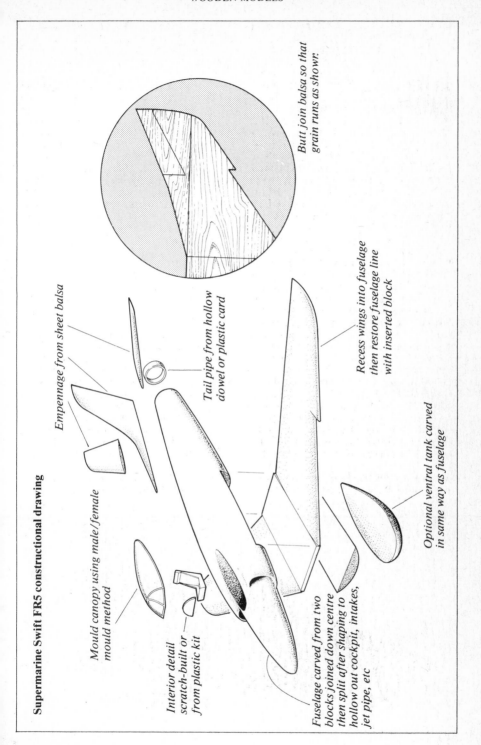

Supermarine Swift FR5 constructional drawing

Empennage from sheet balsa

Butt join balsa so that grain runs as show.

Tail pipe from hollow dowel or plastic card

Recess wings into fuselage then restore fuselage line with inserted block

Mould canopy using male/female mould method

Optional ventral tank carved in same way as fuselage

Interior detail scratch-built or from plastic kit

Fuselage carved from two blocks joined down centre then split after shaping to hollow out cockpit, intakes, jet pipe, etc

Swift FR 5 of 2 Squadron RAF Germany flown by Squadron Leader C. S. MacDonald. This is the aircraft featured in the drawings and shown modelled in wood in the previous photograph (photo via R. L. Ward).

model shop. So it is always worth taking a closer look at the stock in any shop that sells models, for you might also discover some long forgotten product that will give a quick answer to your particular needs.

Making wooden models is a very satisfying facet of the hobby and is one that probably leads to more improvisation and sense of achievement than any other. It is well worth trying at least one model as the experience gained will prove useful when you progress to conversions and scratch-building in plastic card. The plans for the Supermarine Swift will enable you to add this interesting aircraft to your collection by building one in wood or using them as a basis for scratch-building in plastic card.

The Swift was the first swept-wing jet fighter to serve in RAF Fighter Command but is less well-known than its famous contemporary, the Hawker Hunter. Developed from the Attacker and Type 510, it was ordered primarily as a safeguard against failure of the Hawker machine but was issued to only one fighter squadron, No 56, who used the four marks that were manufactured as interceptors. The F1 was powered by a Rolls-Royce Avon RA7 engine, armed with two .30 mm Aden cannons, had no re-heat and a fixed tailplane. It was followed by the F2 which featured a 'cranked' leading edge to its wings, and had its armament doubled to four Aden cannons. The F3 was basically an F2

with re-heat, whilst the final fighter version, the F4, introduced a variable incident tailplane. Throughout its short service career as an interceptor the Swift was dogged by trouble which eventually led to its withdrawal from use in its designed role. One claim to fame is that on September 25 1953 the F4 prototype raised the World Air Speed record to 737.7 mph in the hands of Vicker's test pilot Mike Lithgow. Earlier in the same year the aircraft also captured the London to Paris record in a time of 19 minutes 5 seconds which gave it an average speed of 669.3 mph.

Despite its disappointment as an interceptor, the Swift equipped two squadrons in Germany, Nos 2 and 79, in the fighter reconnaissance role as the FR5 when it replaced the ageing Meteor FR9.

The FR5, which is featured in the drawings, started life as a F4 but was fitted with a lengthened nose in which was accommodated three cameras, as well as increased chord at the tips which gave it a saw-tooth leading edge. The aircraft's already considerable fuel capacity could be increased by the addition of a 220 gallon ventral tank which extended its radius of action.

In the tactical reconnaissance role the Swift enjoyed much more success than it had as a interceptor and proved this by being both the winner and runner-up in the 1957 NATO reconnaissance competitions, a success it repeated two years

Two views of Swift FR 5 XD962 of 2 Squadron RAF Germany at Jever. The squadron leader's pennant and name can be clearly seen on the port side of the nose (photos by Wing Commander C. S. MacDonald, via R. L. Ward).

later when it again won the competition.

A planned unarmed version to be called the FR6 never materialised but a modified version known as the F7, with a longer fuselage and increased span, was produced in small quantities and equipped No 1 Guided Weapon Development Squadron at Valley.

The Swift remained in service until 1961 and was unique in that it was the only re-heat equipped fighter in the RAF until the advent of the Javelin FAW7 and 8. Although the Swift has been consigned to semi-obscurity by the Hunter, it will retain a place in the history of the RAF and is therefore worthy of consideration for inclusion in collections depicting the history of RAF aircraft. At the time of writing it has been ignored by

the plastic kit manufacturers, although the American company Hawk, did release a 1:72 scale model of the F4 some years·ago. This model is inaccurate in many respects but its age must be considered before condemning it out of hand, and if you feel that you do not want to tackle a wooden Swift, but want an example in your collection, then the kit — if you can manage to locate one — can be turned into a presentable example. But before fighting shy of tackling a wooden model, remember that there is little to be lost if your efforts are a failure, but a lot to be gained if they are not. So take the plunge and have a go, you may well surprise yourself, and the sense of achievement if you do is one of the joys of model making.

four

Plastic models

It is not unrealistic to claim that the plastic kit is probably the single biggest factor in the growth of model making during the last two and a half decades. Its pre-shaped components enable even the least skilled to produce a presentable replica of their favourite full-size subject, be it aircraft, ship, car or tank. Naturally, during the war years solid scale modelling was a popular pastime and many of today's well-known modellers cut their teeth on the wooden kits that were available during that period. The return of peace brought a decline as other activities that had been restricted by wartime economies were revitalised. Manufacturers of solid scale kits found it harder to sell their products and by the early 1950s only Veron remained as a major producer of this type of kit, but they were soon to put up the shutters — as far as solid scale models were concerned — and leave the field clear for what one can term the new generation of modellers and their plastic kits.

In the USA Hawk, Revell, Aurora and Lindberg were among the first to use polystyrene to produce model aircraft kits, and in 1953 Airfix in England followed their first plastic kit, which was a Massey-Ferguson tractor, with a plastic kit of the Spitfire. Prior to this Frog had tried to re-introduce their pre-war Penguin kits which were really the forerunner of the plastic kit as we know it, but they met with little success, although they were not too long in rejoining the field with the new materials favoured by their competitors.

It is doubtful if anyone in those early days envisaged the extent to which the production of plastic models was to escalate. The feelings that had greeted the first wooden kits as being a method to short-cut the carving from square one of a solid block of wood, were repeated when plastics first appeared. Modellers who had initially scorned wooden kits, but then happily accepted them, looked upon the newcomers as a form of cheating. A cheap way to make models that required no skill and was strictly for junior, and had no place within serious modelling circles. But gradually these modellers saw in the plastic kit a means to an end whereby the kit could be used as the provider of raw material from which accurate and acceptable models could be produced.

The 1950s can be regarded as the prelude to what was to follow, and from a small trickle has grown a flood which has now washed away the doubts that existed. Those who still have early kits can readily appreciate the enormous steps that have been taken, not only in

Examples of the type of detail which can be observed at air shows can be seen in this and the following photos. This is a close-up of a Westland Wessex helicopter showing fine detail, stencilling and other material which can be used by the dedicated enthusiast.

Canberra TT18. This type of detail picture can be easily obtained at most air displays with even a modest camera. Particularly noteworthy here is the gap beneath the tailplane which many modellers would be tempted to fill in on a kit.

production techniques and overall quality, but also in the care that is now taken in providing authenticity, the number of components, choice of subject matter and not least of all, assembly instructions and transfers. Parallel to the growth of the plastic kit, there has also mushroomed an industry geared to supply the model maker with tools, vast ranges of paints, accessories, conversion components, and many alternative sheets of markings for completed models. Whereas in the early days the modeller was virtually on his own when it came to changing a commercial kit to another version of the basic aircraft, or using paints that were designed for wooden models or toys, he is now able to buy separate parts that, for example, will enable a kit of a single seat Hunter F1 to be converted to a two-seat T7, and authentic quick drying enamel paints designed specifically for use with plastic kits.

Despite all these advances and the ready availability of paints, markings, and other accessories, there still remains the fundamental skill of the modeller concerned in putting together all the available ingredients in turning what is basically a toy into a beautiful scale model.

Many readers will not readily agree that present day injection-moulded kits are toys, but I believe that it is important

to get one's perspectives in the right order so that kits can be looked at in their true colours. Modellers can be divided into several categories; at the top of the tree are those who are experts and use plastic kits as a means to furthering their hobby but would be equally at home with any other medium. There are then those who will spend many happy hours building kits, adding improvements and painting them in authentic colours, as they see in the plastic kit a means to produce a collection of models that they might otherwise not be capable of producing. We then have the person who makes the kit straight from the box and is happy to do so. This type of modeller will, probably, graduate to the next higher level in time, but if he does not, will still obtain a great deal of enjoyment from the way he chooses to model. At the bottom end of the scale are the very young who buy a model and a tube of glue, put the two together as quickly as possible, use the result as a plaything, and within a very short space of time are back at the retailers ready to repeat the process.

Although the second and third categories are a considerable force and the main supporters of the accessory manufacturers, it is the latter type of market at which most manufacturers aim their sights. With this in mind their object is to produce models that have appeal to the young, but at the same time are accurate enough to be bought by the more serious collector. This fact must be kept in mind when kits in general are looked at. The cost of modern injection moulding equipment, not to mention the master tools from which the kit is produced, runs into many hundreds of thousands of pounds, and if the manufacturer is to stay in business he must recover his costs as well as make a profit as quickly as possible.

Modern tooling techniques enable even the most complex shapes to be produced, but there are many occasions when manufacturers take a short cut, producing a part that looks correct on the completed model but is not 100 per cent as it should be when compared with the original prototype. This helps to keep costs down and in many cases is of little importance as far as the completed model is concerned. After all, the aim is to produce a kit that will sell in many hundreds of thousands at a reasonable price rather than a perfect one that will sell at £10 a time to a few hundred enthusiasts.

The many thousands of kits that are sold to what is generally known as the 'schoolboy market' enable the general quality to be kept at a high standard, as will be quickly appreciated by comparison of models available now with those of just five years ago, but it is very unlikely that the true enthusiast will ever be able to buy what he considers to be the perfect kit, although he is now much more often satisfied than he was during the early days of the plastic kit. Facts such as these must be kept in mind when reading review comments that appear in modelling magazines. Unfortunately

Below A useful reference photo of a Saab Viggen showing underwing stores as well as the unusual camouflage pattern (photo by John Carter). *Bottom A T-28 with flaps drooped and engine cowling panels open. This type of picture is always useful for reference purposes, especially if an unusual colour scheme is wanted* (photo by John Carpenter).

A Chipmunk with its engine cowlings open, a modification that could enhance the Airfix kit of this popular subject (photo by John Carpenter).

some reviewers tend to go well outside their brief in an attempt to air their knowledge, with the result that they make comments that most will readily appreciate are beyond the economic control of the manufacturer of the particular kit concerned. This does not mean that there is any excuse for a kit of an aircraft that is well documented to be produced with glaring errors of shape and overall size, but to condemn a model because the camber on the underside of the wings, or the wing-tip washout is not present, reflects a total lack of appreciation of what the manufacturer is aiming to do.

It follows therefore, that even before starting to build a standard stock kit, the modeller who takes his hobby seriously should endeavour to carry out some basic research into the subject himself and decide exactly what his intentions are as far as the project on hand at the time is concerned.

The multitude of aviation books and magazines now available will enable even the most impecunious modeller to collect some form of reference library related to the subject in which his own particular interest lays. An inexpensive scrap book with pages devoted to individual aircraft, campaigns, aircraft that fought in campaigns, or aircraft of a similar type, is probably the cheapest way to start a reference library of one's own. If you subscribe to one or two magazines and do not want to damage them by cutting out pictures or removing pages, an exercise book with a simple alphabetical index in which is noted important points

from magazines showing the edition by date and the page on which the reference appears, will enable quick location of the point noted at a future date. It is as well to start this as soon as you decide that the hobby is to be taken seriously, for if you leave it too long, you will be faced with the daunting task of cataloguing information from a considerable stack of accumulated back issues. Visits to air displays and museums is time well spent as it is possible to note a considerable amount of useful information both in relation to a particular aircraft as well as generally, in nothing more elaborate than a pocket note book. Of course photographs are always useful, and the cost of even a small box-type camera will be repaid many times over. It is not necessary to have a super expensive piece of photographic equipment to take useful pictures, providing you remember to use what you have within its capabilities. Accurate drawings are essential especially when it comes to improving or converting kits, and those published in magazines such as *Scale Modeller, Aviation News, Koku Fan* and *Scale Models* are well worth collecting.

Most towns have free public libraries and invariably these have a reference library within the building they are housed in. Sources such as these are too frequently overlooked by modellers, but they can provide books on every published subject and the librarian will always be pleased to obtain any copies that might not be in your particular library's collection. The usual fee is nor-

Open cockpits and drooped flaps help to add interest to a model and photographs such as this form a useful guide when it comes to carrying out this type of work (photo by John Carpenter).

mally the postage required to obtain the book, and for this modest sum even the most expensive aviation publications can be yours for several weeks. In the event of you not being allowed to remove the book from the library, the ever faithful notebook and pencil is all that you need to acquire the information you need. A sheet of tracing paper can be used to copy drawings published in such works, but be very careful not to damage the book in any way, and as a matter of courtesy let the librarian in charge know what you are doing. To the casual observer it

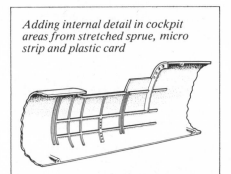

Adding internal detail in cockpit areas from stretched sprue, micro strip and plastic card

Stretching sprue by heating in flame from candle then gently pulling away from centre

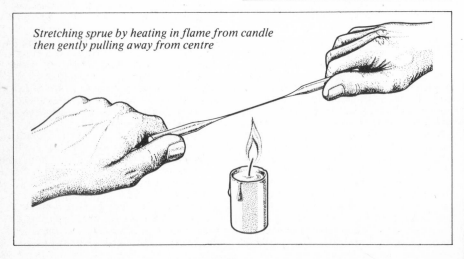

Interior detail such as this on the Monogram 1:48 scale B-17G is now commonplace in modern kits. But it can still be improved by the fastidious modeller and used as a guide to adding such refinements to older kits which do not include such detailing.

may appear that you are writing on pages when all that you are engaged upon is tracing details you want, so if you have made this point clear from the start, embarrassment can be avoided.

Information you have collected in respect of the model you are going to make should be studied alongside the kit components, always keeping in mind whether or not the aircraft featured in the kit is the exact version referred to by most of your material, and if it is not, the changes that have been made. Say for example you have chosen to model aircraft of the Luftwaffe and the kit you have just purchased is the Revell 1:32 scale version of the Messerschmitt Me 109 'G' variant. As good a starting point as any is the book by William Green titled *Aircraft of the Third Reich*, the section on aircraft made by Messerschmitt will quickly reveal that there are many variants of the 'G' so ascertain which one is claimed to be depicted by the kit and compare it with the many photographs and drawings that abound in this book. Once you have decided if the kit is generally accurate as far as external detail is concerned it is a simple matter to check the kit dimensions against those published for the full-size aircraft. If there are any glaring errors in this respect, now is the time to decide how you are going to put them right, and start planning in your mind the work

needed and at which stage of the construction it will be carried out. On a large scale aircraft such as the example quoted a component that comes out one foot too short will need rectifying as in 1:32 scale this will be ⅜ inch, but the same error in a 1:72 scale model will be something less than 3/16 inch. This is still noticeable in this scale but not so glaring as it is in the larger model, and harder to rectify. If you are a perfectionist then you will put it right despite the fact that you will probably be the only one who will know you have done so, but if you are realistic and prefer to spend a little more time in general finishing then you will not bother. Once again we return to the point that any form of modelling is largely a matter of personal choice, and only the individual concerned can make a decision relating to his modelling.

Correcting dimensional errors of this type is not too difficult providing they are confined to major parts such as the fuselage, wings and tailplanes, but they can lead to the necessity of carrying out other work, so everything must first be considered before a decision as to whether or not to do them is taken.

It is comparatively easy to detect any dimensional errors in the wings and fuselage providing comparison is made against accurate scale drawings, but the difficulty is deciding exactly where the error has occurred. If the model measures out a scale foot it is not just a matter of adding a piece of plastic card to correct this, but finding out exactly where the addition must be inserted. Say for example the additional foot is added by cutting off the tail, inserting a spacer, then refixing the tail, although the overall length will now be correct the length from the wing trailing edge to the rear of the fuselage might measure out incorrectly. If the Airfix 1:72 scale kit of the Messerschmitt Me 109G-6 is used as a practical example it will be found that the model is 3/32 inch too short in fuselage length. The error in the kit has occurred just forward of the windscreen so a plastic card spacer has to be inserted at this point. This has the effect of lengthening the nose but it also means additional changes have to be carried out at the wing roots as the cuts in the fuselage will pass right through these. So it immediately becomes evident that a lot of work is needed if this model is to be put right. It can be argued therefore, that in many ways it is best to accept such a small error rather than attempt to correct it in the wrong place, for after all, if plastic card is added near the tail, the length scales out correctly, but the aircraft will look entirely incorrect as the tail section will be far too long. Such an error is more easily detectable than the slightly incorrect and shortened nose which will probably go unnoticed if the model is built as it comes in the kit.

The same rule applies to the wings, as insertion of correction pieces in the wrong places can easily change the leading and trailing edge taper resulting in a model that again might be accurate dimensionally but inaccurate in shape. The only way to discover where changes should be made is to compare each part against the drawing, gradually eliminating those that match exactly, then taking a closer look at those that don't.

This basic research must be carried out before the main construction work starts when there is still time to decide if the efforts involved are possible and will improve the model. It is wise to keep in mind that there are very few people who can look at a completed model and immediately detect dimensional inaccuracies, unless of course, these are so glaring that the appearance of the model suffers, in which case it is doubtful if a serious modeller will even have bothered to consider the original kit as worthy of his attention.

Having decided just how much attention you are prepared to give to the model as far as overall appearance is concerned, further thought must now be put towards any interior details that are to be included, as much of these will need to be made before the main kit components are put together.

Most of the new additions to existing ranges of plastic kits contain a considerable amount of interior detail, this is especially noticeable on kits in the 1:48, 1:32 and 1:24 scales. But in the smaller scales, notably 1:72, although such detail is included it is often very rudimentary and can be improved with little effort.

The area that will need most work carried out on it is the cockpit as nothing looks worse than a well made and painted model which, on close examination, has nothing but a simple seat and plain floor under the canopy.

Photographs and drawings of the interior of aircraft are not hard to find, and any will serve to give the modeller a basic idea of what an aeroplane's cockpit looks like. In cases where parts are provided in the kit these can be used as a foundation on which to build or patterns from which new components can be produced from plastic card.

The first step is to add some of the interior structure of the aircraft where it is not covered by equipment and instrumentation. Stretched sprue is ideal as a medium for making internal fuselage stringers which should be spaced equally around the area that can be seen. It is essential that reference material covering the model being made is consulted as the structure that is being simulated is not always the same on every type of aircraft. In 1:72 scale just the suggestion of internal bracing and frameworks is sufficient but as the scale gets bigger additions such as those mentioned must be as accurate as the rest of the model. It is a good idea to study kits that have such interior detail, and two that were released in 1975 provide just the information that is being sought. These are the 1:48 scale kits of the B17G by Monogram and the Tamiya Lancaster B1/111. Both these models have the interior structure of the aircraft included in the mouldings and enable a good impression to be obtained of what this should look like if it is being reproduced with stretched sprue, or plastic strip. Some

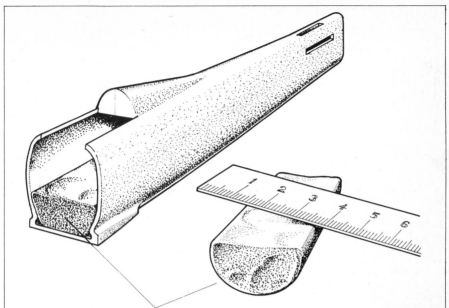

Plasticine block set in fuselage to obtain internal dimensions for making bulkheads, cockpit floors, etc

of the internal stringers that run longitudinally along the airframe are rectangular in cross section, and this can easily be reproduced by cutting strips of thick plastic card then heat stretching them in the same way as is done for sprue. Unlike stretched sprue, which is usually circular in cross-section, such strips of plastic card will be flat and have a rectangular cross-section. It is best to use liquid cement for fixing parts such as these to the interior and the same adhesive should also be used if plastic card bulkheads are fitted.

One of the major problems that modellers seem to encounter when it comes to adding floors and instrument panels, is the accurate measuring of the internal dimensions of the fuselage. If the kit includes a simple floor and panel these can obviously be used as templates, but in cases where such parts are not provided it is all too easy to end up with a floor that is not wide enough to meet both halves when they are joined together. The solution is simplicity itself. Take a block of Plasticine which has been rolled until it is soft, and press it into one fuselage half at the point where the floor is to be located. Make sure that

the amount of Plasticine protruding outside the half is wide enough to fit the total depth of the other half, then press this onto the first component making sure that the join at top and bottom meets. Use a flat spatula, which need be nothing more elaborate than a thickish piece of plastic card, to push the Plasticine across the total fuselage width through the cockpit opening, then carefully separate the two fuselage halves. You will now be left with a block of Plasticine the top of which gives the exact width of the fuselage at the point where it was inserted, and it is now a simple matter to either measure the area or use it as a template from which to cut a plastic card floor, bulkhead, or whatever component you are trying to fabricate. The problem of making instrument panels or bulkheads with sides in which the curves match the exact interior shape of the fuselage can be solved in a similar manner. To do this use a length of soft solder pushed into the interior fuselage curvature then trace the resulting shape on to a piece of plastic card. If the point where the solder protrudes outside the fuselage half is marked the same piece can be used for both the right and left

45

hand sides by simply pressing it into one side, removing it and drawing round the shape, then turning it over, lining up the previously marked point with the equivalent point on the part already drawn, and marking the other half on the plastic card.

Once the cockpit floor has been cut out attention can be turned to the side consols which are built up as three sided boxes along the sides of the floor so that they join the interior fuselage when the cockpit is inserted. When doing this remember that the pilot's seat has to fit in the middle and this will dictate just how detailed the consols can be. This type of cockpit is confined mainly to single or two-seat fighter type aircraft but larger types also have side consols as well as a central pedestal containing the throttles and engine controls. The degree to which such detail can be added depends on the aircraft being modelled and how much will be seen through the cockpit when it is complete. Of course, in aircraft with sliding or hinged canopies, these can be modelled in the open positions, so that the extent of the work you have carried out can be seen. In the case of the two examples previously mentioned, the whole interior is included and can only be improved by the addition of safety harnesses, wiring harnesses and looms of electrical wiring. The B17G has perfectly detailed seats mounted on structures exactly as the real aircraft, the central pedestal and side consols are also provided as are oxygen hoses, radio equipment, bomb sight, navigator's table and the radio equipment. In 1:48 scale such immense detail can be painted very effectively, and when completed the crew positions have an air of true authenticity. With this model and the Lancaster, which is similarly detailed, a lot of the work carried out is lost forever when the fuselage halves are assembled, but at least you have the satisfaction of knowing that it is present and what can be seen through the transparencies will pay testimony to the work done on it. On 1:72 scale models a compromise has to be aimed for, since it is very easy to overdo the detailing with the result that the cockpit will look cluttered and unconvincing.

If the model you are making is the subject of one of the sets of markings available on specialist transfer sheets, such as those produced by Modeldecal and

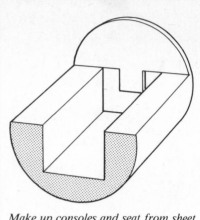

Make up consoles and seat from sheet plastic. Obtain correct widths from Plasticine as illustrated

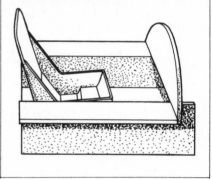

Microscale, a decal for the instrument panel will invariably be included. This should be fitted to the plastic card panel after this has been painted a suitable background colour, then treated to a coat of flat varnish to protect it. Should a decal not be available then the panel will have to be reproduced by an alternative method. Once again the overall size of the model will dictate the best way to do this. One of the simplest methods is to paint the panel matt black or light grey, then with a scriber or pin, mark the instrument outlines and finish by adding switches and warning lights in coloured paint. A more effective panel can be made by using two shapes cut from plastic card, one is painted matt black and the other has holes drilled in it to represent the instruments, this being painted the colour required which will invariably be matt black, dark or light grey. The two are sandwiched together and glued with an epoxy resin, and finished by adding a drop of clear varnish into the holes. If the panel is large enough the matt black interior showing through the drilled holes can be scribed with marks to represent scales and needles before the gloss varnish is dropped in.

Side consols usually consist of removable panels containing switches, lights and instruments, so these should be treated in a similar way if size allows, or simply marked with thin white lines scribed through the painted surface or carefully drawn with a mapping pen and white ink. Throttles, propeller pitch levers, control columns, flap and under-carriage selector levers can all be made from stretched sprue or thin plastic rod with grips and knobs reproduced by using a blob of PVA glue which is then painted. Electrical wiring looms carrying power to the instruments and other cockpit equipment can often be seen disappearing behind instrument panels, bulkheads and consols. Very thin stretched sprue painted red, yellow and green then bunched together and cemented into position will reproduce such looms most effectively. It is not possible to lay down any hard and fast rules concerning such detail as this varies from aircraft to aircraft, so the only way to find out what a typical cockpit is like is to take every opportunity that presents itself to examine either full size

Typical instrument panel detail, in this case of a Scottish Aviation Bulldog T1 of the RAF with no navigation radios (photo courtesy Scottish Aviation via Paul Beaver).

aircraft or photographs. Information can be obtained from the least expected sources, coloured advertisements for RAF aircrew and apprentice recruiting will often yield useful details as will many a film or television programme, so always be on the lookout whatever you are reading or watching.

One of the most neglected components in commercial kits is the pilot's seat. Most kits have now progressed past the stage of a simple 'L' shaped piece of plastic to something that looks more like an aircraft's seat, but there is still a long way to go which leaves the field wide open for the detail enthusiast. In large scale kits these components are often lacking in the detail that is included in other similar parts, but as the scale of the model increases so too does the standard of seat provided.

Perhaps the most noticeable omission in any scale is the complete absence of a realistic safety harness. Some kits include this vital component moulded into the seat back and pan, but this is a far from satisfactory method and is best removed by carving it away with a modelling knife and restoring the seat finish with wet and dry paper. The basic seat should be improved before a replacement harness is fitted and this is easily done by either completely scratch-building a new one on 1:72 scale models, to adding sides, arm rests, adjustment levers, armoured head rests and the like on larger scales. In some 1:72 scale models the seat provided can be greatly improved by carrying out similar work

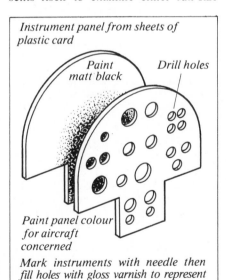

Instrument panel from sheets of plastic card

Paint matt black

Drill holes

Paint panel colour for aircraft concerned

Mark instruments with needle then fill holes with gloss varnish to represent glass

on the kit component and this especially applies in the case of ejector seats. This type of seat is a most complex piece of equipment and has much more ancillary equipment attached to it than the conventional bucket seat. One important part that must be added is the handle used to actuate the ejection gun. On the British built Martin-Baker seat this usually appears as a yellow and black striped handle above the pilot's head and duplicated between his legs. Fuse wire inserted into small holes, held in place with epoxy glue and painted is the best way to reproduce these firing handles, and the same material can be used for the hoses and leads that are to be seen around such seats. Research is important as the ejector seat has been developed over a number of years and latest models look very different from those fitted to early jets. The firing handle mentioned does not appear in the form described on the latest seats such as those used on the Harrier, and American seats are a lot different in design to British ones. So this is yet another area where individual research is essential as space is just not available here to go into the intricacies of every type of ejector seat.

When you are happy that the detail you have added to the seat has turned it

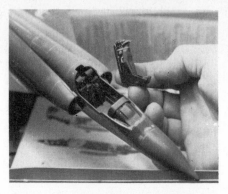

A finely painted ejector seat with additional detail added for the Revell 1:32 scale Mirage kit. Model by A. Taylor.

into a replica rather than just a suggestion of a seat, the safety harness can be added. On 1:24 scale models this can be made from material such as thin linen which is first cut to the lengths required then soaked in polystyrene cement. Buckles and adjusting clips are made from fuse wire and fitted in the correct positions after the linen has been painted in the appropriate colour. This will vary from aircraft to aircraft and period to period. The Sutton harness fitted to most

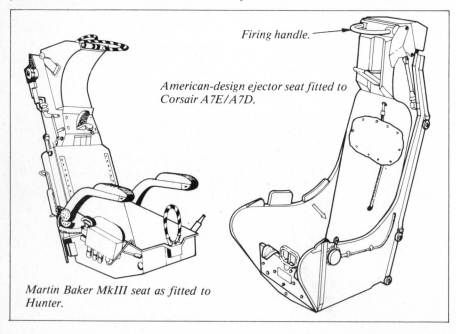

Firing handle.

American-design ejector seat fitted to Corsair A7E/A7D.

Martin Baker MkIII seat as fitted to Hunter.

Extra detail in the form of a map on the navigator's table can add a further dimension of interest. In this case the map came from a small pocket diary, but it would be a simple matter to paint such a map on a small piece of paper.

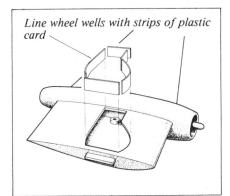

Line wheel wells with strips of plastic card

World War 2 British aircraft was a tan colour, whilst those fitted to American machines were often olive drab or black. On modern aircraft the harness is usually black or very dark grey, with various shades of green also being thrown in for good measure. On smaller aircraft thin strips of masking tape or cartridge paper painted and marked with indian ink for the stitching, and silver paint for buckles, will be adequate. Try to get a natural look by arranging the straps in a careless manner as though the pilot has unbuckled the harness and allowed it to fall back into the seat as he vacated it. If the canopy is open it is a good idea to allow the shoulder straps to hang over the cockpit sill. If you are one of those modellers who likes to include the pilot figure in the completed cockpit, it goes without saying that the straps must be long enough to pass over his shoulders and legs and join around the area of his midriff.

The amount of detail added to the cockpit is governed not only by the scale of the model concerned but also the general overall appearance. A cockpit that is over-detailed and looks cluttered is as bad as one that has no detail added to it. There is no way to describe just how far it is prudent to go but after a few attempts it becomes surprisingly easy to

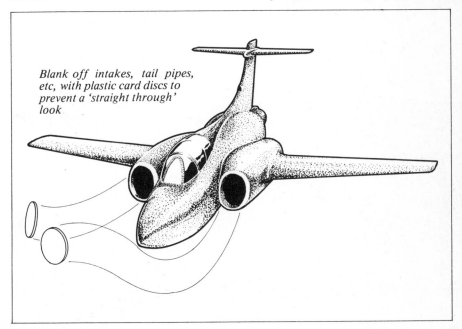

Blank off intakes, tail pipes, etc, with plastic card discs to prevent a 'straight through' look

achieve the right amount of authenticity, so the answer is to practice and experiment until you are satisfied. Other interior detail that can be seen should not be neglected since a model with a super detailed cockpit but having simple 'holes' under the gun turrets would look quite ridiculous. In this respect scale is very much a limiting factor, but a look at the Monogram B17 or the Tamiya Lancaster will show just what should be aimed for. The B17 has a tremendous amount of interior detail within the nose section, with such items as the bombsight, navigator's table, and machinegun butts being readily visible through the clear nose transparency. The addition of oxygen hoses, ammunition belts, or even a map together with instruments on the navigator's table, will all add to the scene the sort of authenticity one would see if a real B17 could be examined at close quarters. Copying of such detail for smaller scale models will enhance their appearance just as much and a good exercise is to build the Airfix or Revell B17 in 1:72 scale adding scratch-built components based on those supplied in the larger kit. When carrying out the addition of such interior detail it is easy to be carried away, and the fact that two fuselage halves eventually have to be put together must not be overlooked, so before every step make sure that any floors or bulkheads that are

added are the correct width and height and will not need major attention when it comes to final assembly.

It is not only the crew's working areas that need detail attention for there are many other parts that will benefit from similar attention. A very good example of such areas are wheel wells. Recent trends in kits have been towards adding etched detail within wheel wells which can look very authentic if it is treated properly. But there are many older kits which the serious modeller will want to make, in which the wheel well is nothing more elaborate than a shaped hole in the wing or fuselage undersurface.

Try a dry assembly run first to find out if it is possible to look straight through the wells into adjacent components or, worse still, right through into the cockpit or daylight through the opposite half. If this is possible the first essential is to provide the well with a 'wall' all round its periphery. This is done by using strips of plastic card, or the same material to make a recessed bulkhead, in some cases both will be necessary. Where the aircraft concerned has a tricycle or nose wheel type undercarriage a simple box made from plastic card can be manufactured in a few moments and inserted into the area where the wheel retracts. A pattern for this can be obtained from the Airfix Phantom or Hasegawa P2V-7 Neptune, both of which have such a part

One of the basic errors. This Frog Buccaneer has a completely hollow fuselage which allows daylight to be seen right through it. The inside should have been filled with cardboard or plastic blanking pieces (photo by John Carter).

The under surfaces of the Revell 1:32 scale Mirage showing additional detail in the wheel wells and air brake areas plus filler in all join lines. Model by A. Taylor.

included in the kit.

Having blocked off the existing wells or made completely new interiors, wiring harnesses, hydraulic lines, reservoirs and the hundred and one other bits and pieces that are to be found in full-sized aircraft's wheel wells can be added. Detailed study of as many aircraft as possible is the best way of finding out what one would expect to find within these areas, so every opportunity should be taken to examine aircraft at air displays and in museums. Photographs will also provide some information so do not confine your reading to just the 'meat' of aviation magazines but also study advertisements for it is here where a great deal can be learned. The same sort of attention can also be given to the insides of dive brakes, and other control surfaces. In many kits these components are provided as separate items and it is often tempting to cement them in the closed positions. But if you look at photographs of aircraft on the ground, you will see that in very few cases are all the separate pieces provided in a kit, always in the closed positions.

Once you have made the interior detail

and prepared all the scratch-built parts that are to be included inside the fuselage and wings, the basic kit components can be put together. Some of the items mentioned will not be added until the basic structure has been completed, so it is as well before even making any sort of start on a new model, to study every part and formulate a plan of how you propose to tackle the additional detail that you wish to add. By doing this it is most unlikely that you will end up having forgotten to tackle a part that you had every intention of adding, then finding that it is impossible to do so.

However experienced you are, time spent in reading the assembly instructions and familiarising yourself with all the components, is time well spent. The complexity of modern kits is such that it is vital to put together some parts in the order specified by the manufacturer, there is always a reason behind the suggested assembly sequence and it is disastrous and disappointing to get halfway through a model only to find that a vital component has been omitted and there is now no way of inserting it. In many cases the instructions are over-simplified

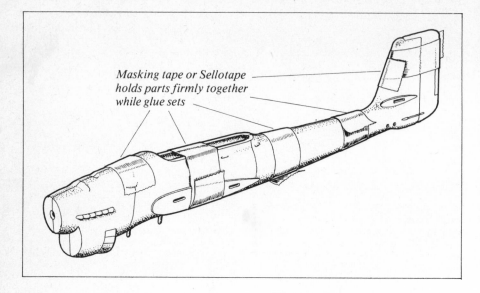

Masking tape or Sellotape holds parts firmly together while glue sets

as they are written to cater for modellers of all ages, there are also steps described in which parts are added without thought given to how they will be painted, as generally speaking the object is to get the model put together before final painting is carried out. Experience will show that small parts such as aerials, guns, pitot heads, underwing weapons and the like, are best left until after assembly of the major components, irrespective of the sequence laid down by the person who wrote the kit instructions. Most modellers will soon find an order of work that suits them and learn to adapt it to any situation, study of the parts and instructions will help to formulate such adaptasituation. Study of the parts and instrucarisen.

The subject of basic kit assembly has been dealt with so many times in other books that there is little point in repeating it again in detail, but it is always wise to reconsider the major points even if they only serve as reminders.

Polystyrene cement is a solvent and should be used with this fact very much in mind, it should not be allowed to get on to outer surfaces of the kit, but if it does it must not be regarded as a major catastrophe. On large components such as the fuselage halves of the B17 or 1:24 scale Harrier, cement must be applied quickly to the areas that are to be joined and this will invariably result in some seepage when the two parts are put together. Under no circumstances attempt to wipe this seepage off the outer surfaces, simply ignore it, tape the two halves together with masking or Sellotape, and leave them well alone until the cement goes hard. There are some modellers who deliberately allow cement to overflow along joint lines as they argue that this will be removed when the joint is sanded smooth and in any case gives a stronger adhesion between the components. Personally I do not go along with this philosophy, but would be the last to say that it is wrong. If you find that this or another method suits you and gives satisfactory results then by all means carry on using it. Any cement that manages to get itself on to surfaces well away from join lines, must be allowed to set hard and then be removed with a sharp knife and the surface restored with careful use of wet and dry paper. Always make sure that the tube of cement you are using is provided with an adequate seal in the nozzle, a type of dress-making pin or mapping pin with a 'beaded' head is ideal as it will effectively stop any cement leaking from the nozzle. Make sure that the sealing pin is always replaced after each application as it is so easy to forget this, put the tube on the work bench, then accidentally lean on it and squeeze cement on to the work surface. When this happens it always seems inevitable that a kit component is underneath the tube and becomes covered in

52

cement, or a part is put down on the resulting puddle of cement. Excess amounts of polystyrene cement resulting from such accidents often cause damage that it is impossible to correct, so it is wise to be safe instead of sorry. The destructive qualities of polystyrene cement must also be considered when it comes to using it for cementing canopies in position or weights within the nose to keep the nose wheel on the ground. It is very easy to insert lead weights then surround them with cement only to find that, (a) it will not stick the weights to the plastic and (b) the volume used has pulled in the fuselage leaving a large 'dent' on the outer skin. Some time ago an accomplished modeller related in a magazine article how he had used this type of cement together with a commercial body putty to hold weights in the

nose of a large scale airliner, and found to his horror that the combination had caved in the complete fuselage where the weights were located. The fact that he was bold enough to relate his error indicates just how easy it is for even the most experienced to make an elementary mistake. The best method of locating weights is the use of Plasticine, which also adds to the weight, or a glue such as PVA white glue or Uhu. The same adhesives can be used for transparencies, but more about this later.

Liquid cement, of which the most effective is marketed under the brand name Mek-Pak, is not nearly as destructive as the tube variety, but it is still a solvent and must be treated with respect. This type of cement is ideal for use with vac-form models and smaller parts on injection-moulded kits. It is best applied

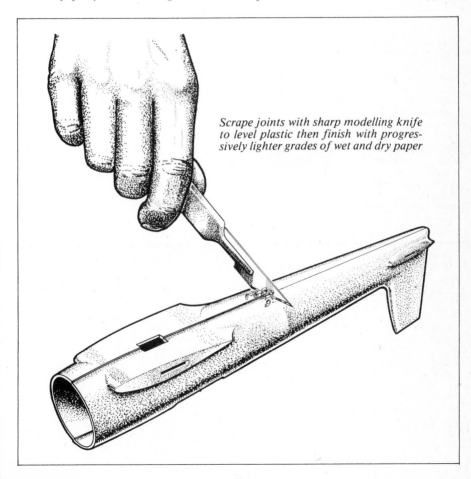

Scrape joints with sharp modelling knife to level plastic then finish with progressively lighter grades of wet and dry paper

with a small brush and the technique is to put the two parts you are joining together then apply the cement with the brush to the area that is to be joined. On fuselage and wing joints the parts should be taped together and the cement allowed to run along the line by capillary action, the areas where the tape prevents ingress of the cement being attended to after the tape has been removed. Liquid cement tends to dry very much more quickly than tube cement and it is therefore imperative that work is carried out quickly if it is used in joining major components. In many respects it is best to use tube cement on kits for the major parts and confine the liquid variety to the addition of small parts such as aerials, pitot heads, undercarriage doors and similar components.

Wing and tailplane parts are cemented together in exactly the same way as the fuselage halves with the components being held under pressure by tape or ordinary domestic spring pegs adapted for the purpose. Before cementing these parts together check the thickness of the trailing edges as these are often over scale as a result of moulding limitations. Should this be the case, reduce the thickness by sanding the *inside* edges with wet and dry by pinning a sheet of this type of abrasive paper to a flat surface and rubbing the kit part across it, making sure that the total area that is being reduced is kept in constant touch with the wet and dry paper. During this operation make constant checks to ensure that too much is not removed, and try to treat each mating component to the same amount of attention, this will ensure that the thinner trailing edge is symmetrical on both surfaces. Similar attention must also be paid to the fin/rudder, and if this is moulded as an integral part of one or both fuselage halves, this must be done before the two fuselage halves are joined together.

Once all the major parts are joined together and the cement has set hard, work can start on removing any excess cement and all signs of seams where joins have been made. There are many ways that this can be done but the one I prefer is the use of a modelling knife in which the blade has become too blunt for cutting duty, but is still sharp enough for use as a scraper. Make sure that the part being treated is held firmly and scrape the knife along the seam, this will shave

An Airfix kit of the Gladiator. This kit was one of the first released by this company and is extremely crude by modern standards. This model was improved by removing all moulded fuselage detail then rescribing it; deleting the poor kit engine and replacing it with one from a Blenheim kit. The cockpit is fully detailed and the pilot's entry hatch opened. Model by Chuck King.

off a certain amount of plastic and in so doing reduce any irregularities between the parts that have been joined. Tackle this work carefully and make sure that at no time is the knife used in a cutting action or the blade is allowed to 'dig' into the plastic. One of the interesting properties of the plastic used in model kits is that it tends to change colour as it is shaved, as both parts are reduced to a common level a distinct line will appear and when this happens, the knife/scraper will have completed its task. Now turn to a fairly fine grade of wet and dry paper and use it to sand the area on which you have been working. As the surface becomes smooth change to a finer grade of paper and use it in conjunction with a lot of water to add the final finish. When satisfied that the seam line has disappeared restore the surface by polishing with metal polish. The best for this is the liquid type which is most effective if it is first poured on to a soft cloth and allowed to stand for several hours. This will allow the liquid to evaporate leaving the cloth impregnated with a very mild abrasive powder, this is applied to the model then polished off with a very soft clean cloth.

All the operations described will have removed some of the surface detail around the areas that have been worked on. Such detail must now be replaced by re-scribing panel lines unless you decide to remove all such detail from the whole model. There are no hard and fast rules about such detail but it is a subject that can lead to much controversy. Whether or not scribed or raised panel lines and rivets add to the overall authenticity of a model depends a great deal on the scale involved, and the aircraft being constructed.

Most aircraft are flush riveted so the tendency among manufacturers to adorn almost every part with impressions of rivets is quite wrong, and it is best to remove such protrusions. In recent years some kits have appeared with riveting being represented by very small holes, this is an attempt to represent countersunk rivets and is certainly much better than the raised variety, but on modern aircraft where this method is used, the centre of the pop-rivet is filled so that the surface is completely flush. It is very difficult to remove this type of rivet representation or to fill every one, so in kits of this type it is probably better to accept the surfaces as they are, since they will not be nearly so objectionable to the eye as the raised type.

Panel lines are also represented in two main ways; one by a raised line, the other by a scribed or etched line. Of the two the scribed line is much the better if it has been produced correctly. It must be remembered that these lines are meant to represent removable panels or joints in the aircraft's skin, they will therefore be flush to each other and not create a raised ridge where they meet, by the same token there will also not be large gaps. So if such panels are to be reduced in scale so too must the area where they meet, with the rsult that a very finely scribed indentation will be much more realistic than a ridge. In view of this I feel that it is best to remove all raised detail and lightly re-scribe it if the model is large enough. On some kits this type of surface detail is represented by very deeply engraved lines, which if enlarged to full-size, would be equivalent to miniature canals, in such cases the only answer is to use filler to fill such detail to the same level as the rest of the surrounding area. The whole question of surface detail can be resolved by a simple exercise on the next occasion that you visit a museum or air display. Try standing about 72 yards away from an aircraft and note just how much surface detail you can see, then view a model of the same subject at a distance of one yard and compare the two. This simple little test will quickly indicate what should and should not be included. However, once again the question of personal preference will provide the answer, and only the modeller concerned can decide what is right for him.

Before finally committing the main assemblies to the application of cement it is important to put the components together in what is known as a dry run, which will immediately show if all the locating tongues and slots are clear from flash or unwanted protrusions, or need attention from a modelling knife or wet and dry paper so that they fit perfectly. If there are any areas where parts do not mate together properly find out what is preventing them from doing so, then correct this and try another dry run until you are satisfied that the fit is as good as you can make it. Now is the time to apply cement to the slots and tongues of the wings, tailplanes and fuselage parts. Do this carefully and try not to use too much as again seepage might occur and this can be troublesome if it gets on to adjacent surfaces. Before the wings and tailplanes set make sure that they are aligned correctly when the model is viewed from both the front and rear, paying particular attention to any dihedral or anhedral that might be present. Leave the model at least overnight in a place where it is safe from accidental knocks as once the parts have fused together it is difficult to take them apart if the alignment has moved. Whilst the major assembly is setting other components such as wheels, long-range tanks, rockets, and similar underwing stores can be assembled. It is important to give as much attention to these components as it is to the rest of the model, as a fuselage centre-line tank in which the join line is not clean, or rocket with overscale fins, will mar the final appearance of the completed model.

Moulding limitations usually result in such components as wheel doors being far too thick, those provided in the kit can be used as templates from which to make thinner ones from plastic card, and jobs like this can be undertaken during any odd moments that become available whilst major parts cannot be worked on.

When the main part of the model has been assembled and allowed to dry any gaps that are present where wings and tailplanes fit should be filled with body putty. The best tool for this job is a dental probe with a flat end but adequate substitutes are a small screwdriver or the spade-shaped tool from a manicure set whose normal function is to push down cuticles. Squeeze a small portion of filler on to a clean piece of cardboard then insert it into the gap with the probe, gradually working it along the length of the area that is being attended to. Try to get the surface as smooth as possible as this saves a lot of time during the sanding operation that follows. Before going ahead and filling all wing root and tailplane gaps study photographs to make sure that the aircraft concerned does not have landing flaps that create a small gap between their edges and the fuselage, or an all flying tailplane. The latter is usually called a variable incident tailplane and this means that the whole tailplane can be moved in relation to the centre datum line of the aircraft, so there will be the smallest of gaps forward and aft of the point where it hinges to the fuselage or fin/rudder. Points such as this must be carefully watched as they all help to create an air of accuracy when the model has been completed and is placed on display. During these filling operations do not neglect any small indentations on the main surfaces of the kit that may be present as a result of a sink in the mould or where cement has been inadvertently placed and removed in the preliminary cleaning up.

The model has now reached the stage where thought must be given to the addition of the transparencies. Some modellers prefer to omit these until after the painting stage but the danger in doing this is that there is little that can be done if they do not fit as accurately as they should. Obviously they can be placed in position and tested before painting is carried out, and if their fit is poor modified accordingly, but these components are often most delicate and it is best to limit handling of them as much as possible. In view of this my own preference is to fit canopies and windows before painting and then carefully mask them whilst this work is carried out. The assembly of some kits will dictate this action anyway, as in most bomber aircraft turrets and fuselage transparencies will have already been inserted within the fuselage halves during assembly, so if you have over-

come the problem of masking such components why not go the whole way and add all similar parts before thoughts are turned to the paintbrush?

Remove the cockpit cover from its sprue and wash it in lukewarm water to which a dash of washing-up detergent has been added. Try it for fit on the fuselage and if there are any points where it does not seat correctly remove whatever is causing the problem by gentle application of wet and dry paper. Always look for irregularities on the aircraft rather than the canopy but where they are on the latter do not be afraid to remove them in the same way. It often helps to bevel the inside edge of the canopy where it is to join the fuselage by using the point of a very sharp modelling knife in the same shaving action that was used on join lines. Once you are satisfied with the fit of the canopy polish the inside with an abrasive paste; powdered toothpaste is ideal for this but the impreg-

The machine-gun on this Revell 1:28 scale Fokker Dr 1 was made by drilling stretched sprue. The removable cowling enables the fine detailing of the engine to be viewed. Model by Paul Roeder (photo Kunze).

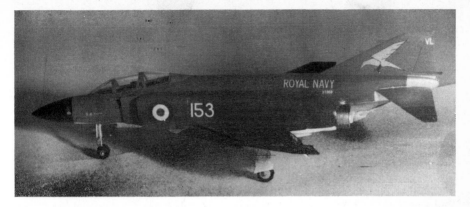

A Frog Phantom with all the heavy rivet detail sanded off and wing leading edge slats extended. The trailing edge control surfaces have also been cut out of the moulded wing and replaced in the lowered position.

nated cloth described earlier will do just as well. Tackle this job thoroughly as once the canopy is cemented in position and the outside has received similar treatment, it will not be possible to correct any blemishes that you missed, and these will prove an eyesore.

Cement the canopy in position using epoxy glue or PVA white glue and allow this to set hard before you attempt any further work. If the aircraft concerned is a fighter that has a sliding rear half to its canopy it is not necessary to merge this into the main structure with filler, but if it is a bomber such as the Lancaster, Halifax, Marauder or any other aircraft where crew entry is through hatches or removable cockpit sections, it is necessary to ensure that the cockpit glazing looks as though it is part of the main structure and not added on as an afterthought.

Fill any gaps with body putty then with a 600 grade wet and dry paper, used dry, sand this until the join between the glazing and the fuselage appears as one. Turn to a lighter grade of paper and continue sanding without worrying about any scratches that you might be inflicting on the transparent part. Once you are satisfied that the cockpit has been made to look as though it is an integral part of the structure, use the finest grade of wet and dry that you can get, and with plenty of water — to carry away the abrasive dust — continue the treatment.

Finish the canopy by wiping it dry with a soft cloth, then polish it with the same abrasive paste that was used on the inside. The result, if the work has been done correctly, will be a crystal clear transparency through which it is possible to see all the interior detail you have added. The final step is to paint the canopy with a clear gloss varnish which will add to the lustre as well as protect it from any further scratching. This attention to transparencies can be a somewhat irksome task but the end result is well worth all the effort that has been expended.

With all seams and gaps filled, the major parts assembled, and the canopies in position the model is now ready for painting, but before this major operation is started there is one more job to do.

During the original moulding a mild form of grease will have been applied to ease removal from the master mould, and also, during the work you have carried out, a certain amount of natural oils from the body will have been transferred to the structure. It is now necessary to remove all traces of this otherwise it can affect the final paint finish. After lightly sanding the whole model with a fine grade of wet and dry paper, wash all surfaces with a lukewarm mixture of water and washing-up liquid, dry the model thoroughly and only handle it in future with a tissue handkerchief between your fingers and the plastic surface.

At this stage the model will begin to look as though it is practically complete, but painting is an art in its own right, and if it is done properly there will still be as much work to be done as you have already carried out.

five

Painting and airbrushing

Patience is one of the biggest assets any modeller can possess, and nowhere is this more important than when it comes to the final stages which involve painting and finishing any type of model. Once the model has reached the stage where the main construction has been completed, it begins to look like the original on which it is based, and the temptation to rush ahead is always present. Such impetuosity must be curbed, as rushed or careless work with the paintbrush can spoil all the careful work that has been carried out. Poor finishing will always mar a well-made model, and similarly, a model on which the construction has been rushed will not be improved by painting however well this may be carried out.

It is important that the best equipment available is used and there is nothing to be gained — except maybe frustration — by making do with inferior brushes and paint. Having spent money on good quality tools a similar investment must be made on paintbrushes, after all these are also tools, and are just as vital to good modelmaking as are quality modelling knives, files and razor saws. Sable brushes, which can be bought in art shops, are very expensive but this expenditure must be viewed in the correct perspective. Cheap brushes in which the bristles are constantly coming out will need frequent replacing, so over a comparatively short space of time the expenditure on them will equal, or exceed, the initial purchase price of a good quality equivalent. The number and size of brushes will depend on the type of modelling and scale that you adopt as your standard, but generally three will be enough. These should comprise a very small size such as 00 for fine detail work; a number 2 or 3 medium size for small areas and a larger size such as a number 6 or 7 for large areas. Three brushes of this type are likely to cost something like £3 or £4 but if looked after properly they will last a very long time.

When you have purchased the brushes wash them in warm water which will remove any loose hairs that might have escaped the manufacturer's quality control department, then smooth the bristles into a fine point and store them vertically in a jam jar or piece of wood in which you have drilled holes, to dry. A good quality number 6 brush can be smoothed into a delicate point that in the hands of an expert will be as capable of painting a fine line as the smallest 000 brush. But this comes with practice so until this skill level is achieved, the use of the three sizes mentioned is recommended. After each painting session clean the brushes with turps or white spirit to remove the paint, then wash them in a brush cleaning fluid, and finally use soap and water to remove all traces of the cleaning fluids used. When this has been done, once again smooth the bristles into a fine point and store the brush in a vertical position. Never simply swill the brush around cleaner of doubtful age, dry it on a rag, then throw it into a box. This is the easiest way of shortening its life, and negates the money spent.

To complement the brushes it is necessary to use good quality paint and nowadays this is available in many ranges at a wide range of prices. Plastic models should always be painted with enamel type paints and it is this type that is marketed in a bewildering number of varieties, most of which have the modeller specifically in mind. Lacquer and 'dope' — as used by those who make flying models — can be used on plastic kits *if* the surface is first prepared with a suitable undercoat, but if painted direct on to the surface they will attack it and cause it to crinkle all over. However, such paints can be used on wooden scale models, and for certain subjects do produce a very good solid finish.

Water soluble paints are becoming popular in modelling circles as is evidenced by the increasing ranges that are being introduced by manufacturers of this type. They are easy to use, give a good finish, and present very few problems with thinning or paintbrush cleaning, both of which are carried out with water. After a period of time most followers of the hobby will find the type that suits them best and stick to this through thick and thin. It is a good idea to approach the subject with a completely open mind and try all types of paint either on completed models, or discarded pieces of models, until you find the one that you like using and which gives you the best results.

Long before you reach the painting and finishing stage you should have already decided on the scheme in which you intend to complete the model concerned. In many cases this will, in fact, have been the very first thing that was decided when the model was started, and the mental picture of how you wanted it to turn out was formed in your mind. With this knowledge foremost in your mind, the colours required obtained, it might seem that the next logical step is to dip the brush into the pot and make a start. But before this there is a vital and necessary step that will only enhance the final paintwork. This is the preparation of the model by applying a neutral colour undercoat, which will serve several purposes. The most important of these is that it will immediately show up any blemishes that were missed during the final cleaning up operations, and allow further work to be carried out with wet and dry or glass paper. It will also show if the grease mentioned in the last chapter has been cleaned off properly, for if the undercoat goes patchy or streaky, it is a good indication that the model was not washed as thoroughly as it should have been. The undercoat will also act as a sealer in areas where body putty has been used, as this material has a habit of absorbing paint and giving a different texture between it and adjacent parts. Finally it gives a key to the top coats and enriches their colours. Matt white or light grey are the best colours to use for undercoating which should be applied in as thin a coat as possible, the best method being the application of two or three coats with a gentle sanding operation between each. But even before the undercoat can be applied attention must be given to masking.

Masking of parts to which you do not wish paint to be applied is carried out at various stages during the painting of the model. The first of these is prior to the application of the undercoat or primer, and is carried out on surfaces that have already been painted during assembly and any transparencies that have been fitted. During the assembly of the model pieces such as the undercarriage legs should be painted while they are still attached to the plastic runners, if they are fitted into the fuselage or engine nacelles during the final assembly operation they must be protected before the final finish is applied to the aircraft. In brush painting it is fairly easy to avoid these components by dexterous use of the paintbrush, but any forgetfulness or slip will put paint of a colour that is not wanted on them, so it is best to mask them completely then painting can be carried out without any further thought being given to such accidents. Similarly, windows, gun turrets, and cockpit canopies must also be protected as it is not easy to remove unwanted paint from these components.

Masking tape which is produced solely for this purpose is by far the best material to use. It is usually a light brown in colour, and is thicker than sticky tape which is often transparent and designed for holding paper together or repairing tears in documents. Proper masking tape has a much lower adhesive level than transparent tape and will not cause any damage to the surfaces it is used on. In some cases even masking tape has too high a sticky factor for modelling but this can be reduced by rubbing its adhesive side between the fingers before it is applied. Another advantage it has over the more familiar transparent tape is that it is far more maleable and will follow complicated shapes much better. There is one form of transparent masking tape marketed under the trade name of Frisk tape, and this should not be confused with the other variety which is generally referred to as Sellotape. This in itself is quite wrong as Sellotape is purely the trade name for a variety of tapes and the company concerned also make a specialised masking tape for painting. But to use the name Sellotape will clear any doubts in the readers' mind as this is the general term by which transparent tapes are known. Frisk masking is sold in rolls of various widths and is used in art studios, it has an extremely low 'tack' quality and is ideal for use in modelling, it is attached to a backing sheet and one of its big advantages — apart from its low 'tack quality — is that very complex patterns and shapes can be drawn on the backing sheet before this is cut out and removed. This tape is ideal for masking such items as undercarriage legs and to do this simply cut a strip the exact length of the leg and wrap it around so that it sticks to itself, forming a trousered protecting shield over the oleo.

For cockpit canopies a form of masking fluid such as Maskol or Micromask is ideal. This is painted on to the surfaces and sets into a solid skin which is simply peeled off when painting has been completed. To ensure that the surfaces are not scratched when attempts are made to remove it, attach a very fine strip of ordinary masking tape or paper to the cockpit and paint the fluid over this, leaving one end exposed. To remove the fluid all that is necessary is a gentle pull on the exposed end.

The method I have found best as far as masking windows and certain canopies is concerned is as follows. Cut very thin strips of masking tape by first attaching a length to a metal surface, a tin lid is ideal, then cut this into strips about ⅛ inch wide with a sharp knife against a steel rule. Peel off a strip and use it to outline the window or lower edge of the canopy making sure that it does not wander on to adjacent surfaces. Cut off any surplus and with the pointed end of a modelling

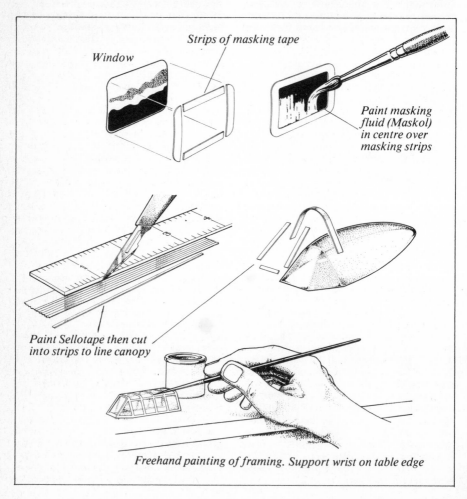

Window

Strips of masking tape

Paint masking fluid (Maskol) in centre over masking strips

Paint Sellotape then cut into strips to line canopy

Freehand painting of framing. Support wrist on table edge

knife or scriber, very carefully push the tape into any corners and the edges where the transparency meets the plastic surrounding area. Once this has been done, the window will appear to have a fine masking tape frame. Now attach another small strip to the centre of the window, leaving the end free, and complete the task by painting masking fluid over the parts of the transparency that are still exposed, making sure that it also covers the edges of the masking tape. By doing this masking fluid is prevented from drying on to areas surrounding the window or canopy and thus stops the annoying situation of finding, when the fluid is removed, that it has also masked small irregular areas around the transparency. Masking fluid can, of course, be used to protect undercarriage legs, gun barrels or even the insides of wheel wells, but this invariably leads to problems when it is removed as it does dry very hard and has a habit of getting into even the smallest crevices from which it is very hard to remove without causing damage.

If the model you are making does not have any internal windows or turrets and you choose to leave the fitting of the canopy until after painting has been done, it is still necessary to mask the exposed cockpit area during the time the model is having paint applied. Do this by using a tissue which should be soaked in water and squeezed dry, then torn into small pieces which can easily be pushed into the hole over which the canopy will fit. The same method is also used for wheel wells and any other holes such as radiators, jet intakes and exhausts. So before applying the undercoat the areas that should be masked are: any canopies or holes that will be covered by them if they are not fitted, wheel wells, radiators, jet pipes, jet intakes and any other areas that will allow the undercoat to get into the internal structure of the model.

The undercoat paint, which should always be matt, must now be mixed well and the whole model painted with it using a number 5 or 6 brush in smooth even strokes which should be in the same direction. When the paint has dried any blemishes that are still apparent must receive attention and a further coat of paint applied if necessary. The model is now ready for its final finish but before rushing into this it is best to leave the

undercoat to set really hard, and a period of at least 24 hours should be allowed for this.

The secret of obtaining a good finish is to use good quality paint that is stirred well and applied as thinly as possible. Start by selecting the lightest colour unless there are any bands or areas of darker colour on the particular model being made. If we assume that the model is of a Luftwaffe fighter with a yellow nose and yellow and red defence of the Reich identifying bands on its tail, the following procedure could be used. Paint the nose and fuselage where the bands are to appear yellow without any regard as to the final demarcation lines of this colour. When the yellow paint has dried mask it completely, making sure that the demarcation lines are straight and all areas that are to stay yellow are well covered. The width of the tail band is scaled off the drawing or reference material you are using, and a strip of masking tape cut to this, is wrapped around the area that is already yellow. Now paint the red over the tape extending it to cover the area that will be a red band. Leave the red to dry then cut another strip of masking tape to the total width of the red/yellow/red band and apply this making sure that all the edges are firmly pressed on to the plastic surface. The light blue undersurfaces can now be applied followed by the two tone green or grey top surfaces. When all painting is complete the tape is removed and the result will be, if the work has been done properly, a perfectly defined yellow nose cowling as well as neat, accurate tail bands. This technique can be applied to any colour scheme, it is just a question of working out first how you propose to tackle the job at hand, the order in which the colours will be applied and accurate masking. As with everything there are exceptions to every rule, so in some cases it will be better to apply darker colours first. A good example of this is if the aircraft has large areas of black such as anti-dazzle panels or wing walks. In such cases paint the black first, mask it to the shapes needed, then apply the overall finish colour.

Every model will require a different approach when it comes to painting, in some cases it is wise to paint components separately before they are assembled but this can only be done if the fit of the parts in the kit is accurate and no

This 1:48 scale Monogram B-17G was built straight from the kit but has been finished to depict a weathered aircraft as it appeared after 52 missions. Weathering has been done with care and can be achieved most convincingly on larger scale models. Some might think that this Fortress is overdone, but it was weathered as per photographic evidence supplied from the United States. It should also be noted that the markings have been weathered, an important point to remember when doing this type of work (photo by John Carter).

filling is needed. The Harrier is a machine that can present problems when it comes to painting the fuselage under the wing joins, so it is best to make sure the wings are an accurate fit, then paint their under surfaces and the fuselage before before they are attached. The F-8 Crusader kit by Fujimi is designed in such a way that the wings slot into the top of the fuselage, so with this model it is particularly easy to paint the whole airframe before the wings are attached without having any worries about gaps or join lines. Biplanes present their own peculiar problems to modellers in many ways, not the least of which is painting. There is really no other way as far as this type of model is concerned than to omit the top wings until the final stages, which enables the top surfaces of the bottom wings and the undersurfaces of the top wings to be painted with ease.

To every problem there is a solution if you care to look for it; if you want to assemble any model completely before

painting is carried out, then you might well find yourself faced with a tremendous masking job that leads to frustration and disappointment. On the other hand you might well solve it very quickly and thus achieve that tremendous feeling of self satisfaction that it is very hard to describe. The only advice that can be given is to try all methods until you find the one that suits you then stick to it.

The secret of success in brush painting is to make sure that the paints are mixed well, are of a thin consistency, applied with a clean brush on to a clean surface. Before even thinking about applying the colours to the model the paint must be thoroughly mixed and this can take some time if it is done properly. A new tin of paint should be thoroughly shaken before the lid is removed as this does help to start the mixing process. A thin flat stick shaped like a canoe paddle then makes an ideal implement for stirring and it takes only a few minutes to cut one from an odd scrap of balsa or

A weathered Me 110D in a winter scheme. The cockpit has been opened to show a fully detailed interior and exhaust stains have been lightly applied over the wing top surfaces. It is important that this type of work is not overdone or the whole effect can easily be spoiled. Model is a combination of Frog and Monogram in 1:72 scale.

plastic card. Under no circumstances use a paintbrush to stir the paint and also avoid disused paintbrush handles as they are entirely the wrong shape and, if they have been sealed with a varnish, there is a distinct possibility of this gradually flaking off and getting into the tin you are stirring.

Most enamel paints will be found to have a thick sediment at the bottom of the tin and this must be stirred into the liquid if the true colour and paint thickness is to result. Once the stirring stick has reduced this sediment into liquid the stirring process can be speeded up by an electric mixer. It is possible to buy for a modest sum a small battery powered mixer used in making cocktails, these usually have a variety of different shaped ends which can be inserted into a simple chuck and such a gadget is ideal for obtaining a good paint mix. Mixers of this type can often be found in junk shops or at jumble sales, in fact the one I use was acquired in this way for 25p! Should you not be able to locate one, it is a simple matter to make a suitable equivalent by fixing a piece of shaped

piano wire to an electric motor of the type that are sometimes included in AFV kits, and connecting the motor leads to a battery. Such types of mixer must be used with caution as they rotate at considerable speed so it is best to stir the paint with a stick first, then pour some into a separate container to reduce the level in the tin, before the electric mixer is used. If this is not done the centrifugal force generated by the mixer will quickly throw the paint out of the tin causing a terrible mess. Always insert the mixer well into the paint before switching it on, and turn it off before removing it from the paint. Once the paint has been stirred and used, replace the lid as firmly as possible, first wiping off any paint that has collected around the lid rim, this will provide an air tight seal and help to prolong the life of the remaining paint.

It is a good idea to occasionally go through all your collection of paints, stir them, reseal them, then stack them back in their container upside down. Jobs such as this can be done when suitable pauses occur during model making and they pay dividends as they keep the paint in a fluid state and make them last much longer. Nothing is more frustrating when it comes to selecting a colour than to find that because the lid was not sealed properly, or the paint has not been used for some time, it has gone solid and is beyond recovery.

The procedure outlined applies equally to water based paints as it does to enamels as these have similar properties as far as their consistency and fluidity is concerned.

The addition of a few drops of thinner often helps when it comes to mixing old paint and the most economical way of buying this is to use White Spirit which can be bought at most chain stores or DIY shops in large cans for a fraction of the price a similar quantity of enamel thinners costs.

It will often be found necessary to mix paints to obtain a specific colour or to lighten or darken existing colours to obtain special effects. This is done by first thoroughly stirring all the paints concerned then taking a brush full from each tin making sure that the brush is cleaned between each colour, and dropping the brush load into a mixing pot. Blend the colours with a clean brush adding more of each one as required with another brush, until the correct colour is achieved. It is possible to buy from art shops proper mixing pots but ideal substitutes are the plastic covers that can be found on aerosol containers containing anything from shaving cream to deodorants. These plastic pots come in many sizes and it does not take very long to accumulate a good quantity, they can be used not only for mixing but also to contain thinners for diluting, brush cleaning and the 101 other tasks that occur during model making. If they are cleaned after each painting or modelling session they will last for a very long time.

Most readers will be familiar with normal brush work so there is little point in repeating this in detail. But it is as well to mention the major aspects that must be kept in mind if a good finish is to be achieved. It goes without saying that the most important requirement is a clean brush which should be kept full during painting. Always apply paint in one direction and try not to overpaint areas that have already been covered. Most paints now used in model making dry very quickly so if you do go over an area

that was painted only minutes before the first coat will already have started to dry and the new paint will tend to pull this resulting in brush marks and an uneven surface. Use the paint as thinly as possible and leave each coat to set hard before the next is applied. Although paint seems to dry quickly it does take some time to set hard and it is essential that it reaches this state before additional coats are painted over it. This is where patience plays a most important part in model making, as the temptation to test surfaces to see if they are ready for the next colour or coat is very hard to resist. To be absolutely sure it is best to leave a painted model for at least 24 hours before attempting any further work; this might seem to be time consuming but the end results will more than pay for itself in the quality of finish achieved.

As modelling is a very individual pastime, the various methods used to obtain the variety of finishes that are needed on aircraft are quite considerable. When it comes to a camouflage scheme there are many ways of obtaining the desired results. If a standard World War 2 scheme for RAF aircraft comprising Dark Earth and Dark Green is considered there are those who recommend that each coloured section is painted only over the surfaces to which it is applied. There is another school of thought which recommends painting the lighter colour, in this case Earth, over the whole of the top surfaces, then lightly marking the Green areas in pencil before applying this colour. Of the two I personally find that the second method is the best apart from the marking in pencil which I feel is not necessary. I prefer to paint the Earth first then paint the Green in the disruptive pattern without the aid of any pencilled guide lines, simply using a normal number 6 brush with a fine point to first mark the demarcation line then carrying on from there.

Whilst on the subject of camouflage patterns one must remember that these are usually painted to a definite plan that was laid down by the authorities of the air force or Government to which the original aircraft belonged. They are not just a variety of disruptive shapes painted at the whim of the person detailed to paint the aircraft concerned. Reference material on such schemes is plentiful and should be studied in detail before a model that requires a camouflage finish is constructed, some of the more readily available material is listed in the appendix at the rear of this book. It is also worth remembering that colours used were and are specified and related to British or Federal standard paint numbers. But what is often overlooked by modellers is that these specified colours can vary, and this is especially true of wartime aircraft. It is one matter to state what colour a particular scheme or aircraft must be painted in, but quite another when it comes to the front line availability of such colours. The effects of service use and exposure to weather should also be considered but matters such as this will be discussed later in this chapter.

One of the hardest tasks confronting modellers is the painting of straight lines, especially those that are needed on cockpit framing. The method described during masking can be used successfully when it comes to painting such items as fuselage cheat lines, invasion markings, or leading edge de-icing boots or identification colours. All that is necessary is to paint the colour required over the area where it is to appear then cover this with strips of masking tape cut accurately to the widths and shapes needed. But cockpit framing presents different problems. On large scale aircraft such as the Lancaster and B17 it is possible to cut small sections of masking tape and cover the whole canopy in the areas where framing does not appear. This can also be done on some 1:72 scale models, but it is an onerous task that can take a very long time and the slightest slip in cutting the masking tape or not pressing it down hard enough will stick out like a sore thumb when it is removed. Alternative methods are the use of a fine brush used freehand, which is not as difficult as it at first sounds, or thin strips painted on to a

The most simple airbrush available, a Badger Model 200. This is fine as an introduction to airbrushing but is limited to overall one-colour finishes as there is no adjustment on the paint and air nozzle (photo courtesy Morris & Ingram).

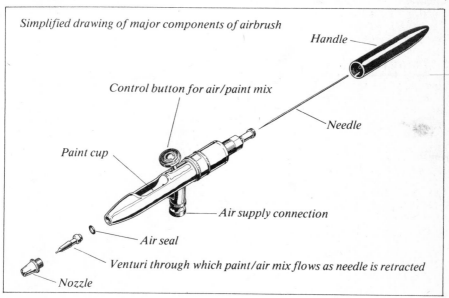

Simplified drawing of major components of airbrush

Handle

Control button for air/paint mix

Needle

Paint cup

Air supply connection

Air seal

Venturi through which paint/air mix flows as needle is retracted

Nozzle

decal sheet then cut out with a steel rule and modelling knife. If the freehand method is used it is essential to have the paint as thin as possible, keep the brush full and finely pointed, and follow the etched lines that are on most canopies. The model must be supported firmly on the work surface and *not* held in the hand, the reason for this is that however hard you try there will always be some movement by the hand holding the model, if the hand wielding the paintbrush also moves then the chances of error in making the line that is being painted straight are doubled. By supporting the model on blocks to keep it in the right position and using masking tape to hold it steady, the chances of success will be greatly increased. Use the edge of the painting surface as a support for the wrist holding the paintbrush, breathe evenly, and apply the paint in steady vertical or horizontal strokes, trying not to complete too much of each frame line each time the brush is applied. Work to a pre-arranged plan, for example on the Lancaster paint all the vertical frames on one side, then the horizontal frame, turn the model round and do the same the other side, then complete the top framing. If the paintbrush should wander outside the frame line, do not attempt to compensate by making the line wider as this will only result in multiplying the error as you progress; leave the area outside the frame line to dry, then with a pointed cocktail stick soaked in thinners, gently remove the unwanted paint. This method requires some practice but a fairly high skill level can be achieved if you concentrate and do not rush.

The other way is to paint the colour you want the framing on to a sheet of white transfer, cut strips into the correct sizes then apply them as you would normal water slide transfers. Transparent tape can also be used in this way but it does add a thickness to the canopy framing and is prone to coming adrift after the model has been completed and displayed. Letraset coloured lines, and Letratape as well as a very thin material called Chartpak can also be used for framing but they can rarely be obtained in the correct colours; where they are particularly useful is on models of modern jet fighters where the canopy sealing is often in white or yellow.

Providing adequate care is taken of paintbrushes, the paint is mixed well and applied carefully, there is no reason why any model should not turn out perfectly, but in recent years more and more modellers have turned to the airbrush as a means of obtaining a really smooth and authentic finish. Some of them have mastered it but others have quickly become disillusioned. There is no mystery about this invaluable piece of equipment but there is no easy way to master it and despite what some may have been led to believe it will only be as good as the person using it. The airbrush is *not* a passport to competition winning models, it will *not* improve a poorly made model nor will it turn a mediocre modeller into an expert overnight. But if used properly it will certainly enable much more authentic finishes to be applied, will widen the scope of finishes that can be

Below *This is a venturi-fed Badger 100 airbrush with a rather cumbersome paint jar behind the nozzle. This is a versatile beginner's airbrush and is capable of fine lining work if used carefully* (photo courtesy Morris & Ingram). **Bottom** *A Badger 100XF. This is a versatile airbrush with a side-mounted paint cup, available in two sizes. The air and paint nozzles can be adjusted to obtain a very fine spray* (photo courtesy Morris & Ingram).

A Badger 160GKF. This is a gravity-fed airbrush similar to the DeVilbiss model also illustrated. The paint cup is permanently mounted to the top of the 'brush. Air and paint flow are controlled by the single-action push button which can be seen behind the paint cup (photo courtesy Morris & Ingram).

obtained, and will also add a completely new dimension to modelling.

From the start it is well to remember that a good airbrush is a precision made piece of equipment, it is therefore a costly item and should be treated as such. Basically it is no more than a very fine spray gun operated by compresssed air; it usually has an adjustable nozzle as well as a finger-tip air control, both of which enable most delicate work to be carried out. Since it reproduces in miniature the exact way in which full-size aircraft are painted it is carrying scale finishes to the ultimate.

For many years American modellers considered the airbrush to be an essential part of their equipment and had a very wide range of types made by a variety of manufacturers from which to choose. It is only during the last five years that British modellers have had the same variety of choice as prior to the introduction of some of the American-manufactured airbrushes, those available in England where extremely expensive and confined to use in art studios and professional model makers.

The two most popular and well-known models currently readily available in England are those manufactured by the Aerograph DeVilbiss Company of England and Badger of America, the latter

being imported by Morris and Ingram (London) Ltd who have been in the paint spraying business for many years. In America there are brushes made by Paasche and Binks as well as Badger. Although all these makes perform basically the same functions there is a marked difference in the design parameters used, with good and bad points — as there are with most things — in all of them.

As my experience has been confined to only the Aerograph DeVilbiss and Badger models, apart from a very short session with a Paasche which worked admirably, my comments must be confined to these two manufacturers.

The main difference between them is that the Aerograph DeVilbiss models have the paint reservoir on the top and are gravity fed, whilst the Badgers use a venturi to suck the paint from its carrier into the spray nozzle.

The most economical model produced by Badger is the 250 which in the truest sense of the word is not really an airbrush at all. When compared with other models the 250 can be considered as no more than a small spray gun but it must not be dismissed as a toy, for although it has its shortcomings, it does enable good one-colour finishes to be achieved and allows the younger modeller to 'cut his teeth' before progressing to more expensive and sophisticated products. The 250 consists of a paint container and a very simple air control; it does not have an adjustable nozzle and the amount of paint being sprayed cannot therefore be controlled as it can with the more expensive brushes. It is a step beyond using aerosol paint sprays since it is possible to mix the paint used to the colour and consistency required. But it must be stressed that it cannot be used to obtain very fine lines or gradual blending of colours that are essential on some finishes.

One fact that must not be overlooked on any account is that the airbrush is a precision instrument and as such is costly to produce, and must be well looked after if it is to maintain peak performance. The engineering of the Aerograph DeVilbiss is absolutely first class and their quality can be appreciated as soon as one is removed from its box. Of course such quality must be paid for, hence this manufacturer's products are more expensive than their Badger counterparts, but once one has been purchased it should, if taken care of, give many years of excellent service.

The major difference between the Aerograph DeVilbiss and the Badger Model 200 series is that in the former both the air and paint flow are controlled by a single push style lever on top of the brush. Push the lever down to allow air to flow, and pull it back to regulate the needle that controls the amount of paint being sprayed. The Badger 200 has two controls, a button on the top to release air and a threaded nut on the end of the handle to adjust the needle, this means that with this model one really must set the width of the spray before commencing work. With practice the needle can be adjusted whilst spraying is being carried out but this has to be done with great care. The Badger model 100XF is very similar in design to the Aerograph DeVilbiss as it has both the air and paint controls incorporated in one lever. The main difference between the 200 and 100XF, apart from the mentioned paint control, is that the 200 carries its paint supply in a glass jar underneath the brush, whereas the 100XF has a paint cup attached to the side. In some operations the jar of the 200 can be troublesome as it tends to restrict the areas into which the brush can be inserted, but similarly the 100XF and Aerograph DeVilbiss — which has the paint container on the top — have to be used with the angle of the container in mind as it is easy to get carried away and tip the paint

A DeVilbiss Super 63 airbrush. This picture clearly shows the large capacity paint cup of this gravity-fed airbrush, which is a unit of the highest quality and superb for modelling. The 'test sheet' in the foreground illustrates the fine control which can be achieved with this type of 'brush, the range varying from small dots through wide to very fine lines (photo by John Carter).

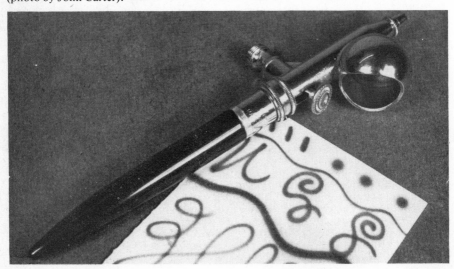

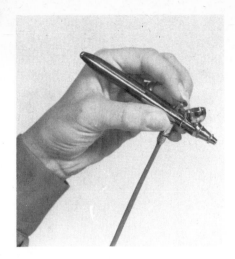

A Badger 160GXF with air hose attached and held ready for spraying. The forefinger presses the button to release air and is then drawn back towards the handle to allow paint into the air stream. This 'brush must be handled with care when in use as it is easy to tip the paint out of the paint cup (photo courtesy Morris & Ingram).

out. The 100XF paint cup is available in two sizes, 1/16 and 1/8 oz capacity, and simply pushes into a hole in the side of the instrument. This makes cleaning very easy and also enables different colours to be interchanged quickly by using two or three different cups that are already primed with the colours that are to be used.

In operation the 100XF, 200 and Aerograph DeVilbiss Super 63 models are all very similar but a lot of practice is needed before they will produce the type of finish most modellers admire, and which is usually the main reason why an airbrush is purchased in the first place. So before any attempt is made to finish a model with airbrush painting it is wise to get to know the feel of the instrument, the paint mixes required and how different effects can be achieved, and there is no better way of doing this than by trying the brush on odd scraps of plastic or even pieces of old models. But before doing this another very important aspect must be considered; this is the form of motive power. Every airbrush requires some form of compressed air to force the paint through the spraying nozzle and this is available in a variety of forms.

The most commonly used propellant is the aerosol container which can be connected direct to the brush via a special adaptor — supplied as part of the basic Badger kits and available as an extra from Aerograph DeVilbiss — or through a similar adaptor fitted with a pressure regulator. Aerosol cans are relatively expensive and can lose their power during prolonged spraying, they also tend to expire at the most inconvenient times without any prior warning. Since air must be sprayed through the instrument during the cleaning operation the can must also be used for this, and it is non-productive as far as painting is concerned. There is no doubt that a proper electric compressor is the most effective form of propellant but since these are expensive, many will cope quite happily with aerosol cans. But before dismissing the electric compressor as an expensive luxury basic economics must be considered, for there can be little doubt that if a lot of modelling is undertaken the saving of the £30-£40 necessary to purchase a compressor is sound common sense; after all, this amount is approximately what will be required to purchase 35 cans of propellant and if each can sprays an average of four models, it does not take a mathematical genius to work out that a compressor which will last for a lifetime is a wise investment. As an alternative to the electric compressor there is available a foot operated compressor. This consists of an air reservoir which is replenished by a car type foot pump attached to it. The reservoir is fitted with a pressure gauge and safety nozzle and all that is required is some leg work to fill the tank up to the required pressure and keep it replenished as the air is used. The foot operated compressor is less expensive than the electric type and is certainly more economical than aerosol cans, it has the added benefit of keeping one's leg muscles in first-class condition!

A final solution is the use of a spare tyre for which a special adaptor enabling the airbrush to be connected to it is available. The adaptor fits on to the tyre valve and gives an inexpensive supply of compressed air. This is really the same principle as the foot-operated compressor as a foot pump is required to replenish the tyre as the pressure falls off. The tyre, which is only acting as a reservoir, must be attached to a wheel, so there are of course problems unless one has a room or shed exclusively devoted to modelling activities. Most wives, mothers and girl friends, are usually prepared to tolerate most things connected with modelling, but when it comes to introducing the spare wheel off the family car into the house, such tolerance is likely to be stretched to the limit.

Whatever form of motive power or airbrush is finally selected the work produced will only be as good as the operator using it can produce, and this in turn will be reflected in the condition in which the equipment is maintained. Airbrushing is not easy and there is little point in adding to one's problems by neglecting the instrument; it must be kept in tip-top condition as this is one of the secrets of getting good results.

After each colour is sprayed, always clean the brush by spraying thinners through it and at the end of a painting session repeat this more thoroughly than ever and end by spraying Polyclens to remove the last vestiges of paint, followed by a further application of thinners to remove the Polyclens.

Never take the airbrush to pieces unless you are absolutely sure of what you are doing. Remember that it is a precision made piece of equipment and great skill has gone into making it. If the needle is removed do this very carefully making sure that the tip is not damaged in any way, and never, never attempt to clean the nozzle by poking any form of wire through it. Any damage to the tip will almost certainly mean the purchase of a replacement, and in some cases, such as the Aerograph DeVilbiss model, this also means a new nozzle as the needle and nozzle are sold as a matched set. Cotton wool ear buds, pipe cleaners and tissues are the best cleaning mediums and even these must be used with care as the slightest piece of cotton wool or tissue entering the brush can cause endless problems when it is next used.

Having become familiar with the operation and maintenance of the instrument thought can now be given to using it to spray a model, but before doing this the basic finish of the model must be carefully looked at.

The airbrush produces such a fine finish that even the slightest blemish or imperfection in the application of filler or general inattention to the model's construction will become very apparent. The cleaning-up of the model and the

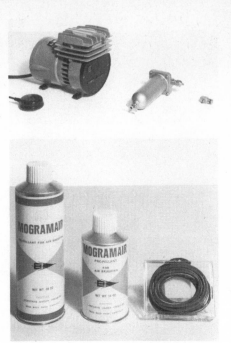

Top *The ideal form of air supply for airbrushes is an electric compressor. This is simply plugged into a mains electric supply, the 'brush connected to its airline by the adaptor seen on the right, and air is 'on tap'. The device in the centre of the picture is a water trap which fits between the airbrush and compressor and traps compressed water before it can get into the air line and spoil the paint being sprayed* (photo courtesy Morris & Ingram). **Above** *Two sizes of propellant for the Badger range of airbrushes. These propellant cans are a convenient way of obtaining motive power for an airbrush but are expensive if a lot of spraying is to be carried out* (photo courtesy Morris & Ingram).

washing of it in detergent as outlined earlier must be done thoroughly and it cannot be stressed enough that patience and work in this respect will be rewarded when it comes to spraying.

Once satisfied that the model has been completed to the best of your ability and the colour scheme chosen is available in suitable reference form, attention can be turned to preparing the airbrush for use. Make sure that all the paints needed are available, as well as having a ready supply of thinners, tissues, pipe cleaners and cotton wool earbuds, not forgetting some clean mixing pots, and perhaps most important of all a good quality eye-dropper.

When an airbrush has been standing without use, condensation can form inside the air venturi, although some models can be fitted with a water trap; it is wise to connect the brush to its air supply and blow it out before attempting to mix paint in the colour cup or jar.

Having tried the brush and made sure that everything is to hand, decide on the first colour to be applied. Generally speaking, it is wise to attempt a very simple scheme first before proceeding to more complicated finishes, and with this in mind a useful rule is to apply lighter colours first. Assuming that an RAF fighter of World War 2 is chosen, apply the undersurface blue, light grey or Sky, followed by the Dark Earth and Dark Green. The paint should be mixed in the colour cup or jar by putting some in with a No 6 brush, then gradually adding thinners with the eye dropper until the correct consistency is achieved. If the paint is too thick it will not pass through the nozzle when air is applied, and if it is too thin it will tend to run and not cover. As paints vary in their make-up it is not possible to state any hard and fast percentages of thinners to paint, but a general guide is that if the colour cup is slightly tilted and then returned to the vertical position, the paint remaining on the side will have kept its colour and not appear transparent. Experimentation and practice is the only answer but once

a colour has been mixed successfully the knack will soon be learned and retained.

It is absolutely vital that the paint is stirred thoroughly, as any small particles will soon block the brush resulting in the need for extensive cleaning operations before work can proceed. The instrument must be cleaned between each colour as already described and it is in this operation that use is made of the ear buds, tissues and pipe cleaners.

During spraying keep the brush moving evenly across the surface and try to keep it the same distance from the surface the whole time. If the brush you are using has an adjustable nozzle, set this to your requirements first but remember that the spray from it will be in a cone shape, so the closer the instrument is held to the model the finer the spray will be. Once the air is on and the brush is spraying it must be kept in constant motion, hesitation in strokes will produce uneven coverage or worse still, big blobs of paint where the spray is too concentrated. A rule that most airbrush users follow is, 'air on first and off last'.

When sufficient skill has been acquired in simple finishes, consideration can be given to more complicated schemes and one that comes readily to mind and is always eye-catching, if done correctly, is the Luftwaffe mottle style camouflage. The easiest way to describe this is to take a model through every stage. Let us assume that you are making a model of the Bf 109G of Jg 2 illustrated in Profile 184.

The old enemies in model form. A Bf 109E and Spitfire II, both in 1:72 scale. Both models have been airbrushed and finished with Letraset rub-down type transfers.

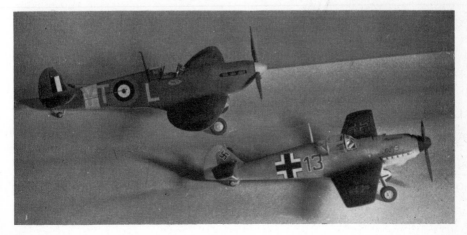

First spray the rudder and nose red; when this is dry mask the areas that are to stay red with masking tape. When this has been done, clean the brush and mix some Hellblau, spray the undersides and fuselage sides with this colour, then change to Dunklegrun and spray the top surfaces of the wings and tailplanes. Using the same colour, first run a line along the spine of the fuselage and gradually merge this into the blue sides. The mottle is achieved by short sharp bursts on the brush with the spray set fine, varying the distance away from the fuselage to achieve the subtle differences that are apparent in the mottle. Now mask the splinter camouflage on the wings and tailplanes, using masking tape to obtain the sharp edges this pattern had, and spray the exposed areas with Schwarzgrun; intermingle this with the fuselage mottle, making sure that it is darker at the top of the fuselage but at the same time ensuring that the Dunkel-grun is not completely covered. Now return to the Hellblau and touch up any areas where undesirable overspray has occurred, at the same time merging this colour into the two greens on the fuse-lage. Finally paint the spinner white, the original undercoat should be sufficient here if it has covered well, remove the masking tape, add any parts that have so far been omitted and the model is ready for application of the transfers.

During all spraying operations try to keep in mind any parts that you have left attached to the kit sprues which need to be painted in the colour you are using at the time. A good example of this in the model just described are the under-carriage doors, which should be sprayed Hellblau whilst this colour was in the brush. Failure to do this then instead of setting up the airbrush again and using a paintbrush instead, can mar all the work that has already been carried out. Touch-ing up an airbrush finish with a paintbrush is never very satisfactory as it is not possible to obtain the same smooth finish, so work of this type should be avoided wherever possible, but if this is not so, then confine it to edges of wheel wells, trailing edges of wings, etc, but never surfaces; it is far better to respray the whole model than try to repair a damaged or missed area with a paintbrush.

The airbrush enables the feathered edge that sometimes appears between camouflage colours to be reproduced with ease, but make sure that the model being made did in fact have such a finish, if it did not then use masking tape to achieve a sharp demarcation. The whole question of feathered edges is one that is discussed and viewed by modellers in different ways. One argument is that on small models such feathering will be well out of scale, as on full size machines this will only be something like an overlap of two inches. So a full size aircraft viewed from a distance where it represents 1:72 scale, will appear to have sharp demar-cation lines even though they are in fact feathered. My own thoughts on this are that if a fine feathered edge can be reproduced, even though it may be out of scale, it does give the model a more authentic look and should be done. Feathering does require a certain degree of skill and a brush that can be adjusted to a fine line, the technique being to use the brush to 'draw' the edges of the pat-tern first then fill these with it set to a wider spray or moved further away from the surface. As the scale of the model increases so too does the scale effect of the feathered edge, but it must still be done with care and the same fine line used. It is possible to cut re-usable masks from thin paper for all camouflage patterns, which does ensure that every model in a collection of the same period has identical camouflage patterns, but I find such masks more trouble than they are worth and much prefer to use the air-brush freehand.

Although the airbrush is as happy spraying matt as it is gloss paint, it is better to use matt throughout as this dries quicker and is therefore not likely to pick up any dust particles or be inad-vertently marked before it is dry. If the original aircraft had a gloss finish this can easily be achieved by spraying the whole model with gloss varnish which can be used in an airbrush equally as well as paint.

Water based paints such as Polly S or Pelikan Plaka are ideal for airbrush use but the initial surface of the model must first be sprayed with matt varnish or white enamel paint to give the water col-our paint a 'key'. A big advantage of water based paints is that it is much easier to thin them by simply adding water, and similarly cleaning the air-brush is not such an onerous operation as again water is the only cleaning

A simple spraying booth for use with airbrush. This prevents overspray and unintentional spraying of adjacent components, equipment, etc

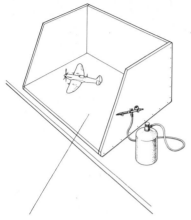

For ease of turning model a disused gramophone turntable or wooden disc on spindle can be fitted to base

medium necessary.

There is little to be gained by once again raising the for and against arguments that occur in relation to authentic colours. Colour reproduction on a scale model is something that has been argued about for years, and is likely to continue to be as long as modellers meet or write to magazines. Obviously it is necessary to aim for the most authentic colour you can obtain with the paints available, but discretion must be exercised. The exact colours used on full size aircraft, would in many cases look far too dark if they were transferred to a 1:72 scale model, as it is not possible to reduce the tonal qualities by the amounts we are concerned with. Many manufacturers of paints used specifically in model making market what they term authentic colours, and generally these are fine for the size of models we are mainly concerned with. Due to the vagaries of paint manufacture, batches made at different times can be quite different in their tonal qualities, so tins bought at different times should be matched before they are applied to a model. Dark colours can be lightened by the addition of a touch of

white and light by a touch of black, so once again experimentation is required. In painting real aeroplanes a certain amount of tolerance has to be allowed, in addition to which a newly painted aircraft that has just left the factory will look a lot different, colourwise, than one which has been exposed to all sorts of weather conditions and service life. So a general rule is to research your own subject and try to the best of your ability to finish your model in the colours that you interpret as being accurate.

While on the subject of paint it is well worth taking a look at some of the faults and problems that can occur during airbrushing, as a high percentage of these can be directly attributable to the paint being used.

It has already been stated that well stirred and mixed paint is essential, so if the brush fails to spray, the propellant and mechanism is known to be in working order, then the fault can often be traced to something connected with the paint mix. If the consistency appears to be correct then the brush nozzle must be blocked, and this will often be found to have been caused by a tiny particle of pigment that has eluded the mixing and stirring operations. The only sure way to prevent this is to filter the paint before use through a fine mesh such as part of a lady's pair of tights or stocking. Another fault is that sometimes the paint will spurt or spray unevenly, this is caused by air bubbling into the colour cup which can be caused by the paint being too thick and building up on the needle or around the nozzle outlet. It can also be caused by the rubber gromet on the Aerograph DeVilbiss, or the wax seal on the Badger, not having been replaced after the brush has been stripped for cleaning.

A grainy texture to the paint or the brush causing spattering can be the result of a number of things. One is the old favourite of too thick a paint mix, but the more common is insufficient air pressure or a bent needle. The former is more often associated with aerosol propellant cans as the pressure falls off, or being used for too long a period. If this happens change the can or take a break and stand the can in warm water for a while to help it recover. If a compressor is being used, then check the connections between the brush and the compressor and the compressor and air line.

If the needle is bent it is possible to very gently straighten it but this is difficult so it is advisable to have a spare handy, and make a note to be more careful with this part in the future.

A colour fleck at the commencement of spraying is invariably the result of poor cleaning of the previous colour, sometimes this can be put right by spraying on to a spare piece of plastic or card until the correct colour starts to flow, but it is usually better to clean the brush and start again.

If the paint is too thin it will simply run as it hits the surface that is being sprayed and not cover the undercoat or surface, so just add more paint until colour adhesion is achieved. One problem that is often encountered is that certain colours mark easily after they have been sprayed. This fault is confined to paints using certain pigments and in simple terms what is happening is that the mix is not quite right. It is thin enough to spray but dries too quickly, in some cases as soon as it touches the model's surface, so although the colour looks right, if it is handled the fingers will lift the paint, which is by now more or less coloured powder, from the surface. Of course all airbrushed paint dries extremely quickly, but even so it should not be handled for at least 24 hours, except during other spraying operations — for example a two or three colour camouflage — when a tissue should be used to protect the surface. It is not always appreciated that the fingers absorb a great deal of moisture, can easily become very greasy and this can be transferred to a model with disastrous results.

A final problem that is confined in the main to users of electric or foot-operated compressors, is that of water in the air line. When air is compressed the moisture in it is also compressed and forms little droplets which will easily filter into the air-line and brush causing blemishes on the model. This is particularly noticeable when high humidity is present, and the only satisfactory cure is the use of a water trap fitted to the compressor which extracts the offending moisture before it gets into the brush.

These few points on fault finding are the most common ones that will be encountered, but there are others and the majority of them will all be traceable back to the common point of cleanliness and maintenance. A properly looked after airbrush will give no headaches so meticulous attention to careful cleaning and following of the manufacturer's instructions in all respects will pay dividends in trouble-free use.

To wind up this chapter a word about the environment in which airbrushing is carried out will not be amiss. Always make sure that the room is well ventilated and, since a certain amount of paint is going to be absorbed into the atmosphere, it is advisable to use a small mask to protect the mouth and nostrils, especially if prolonged periods are to be spent in this atmosphere. The airbrush atomizes paint to a very fine degree and whilst the body's natural juices will absorb such small quantities without ill effect, certain paints can cause severe irritation if precautions are not taken. To spray in a room with poor ventilation is likely to lead to headaches, runny eyes, and clogging of the small hairs in the nostrils. Whilst the danger to health is by no means as likely as it is to those engaged on full-size spraying, it is best to be wise rather than suffer any chance of discomfort. It is also wise to read the paint manufacturer's instructions which are printed on some tins as these clearly state when airbrushing in a confined area can be dangerous. A small spraying booth constructed from odd pieces of wood with one side open — even a cardboard box suitably adapted will do — is a useful asset and will give protection to any adjacent walls, especially during the early days of experimentation when paint can end up everywhere. This type of booth can be extended to include a simple turntable on which the model can be rotated without it being touched, and even a lid that can be shut when spraying is completed to give a completely dust-free enclosure in which the model can be left to dry.

six

Authentic finishes and special effects

There is no doubt that the use of an airbrush is really the only way of producing truly authentic finishes since, as we have already learned in the last chapter, it duplicates in miniature the way in which real aircraft are painted. However, there are some finishes that this equipment produces too well and in so doing fails to reproduce the effect the modeller is seeking. The most common of these is overall natural metal or alternatively a silver finish when the aircraft concerned is painted with some form of aluminium coloured paint.

Most metallic paints such as silver, copper, steel, brass and gold have an entirely different consistency than normal enamel paints. When they are used in an airbrush the end result is a model that looks as though it is chromium plated or finished in pure gold or brass. The occasions when colours such as those mentioned, apart from silver, are used are very rare, but it is with silver

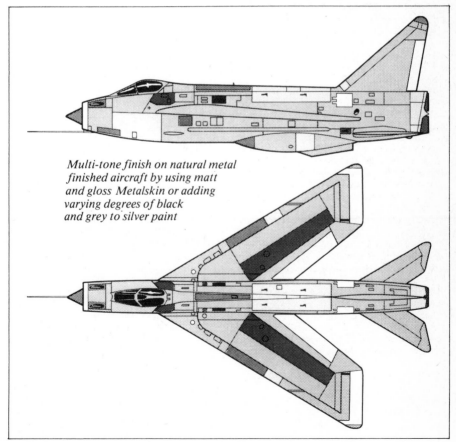

Multi-tone finish on natural metal finished aircraft by using matt and gloss Metalskin or adding varying degrees of black and grey to silver paint

that most modellers encounter problems.

Most silver paint will spray from an airbrush with little difficulty and produce an overall finish that is smooth and even, but it lacks the 'feeling' of the real thing and the resultant model will look far from authentic.

If a study is made of aircraft that carry a natural metal finish it will quickly be observed that the overall effect is very akin to a metal patchwork quilt. Panels made from different batches of aluminium, those cut with the metal's grain going in different directions, and those frequently removed for routine servicing, combine to achieve this effect which can be very difficult to capture on a model.

As it is difficult to mask silver without damaging the surface already painted and covered, the use of an airbrush is a long irksome business but it can be used in the following way. First spray the model silver overall then, when this is dry, seal the finish with matt varnish. When the varnish has dried hard, work out the panels that have to stay in the original tone and cut masking panels for these. The masking is then applied and will not damage the finish when it is removed as this is protected by the varnish. Mix a different shade of silver by adding light grey, then spray again. Once more it is necessary to repeat the sealing process with varnish before cutting out further masks for additional panels then spraying with another silver mix. This process is repeated until you have used as many silver mixes as required, then the masking tape is removed. The danger of this method is that the final panels will have received as many colour values as have been used, and if these have not been sprayed very thinly the separation between all the panels of different tonal qualities will be evidenced by a sizeable ridge. In view of the problems that this method can produce it pays to look for an easier alternative, the simplest of which is the use of brush painting. The secret of applying silver with a brush is to ensure that the paint is mixed very well and is continually checked during painting. Always paint in one direction and avoid going over areas that have already been painted.

Most of the enamel paints sold for modelling tend to have too high a lustre as far as silver is concerned and are prone to drying 'streaky' when brushed.

They are very useful for a base from which to mix different tones but it often pays to look further afield than the model shop in the quest for a good aluminium-based paint. One such paint is the heat resisting aluminium paint sold under the 'Household' brand name in some chain stores and DIY shops. This particular brand dries very flat with a most convincing natural metal appearance and can be mixed with normal modelling paints to achieve the multi-tone finish under discussion. One tremendous advantage, especially to the modeller who choses to specialise in aircraft with natural metal finishes, is that a half pint tin costs less than 50p, thus saving considerably over the normal tinlets that are associated with model making.

Assuming that you wish to try this type of paint in obtaining a natural looking natural metal finish, the first step is to find as many references in the form of photographs of the model being painted, then simulate these into a mental picture of how you want the model to look. On small 1:72 scale models it is very easy to overdo the tonal mixes and end up with a model that really does look like a patchwork quilt, so in cases like this a compromise has to be sought. Generally speaking the larger the scale of the model the easier it is to get away with a multitude of different toned panels. Having worked out the panels that are to be painted with the mix straight from the tin, apply this with a number 4 or 6 brush making sure that the edges are straight. Whilst these panels are drying take several drops of paint from the tin and transfer them to a mixing dish then add a touch of black, stir the paint well until the silver and black are thoroughly mixed and not too dark, then paint the panels that are to have this tonal value. Now repeat the process using light grey with a touch of white and paint more panels. By experimenting with different colours you will quickly find those that look right and those that don't. If the aircraft being modelled has some high gloss panels these can be painted with Humbrol, Pactra or Airfix silver to make them contrast with those that are in the dull flat aluminium. During this type of painting remember that silver is not in fact a colour and tends to reflect those colours around it. Quite clearly it would be incorrect to try to simulate the reflection of colours that might affect the aircraft when it is in its hangar or parked on a hardstanding, but on the other hand, a high gloss panel on the fuselage will absorb some of the duller panels that might reflect in it from the wings or tail-planes, and will therefore tend to look a little darker.

This type of finish is very rewarding if it is done correctly, there are no short cuts and the only answer is practice, practice and more practice.

If painting a model by this method does not appeal but you still yearn for a natural finish, there are other ways of achieving it.

Liqu-A-Plate is the trade name of a special type of paint developed in America specifically for obtaining authentic looking metal finishes. It is available in a variety of metallic colours including silver which can be used to achieve the sort of finish that has been outlined. This type of paint *must* be sprayed on to the model with an airbrush in one overall coat. Once it has dried it is possible to polish it to a very high degree

of lustre, so the obvious step in achiev-ing a multi-tonal finish is to regard the normal sprayed finish as the base or pre-dominant colour, then select panels which can be polished to various tones until the result aimed for is achieved. Masking tape must not be applied over Liqu-A-Plate so it is essential that indi-vidual panels or areas are polished with care making sure that demarcation lines between adjacent panels are straight and true. Once the model has been finished in this way it must be sprayed with the special Liqu-A-Plate sealer otherwise the finish will gradually be removed. This sealing is done after the decals have been applied so during the application of these the surface must be protected by a tissue held between the fingers otherwise the areas where the model has been handled will be polished or worse still the finish will be removed.

A similar method but not using any form of paint is the use of a tube of silver paste which is marketed in modelling circles under the name Rub 'n Buff.

This 1:32 scale F-86F from a Hasegawa kit has been finished entirely in Rub 'n' Buff. Some panels have been polished to a greater degree than others to give a toned contrast seen on natural metal finished aircraft (photo by John Carter).

This material is similar to that used in the restoration of antiques and picture frames as well as other artistic fields. In England the company famous for artists materials, George Rowney & Co Ltd, produce a product under the trade name of Goldfinger which it is possible to use with the same result as Rub 'n Buff. Both these materials come in tubes similar in size to a normal toothpaste tube and they are applied to the model by squeezing a small portion on to a card then applying it to the surface of the model with a soft rag held over one or two fingers. They can both be thinned with turpentine or White Spirit and applied with a brush in the same way as paint, but for the purpose of modelling only the finger-rubbed method will be considered.

Before attempting to apply Rub 'n Buff it is essential that the major components of the model are prepared by lightly sanding and all blemishes removed, since if they are not even the smallest scratch will prevent the Rub 'n Buff from being polished in that area and it will stick out like the proverbial sore thumb. Once the basic preparation has been done assemble all the major parts but leave off components such as underwing stores, the undercarriage, aerials, and similar small pieces that can easily be knocked off. Now wash the plastic with thinners and allow this to dry before starting to polish. The technique used is quite different to any other so forget all that you may have learned about painting and instead study the methods used by any female members of the household when they are polishing the furniture.

Squeeze about ⅛ inch of polish from the tube on to a piece of soft plastic sponge, the type used for cleaning baths and sinks is ideal, then apply it to the model. Aim to spread the polish thinly and evenly over the surface, working quickly but not rubbing too hard, if you do, the pigment from the polish will be removed and the net result will be a piece of highly polished plastic still in its moulded colour. When the polish stops spreading repeat the process with another application making sure that this blends into the area that has already been treated. When the whole area that has to be treated has been covered with this initial coat you may notice that it has highlighted work where you were not as careful as you might have been, especially around join lines. If this is the case give these areas further attention from filler and/or sanding, then restore the initial coat of Rub 'n Buff in the way already described. The final coat is applied in exactly the same way using the plastic sponge but this time it is applied a little thinner and polished by gentle rubbing as you proceed. The finish achieved can vary from the gleaming panels seen on the engine panels of 'between-the-wars' biplanes, to a dull lustre more associated with a battle weary P-47 or P-51. The extent of shine required is achieved by frequent gentle rubbing over the same area and not hard pressure which will only remove the pigment. During the final polishing make sure that the sponge is kept well filled with Rub 'n Buff as this acts as a lubricant and prevents the surface that is being worked on from being scratched. It will be realised that by varying the amount of attention given to individual panels these can easily be made to contrast with each other in a most effective way. A final overall polish with a soft rag will pay dividends but make sure that this is nothing more than a gentle passing of the rag which should be something like cheese cloth and not a lint-like material which will only leave small pieces adhering to the surface. Once the finish you want has been obtained the quickest way to spoil it is by constant handling, especially if your fingers are still impregnated with silver pigment, so be sure to handle the model with a clean soft cloth. If at any time the finish does not seem to be going the way you want it to, a drop of thinners will quickly remove all traces of that which has been applied leaving the surface ready for another attempt.

Component parts are treated in the same way but to prevent excessive handling first fix them to double-sided tape then treat them in the same way as the major parts. Contrast on undercarriage legs can be achieved by giving the oleo sections a very high gloss finish to simulate their constant sliding, and not polishing the non-sliding parts to the same degree. On such components as these Rub 'n Buff can be diluted with thinners and applied with a paintbrush in the normal way.

Before fitting all the accessories to the model make sure that any residual polish is removed from locating points as it remains completely unaffected by polystyrene cement and will thus prevent such parts from staying attached. Rub 'n Buff can be used in conjunction with normal painted areas but it is best to paint such areas first then mask them out as masking tape applied over Rub 'n Buff can damage the surface when it is removed. Decals can be applied in the normal way but it is best to avoid the rub down variety as these do not adhere very well and efforts to make them do so can mark the polished surface where they have been rubbed.

The variation in surface finish will produce the tonal effect to a fairly authentic degree, but by mixing various shades of the basic silver polish even better results can be produced.

It is now possible to obtain Rub 'n Buff in a variety of colours including Frosted Blue, Olive Bronze, Gold and Copper. These can all be mixed with each other and silver to produce a variety of tones which look most effective. Ordinary enamel paint can also be blended with Rub 'n Buff by blending the paint and polish with thinners then applying with a brush. This combination will not polish as well as the straight from the tube material but, if it is applied in small quantities in the right areas, it will produce results that can be difficult to obtain by other methods.

A mixture of silver and gold in proportions of about 60/40 is ideal for producing the finish often seen on panels that are affected by heat such as those around the tail pipes and rear fuselage of the F-100 Super Sabre.

In addition to applying overall finishes this material also has an infinite number of uses when conventional paint has been used. It can be used to add highlights to gun barrels, the simulation of wear around removable panels, wheel centre-hubs, polished pitot heads and in weathering; a subject that will be dealt with later in this chapter.

If your first attempts do not work out right it will probably be because you have applied the polish too thickly, trying to make one thick coat do instead of two thin ones; rubbed too hard and removed all the pigment, or failed to prepare the surface properly before starting. Whatever the cause it is a simple matter to start again and worth persevering with as a well finished model can look very authentic.

Many modellers will argue that the only real way to produce a natural metal finish is to simulate the full-size aircraft by making models in metal. This method is one that requires a great deal of skill and equipment and is probably beyond the scope of the modeller who wishes to build-up a collection of some quantity over a reasonable period of time. But there is a method of getting very close to reproducing the real thing in miniature and that is by covering the model in metal foil which is cut to represent the panels that would go into making a modern aeroplane.

The metal foil that is used to obtain this type of finish is available from specialist model shops, most of whom will supply by direct mail, but in addition to this there is an equally as good material available in most kitchens in the form of baking foil. The sheets that are produced specifically for modelling are marketed under the name of Metalskin and Baremetal, both of which originated in the USA, and although their use has declined in popularity during the last two years they are still available from the sources mentioned. These two products are self-adhesive paper laminated to a smooth metal surface which can be bought with a gloss or matt finish. This type of metal finish is fairly easy to apply but the thickness of the material can lead to a model that does not look exactly right despite the claims of the manufacturers and those modellers who feel it is the only answer to true metal finishes.

In many cases the scale of the model concerned is the paramount factor, for a 1:72 scale fighter such as the P-51 can end up looking as though it has been made either from old scraps of aluminium or cast in solid silver, neither of which is truly representative. On larger models the size does enable this type of finish to be carried much more convincingly but there is still a very real danger of producing the same effects as those mentioned in the P-51 example. The best method to employ if any form of metal skinning is to be tried, is to first assemble all the components as separate items and cover them up before they are put together.

Before making a start make sure that all interior detail such as wheel wells and cockpit interiors are painted in appropriate colours then, to get the feel of the technique and material, select a fairly

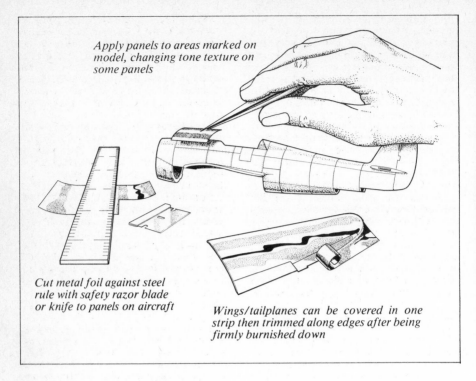

Apply panels to areas marked on model, changing tone texture on some panels

Cut metal foil against steel rule with safety razor blade or knife to panels on aircraft

Wings/tailplanes can be covered in one strip then trimmed along edges after being firmly burnished down

simple part such as a wing on which to apply the first panels. The first step is to sand off all the rivet detail and panel lines from *one* wing only. Now, using the other as a guide, cut out panels from the foil to match those marked on the moulding. Always use a sharp knife and a steel rule as a guide and cut the material on a smooth clean work surface or alternatively a thickish piece of cardboard.

When a panel has been marked and cut out apply it by gently peeling off the backing paper then making sure it lines up correctly on the wing that is being covered, press it into position ensuring that the panel is laying in the exact position you want it. The adhesive is quite strong so it is essential that the panel is completely square to its datum lines before it is pressed into position. When this has been done smooth the panel over the contours with a soft handkerchief wrapped around the fingertips starting from the middle and working towards the edges. When the adhesive has bonded burnish the whole panel with a rounded wooden stick, the small end of a paintbrush is ideal for this. Always work backwards and forwards in the same

direction paying particular attention to the edges of the panel. Adjacent panels are cut and put on in exactly the same way until the whole surface is covered.

Avoid making joins at the leading and trailing edges as this may cause the material to lift. The best method of tackling these areas is to employ small panels that wrap around the edges with the joins coming back on to the top and bottom surfaces at the main spar point or edges of trailing edge control surfaces. By studying the texture of the foil it will be noticed that it has a definite grain so use this to obtain texture by alternating the direction in which it runs on adjacent panels. A mixture of gloss and matt panels always produces a more convincing effect but do not fall into the trap of varying these to a set pattern. A good method is to apply matt panels to the centre areas of the wings and cover the leading and trailing edges in gloss. When the tip is reached do not try to follow the outline of the plastic by cutting the foil close to this, simply allow a generous overlap then press the top and bottom covering together until the shape becomes apparent. Take a pair of sharp scissors and trim the excess off following the line of the wing tip, the shearing action of the scissors will bond the two pieces together and a final burnish with the wooden dowel will complete the job. On some tips there might be a tendency for the foil to slightly part company at the leading and trailing edges, if this happens fill the gap with thick silver paint and leave this to dry before attempting any more work. When one wing has been completed the other one can have its surface detail removed and covered in the same way using the panels on the first wing as a guide.

On some small aircraft an alternative method is to cover the whole wing surface with one piece of foil. To do this cover the top first and cut a piece of foil to the shape of the wing, again leaving generous overlaps all round. Peel off the backing paper and starting at the trailing edge gradually pull the foil tight over the whole surface smoothing it flat towards the leading edge. Burnish it with the finger tips wrapped in a handkerchief until all the detail such as control surface joins show through then roll the surplus material underneath and trim it at a convenient point. The uncovered area on the undersurface is then covered with one piece of foil cut to the shape needed. This method prevents the use of alternation of grain or the combined use of matt and gloss foil and only works satisfactorily on wings that have fairly straight edged planforms. Since it is not possible to introduce any variations in texture the one piece covering method should be confined to small fighter aircraft where the one tone finish is not so glaring as it would be on, say, a B-47.

Fuselages must be tackled by the individual panel method so to obtain a working guide for the panel lines it is necessary either to have another kit of the same type available or make a detailed plan of the panel layout before removing this detail. Another way to do this is to sand off the detail on one half, cover this using the unsanded half as a guide, then sand this smooth and use the covered side as a guide from which to cut the other panels.

The application of panels to the fuselage is straightforward until it comes to areas where there are compound curves. The best way to cover these is to skin the area with small pieces of foil, cutting them to shape once they are in position.

But be careful not to cut too deeply otherwise there is a danger of the surface being damaged to a degree where the cut will show up as a definite line on the finished surface. Any small creases that appear on curved panels can usually be burnished out unless you have tried to cover too large a curved surface, when the only solution is to remove the panel and start again with a smaller one. Make sure that all joins butt together neatly so that after burnishing these appear as mere hairlines. Additional panels such as inspection hatches can be scribed into the surface with a scriber or the pointed end of dividers, and rivet or cowling fasteners can be simulated in the same way. Rivets and fasteners are nearly always spaced equally so accurate measuring and marking of these is essential. However, there is a foolproof method which does not involve any form of measuring; this is the use of a small toothed gear from a broken clock. By fixing such a wheel to a cocktail stick then running it along a straight edge in the position where the rivets are to appear you will obtain perfectly spaced impressions which look much better than those applied in any other way. Another method of adding inspection panels is to cut these from a contrasting strip of foil and position them over the already skinned surface in appropriate places.

Tailplanes are covered in the same way as wings but these components, often being smaller than any other part of the major assembly, can usually be covered by the one piece method.

Once all the parts are covered as individual components, assemble them in the normal way then finish the model by adding thin strips where any joins have not butted together as accurately as they should have done. The foil is fairly thin so small pieces such as this can usually be pushed into areas and burnished down without appearing obtrusive. Aerials, exhaust ports, wheels and other accessories, painted in appropriate colours are added to finally complete the model and it is at this stage that the full impact of a metal skinned model will have its true effect. If done properly this method of obtaining a natural metal appearance can work well, but it is very easy to mar it by trying to be too ambitious in alternating the grain and colour of the panels, and on smaller models making them look clumsy due to the overall thickness of the skin.

Ordinary domestic kitchen foil is much thinner than most other types of metal skinning but the method of applying it is very much harder. This material does not have any form of adhesive backing so this must be added by the modeller. Basically the same techniques as described are used but instead of trying to cut panels by measuring and tracing existing ones an alternative method has to be used.

Cut a small piece of kitchen foil from the roll and place the brightest side on the surface of the model, hold it firmly in place then gently rub it with a soft cloth. The foil will quickly adopt the shape of the component over which it is placed and the panel lines will quickly become very evident. Now remove the foil and with a small pair of sharp scissors cut out the shape that has been impressed in it. Cover the area to which the panel is to be attached, and the inside of the foil panel, with Uhu or matt varnish, leave this several minutes until it is tacky, then bring the panel and component together. Both parts will stick almost instantaneously so it is impossible to remove the foil for another attempt if it was not lined up correctly. The material is burnished in the same way but special care must be taken to ensure that the adhesive is applied evenly and thinly otherwise it will cause blemishes that it is impossible to remove without splitting the covering foil.

Kitchen foil is grained in a similar way to the products mentioned earlier so it is just as easy to obtain a varied texture with this; but as one side is far too glossy for realism it is not so easy to achieve the variations in tonal quality. The big advatnage of this domestic material, apart from its availability and price, is that it is so much thinner than the specially produced products and therefore produces a much more delicate finish. Although there is some merit in the use of any type of metal skinning my own personal view is that it is much better and more realistic when it is confined to small areas such as the cowlings of aircraft like the Hawker Hart and Fury. But we have learned many times that modelling is very much a matter of personal choice and what pleases one modeller does not necessarily have the same effect on another.

It is not only in natural metal finishes where the search for true authenticity is a difficult one as aircraft painted in camouflage schemes can also present many problems.

The biggest trap that many newcomers to the hobby fall into is the continual quest for absolute accuracy, which in any paint scheme is impossible to attain. Any full size aircraft reduced to the dimensions of a scale model would look entirely wrong if such a reduction included exact reproduction of the original scheme. The tonal qualities of paint must also be adjusted in scale if a model is to look right. Large areas painted in dark camouflage colours absorb and reflect more light than smaller areas, so if the same paint mix that was used on a full size Phantom was applied to a 1:72 scale model the result would be a very dull and incorrect looking model. To overcome such problems it is wise to lighten such colours to a degree where, although they retain their basic shade, the tonal value is reduced.

There are too many self-appointed experts who try to stick rigidly to laid down paint specifications without any thought of the various effects reduction in size can make. Similarly it can also be very convenient to accept the unwritten law of the specification without any regard to local conditions or operational short cuts.

Before any model is started a picture must be formed in the mind as to exactly how the finished product is to look. This is especially important as far as the colour scheme is concerned and parallel to this must be the consideration of the period of the aircraft and its function. Very few aircraft retain a pristine factory fresh finish for very long although there are obviously exceptions to this which must be considered. A World War 2 fighter would have been kept serviceable to a very high degree but those responsible for its maintenance would have been more concerned with its mechanical serviceability than its outward appearance. This does not mean that it would have been neglected to the degree that is sometimes seen on models where the builder's enthusiasm has been given too much rein, since a conscientious ground-crew would always make sure that damaged areas were repaired and the canopy polished. But overall the aircraft would not be kept in the same condition as, for example, those highly polished biplanes of the RAF in the 1930s. Thought must also be given to operational environments, since the effect of the sun in hot climates, mud, snow and rain in other situations, would all combine to not only wear the applied finish but also change its colour quite dramatically. Aircraft that are frequently parked exposed to the elements will show much different tonal qualities to their paintwork than those which enjoy shelter. The paint used on modern aircraft is of far higher quality and an entirely different make-up than that used during the two major world wars, similarly a peacetime air force generally has more time available in which to ensure that their aircraft do not become 'scruffy'. Points such as these are well worth considering and experimentation in obtaining the correct paint mix can be as much fun as actually painting a completed model. The colour references for different camouflage colours is obtainable in many specialised books and these are useful guides which should not be ignored, as wherever possible these were adhered to by the personnel concerned. But there were, and are, many instances where an official paint mix was not available and the nearest equivalent was pressed into service. To obtain the sun-bleached effect that is apparent on many aircraft used in the Middle East, existing authentic colours can be lightened by adding matt white or light grey, starting with the basic colour and adding these in very minor quantities until the effect that is being sought is achieved. Black and dark grey will add depth and darkness to colours but again the watchword must be caution.

Any hard and fast mixes and techniques would only serve to confuse the reader who is much better off if he uses his own proven methods to get the finish that he wants and seeks. The last comment is really the only one that matters as every model is made to please the person who is constructing it, and if this goal is achieved then the model has fulfilled its object.

Variations in colour tones and finish are basically a mild form of 'weathering' which is an art in itself and is either liked or despised by modellers or those who derive pleasure from looking at models. There is an old saying that claims 'beauty is in the eye of the beholder', and this adage can be applied to most things including modelling aircraft. For example, McDonnell's F-4 Phantom II, which caused one Fleet Air Arm pilot to question whether or not it had been delivered the right way up or not, is not perhaps one of the best-looking aircraft ever made, but to many its purely functional shape is a thing to be regarded as the ultimate in aeronautical beauty. Similarly, a model finished without a blemish and looking as though it has just rolled off the production line is the ultimate in some modellers' eyes, whereas an equally well-built model painted deliberately to look as though it has stood out in all weathers and thoroughly neglected appeals to others. Basically one can boil the whole thing down to one question which is, 'are you making a model or a replica?' A model of say a Spitfire, finished in the correct colours, carrying correct codes and accurate insignia, will show that aircraft as it should have looked, whereas the same model with paint chipped, oil stains and exhaust tarnishing will be a replica of what the original probably looked like.

However clean an aircraft may look both in reality and in photographs, close examination will invariably show that panels are dented, paintwork is worn, fuel and oil spillage has marred the paintwork, and some areas have been repaired and painted in slightly different colours. As with many other points mentioned, the finish required is a matter of personal choice, but experimentation is always worthwhile, and even if a weathered model does not appeal it can be rewarding to try at least one.

Before trying to obtain a realistic weathered finish it is advisable to study photographs or full-size aircraft to get some idea of the effect wanted. One word of warning: discretion must be used, as it is all too easy to go too far and then the only result is disappointment.

A 1:72 scale model must be viewed as though it is the real thing viewed at a distance that would give the small size of the model; with this in mind it is easy to appreciate that a lot of the scruffy appearance seen close-up would not apply to the model. One of the easiest things to reproduce is the chipped paintwork around panels, wing and tailplane leading edges, and crew entry points. When the model has been finished and prepared for painting, apply silver paint or Rub 'n Buff in the areas where wear is to be depicted, then mask out small areas with pieces of masking tape or Magic Masker, and paint in the normal way; when the paint has dried, remove the masking and gently rub the worn areas with a tissue. This method avoids the unrealistic look that is achieved by dabbing silver paint over the complicated model; after all, the final paintwork on the original is applied over the metal skin and then wears off, so why not do the same thing in miniature?

Rub 'n Buff is very useful for simulating wear around panel joins where paint tends to rub off rather than be chipped. To do this first simulate any chips by the method detailed then paint the final coat and when this is quite dry put a small dab of Rub 'n Buff on the end of a cotton wool earbud and gently rub it down panel lines. The operative word is gently; hardly any pressure is needed as a simple dusting will be enough to deposit just the right amount of Rub 'n Buff in the indentations between the joining panels. This method can be used very effectively on cowlings and removable access hatches to highlight the screw type fastenings as paint is quickly removed from clips and screw heads that are frequently removed for routine maintenance.

Exhaust stains are quite common on most aircraft, except of course, jets such as the Lightning and F-80, where the efflux does not pass over any surface, and these can be reproduced by using thinned black paint applied with a brush that is almost dry or an airbrush. Matt black is usually too coarse to produce the effect that is wanted so it is advisable to add a touch of light grey. Such stains tend to get lighter and spread as they are dissipated by the aircraft's slipstream, so try to concentrate on getting a fairly dark colour at the point where the exhaust emits and lighten and spread it as it moves down the fuselage or across the wing surface. The exhaust gases from a jet are very hot and can cause paint to blister and discolour in the area around the tailpipe, one aircraft where this is particularly noticeable being the North American F-100 Super Sabre which is more often than not seen with a tail end that looks as though it has been inside a furnace. Applying exhaust stains so that they look right takes a lot of practice and it is very easy to overdo them so that the model ends up looking as though it has

only just survived a fire, so care and practice are needed as well as a long study of the effect that is being aimed at whenever the opportunity arises at air displays or visits to airfields.

Soot and pastel chalks, which can be powdered by rubbing them on paper, are useful for obtaining staining of this type and these materials can be applied very effectively with a cotton wool earbud, soft paintbrush or tissue; once the correct effect has been achieved with these it is necessary to seal them with a spray of varnish. The same methods can also be used to show stains around gun ports but remember that such stains have a peculiarity of being thrown forward initially therefore creating a darker stain at the front of the port than at the rear, this is especially noticeable on aircraft such as the F-86 with nose-mounted guns.

Quite frequently aircraft that have suffered battle damage are repaired with panels taken from other machines or with new patches doped on, in the case of fabric-covered aircraft. This effect can be obtained by painting the area concerned a different colour — red oxide being a familiar finish on World War 2 aircraft; but this must be done with extreme thought and care, and under no circumstances overdone. After all, an aircraft that has so many patches that it begins to resemble Jacob's coat, is hardly likely to be in a flyable condition.

Stains from fuel spillage are fairly easy to reproduce by filling a small brush with a mix of matt black and thinners; the latter being about ten times as much as the paint; then allowing the mix to flow from the brush around the areas where fuel caps and dump pipes are located. If the mix is right the thinners will carry the paint in an ever lightning shade away from the area, along adjacent panel lines, and down the nearest curved surface, just like the real thing.

Wheels and undercarriage legs should not be forgotten during any weathering exercise as these parts are as prone to the effects of weather as the rest of the machine. Never, never, paint wheels matt black; a quick look at the family car will indicate that rubber tyres are rarely jet black in colour, but more of a dark grey. One of the best colours to use for rubber is Humbrol Panzer Grey (HM4) which seems to capture the exact texture of the material. Areas where the wheels come in contact with the ground should be highlighted by mixing a slight touch of light grey to the Panzer Grey, or alternatively, if the aircraft concerned has been operating from a grass airfield, pick out these areas and the treads with a mud colour.

Pactra produce a set of weathering paints all of which can be applied to achieve various effects ranging from mud to black and white tinting, among which is one colour simply titled 'Weather' which does achieve an overall worn effect when it is applied correctly in the right amounts.

When all the weathering that is desirable has been applied to the model, it is advisable to mix a very thin solution of the base colour and spray this lightly over the whole model. If for example an Olive Drab B-17, as shown in the photographs, has been made to look as though it really has done 50 odd trips over enemy territory by applying stains, chipped paint and patches, finish it by mixing Olive Drab and thinners in a ratio of about 10:1 and spray the whole model with this. The effect will be a general toning down of all areas, including the markings, which it is easy to forget when weathering with the result that they look too bright and painted on after the aircraft has been made dirty rather than as an integral part of the paint scheme that would be as subject to the elements as the rest of the airframe.

Gun barrels are items that seldom suffer from the effects of weather or operational conditions as they are more often than not covered when the aircraft is on the ground, or in the case of multi-engined bombers, removed completely from the turrets. The gun-metal finish associated with barrels is easy to simulate and can go a long way towards making a model look authentic. First paint all the barrels matt black and while this is drying take a soft pencil (2B or 3B) and rub its point on a light grade glasspaper; shake the resulting graphite dust on to a clean piece of paper or card, and when the paint has dried, rub this dust into the barrels with the fingers. The graphite will polish the matt black paint and add a lustre that really does look like gun metal, a coat of varnish will seal the finish and prevent it from coming off although this is not 100 per cent essential as it is unlikely that parts such as these will be the subject of very much handling when the model has been completed.

Indian ink diluted with copious amounts of water is also a useful medium when it comes to obtaining special effects, and one of the beauties of this is that the water evaporates and leaves very convincing diluted streaks.

There are many other methods and materials available including an oven polish marketed under the name Zebrite which will produce the most realistic metallic effects when rubbed over black and silver paint. Every modeller who likes to finish his models in a truly authentic 'service' condition will eventually find his own ways and materials to do so, but if you have never tried this type of finish before, those briefly described will set you on the road from which you can branch out to discover your own.

One thing about this type of finish is that if you don't like it you can always follow the path of the original; return to a maintenance unit for a re-spray . . .

One of the most important aspects of obtaining a good finish to any model is the application of the transfers, or to give them their more modern name, decals. However well painted a model may be, if the decals are not applied in the correct positions, lined-up accurately and the carrier film, if applicable, not hidden, then all the hard work that has gone into it will have been wasted.

In the early days of plastic kits the decals contained in the box were usually confined to the bare essentials such as the national markings, serials and code letters. Colour was more often than not incorrect, symbols were oversize, register was bad, and the markings were far too thick. However, in the same way that the basic kit components have improved, so too have the decals sheets, although until recent years these still tended to drag a little way behind the standards achieved in injection moulding. The result is that today many of the markings contained in kits are produced to a standard that is high enough to make them equal to those produced and sold by specialist manufacturers. Alternative markings are frequently supplied and now include such refinements as stencil markings, rescue arrows, fuel and oil points, serial numbers, squadron badges and many other items that were once the prerogative of the custom produced decal sheet.

Long before the present high standard

of kit decals was reached the enthusiast was able to discard the kit markings and use sheets produced by specialist companies who had recognised the potential of the market and catered for it by producing a variety of sheets covering almost every need. Most of the sheets produced by the early pioneers in this now extremely specialised field would be considered of poor quality when compared with today's standards, but they were an improvement over the transfers included in most kits. The trends established in the early days have not really varied, the tendency being towards producing either complete sheets of national markings, supplemented by other universal sheets containing unit and squadron insignia, serial numbers and stencil markings, or a composite sheet containing sufficient markings to complete, for example, three versions of one particular aircraft. In many cases specialised sheets of decals were, and in fact still are, more expensive than the kit to which they are to be applied. But this is only to be expected as their production runs do not even remotely approach that of a popular kit.

Development of the specialised sheet of decals has run parallel to the improvement now evident in modern kits, with the result that the modeller of today is able to purchase markings of the highest standard covering almost any field in which he is likely to be interested. Such sheets are accurate in colour, register, scale thickness and basic research, which is really the most important aspect of any set of markings.

As standards improved and modellers became more aware that it was no longer necessary to 'make do' with the best of a mediocre selection, the wheat was sorted from the chaff, with the result that of the many companies who more or less mushroomed overnight, only those producing first class products survived.

In Britain there are only a handful left and competition between them ensures that standards set are of the highest. Thus the user gets good value for money. Competition from overseas is very strong with the development of the custom-designed decal sheet following a similar development pattern as the UK.

The range of specialist decal sheets available to modellers is now vast. These few examples adequately illustrate the choice available from such manufacturers as Modeldecal, Microscale, ESCI, Letraset and Aerodecal. In the case of the latter these are for 1:32 scale models which, until recently, was a neglected field as far as specialist decals were concerned. All those illustrated with the exception of the rub-down dry transfers of the CAF are conventional water-slide type (photo by John Carter).

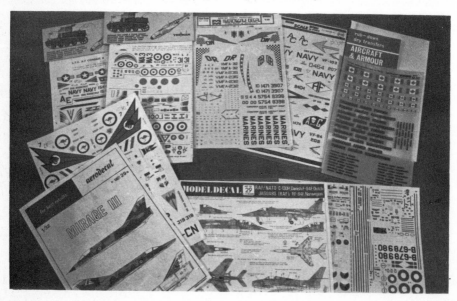

Generally speaking there are only two types of decals available to modellers, these being the conventional water-slide type and the more recently introduced rub-down or pressure decal. Both have their advantages and disadvantages so, as with most things, the final choice as to which type to use remains with the individual modeller.

Looking first at the water-slide type one finds the familiar and easy to use method known to the youngest schoolboy, where the symbol is soaked in water and then transferred to the object that it is to decorate. The basis of this type of sheet is a varnish and solvent, the insignia being painted on the varnish and then carried by this to the model when the solvent has been dissolved in water. Such sheets in their basic form are economical and easy to produce, hence the almost total use of this form of marking by kit manufacturers, where vast quantities of markings of the same type can be made to a not too demanding standard at a reasonable price (actually a fraction of a penny per sheet).

However, once an improvement in standards is called for, the cost rises. Use of more sophisticated varnishes, solvents and top quality printing tends to make costs escalate, though resulting in far better quality markings. The process is slower and demands more care, while the production run may be as little as 2,000 sheets. One of the most important advantages of the water-slide decal is that it is extremely easy to use; once the selected symbol has been cut from the sheet it is only a question of applying enough water to remove it from the backing sheet and slide it into position, a technique familiar to all who have ever made a kit. Providing the markings are kept damp enough they can be slipped into any position before they are finally pressed into their correct positions by a soft rag or tissue. If care is taken in trimming the carrier film this will be less noticeable when the marking has dried. In fact some of the sheets now available have such fine carrier film and are printed on such thin paper, that even if the film is not trimmed as carefully as it might have been, the surrounding film that so often mars a model, is almost unnoticeable.

The best way to apply water-slide decals is the use of solvents and varnishes in addition to water. First prepare the surface that is to receive the marking by spraying (preferably) or painting the whole model with a gloss varnish after the finished paintwork has dried. Allow the varnish to dry then cut out the marking that is required and, holding it with a pair of tweezers, gently touch it on to the surface of a bowl of clean water to which has been added just a drop of washing-up detergent. Remove the marking and place it on a clean tissue which will absorb the surplus liquid. Now paint the area where the marking is to be applied with Solvaset or Microsol, lift the marking with the tweezers and place it in position. Try to get this correct first time as it is not too good an idea to slide it about too much when it is on the model's surface. Take a clean tissue or soft rag and gently press the marking down starting at its centre and working towards the edges, this will expel any water that is still trapped underneath and also remove trapped air which can cause air blisters. When the marking is correctly placed paint a thin coat of Solvaset or Microsol over it and do not touch it again. It is best to position all markings first and then apply the thin solution of solvent, the model can then be left for about six hours until this has dried. The solvent will soften the markings and help them to set properly over any panel lines, etc, over which they are placed. When all the markings are thoroughly dry give the whole model a coat of gloss or matt varnish, whichever is appropriate for the finish desired. The American company Microscale market a complete set of aids for decal application which go under the names of Microsol, Microcoat Flat and Microcoat Gloss. These are obtainable from large hobby shops, but if you have any difficulty then ordinary matt and gloss varnish will do.

The benefits of the method described are that the markings are given a good protection against peeling or breaking as they dry out, they will not fade or discolour as the model ages, and furthermore, if the work is carried out properly the carrier film will be rendered invisible. With some water-slide transfers it is advisable to trim this film before application but this needs a sharp knife and steady hand and should be done with caution as it is easy to cut out too much carrier, especially in Bs, 8s, and Hs, making such markings difficult to handle and very prone to breaking.

Apart from the marring effect of carrier film, one other major disadvantage of the water-slide type transfer is the fact that, unless it is treated in the way described, it will eventually show signs of age by cracking and peeling. Because of their nature water-slide transfers are usually printed on fairly heavy paper — although there are some exceptions — with the result that unless some form of solvent is used, they will not always follow curved surfaces as well as is wished. But overall, the water-slide transfer will always be popular and the range available is so vast that markings to suit every need can usually be found.

For many years modellers who, by their very nature, are often great improvisors, have used standard sheets of rub-down letters and figures produced for use in art studios by Letraset, Blick, Rexell and Presletta. These sheets are standard alphabets and figures produced in a variety of styles for use by printers, graphic designers, engineers, and draughtsmen, and their use in modelling has been to complement the water-slide type of marking. Typical uses include serial numbers, small codes, and unit markings as well as walkways, where black stripes are much better then an unsteady hand and black paint, camera ports and foot holds when black dots always produce and repeat symmetrical circles much better than even the most skilled painter can.

Coloured circles and dots can also be used for minute roundels on 1:144 scale models where red, white and blue ones are superimposed on each other. These and many other of the normal commercial sheets have a vast potential as far as modellers are concerned, but about eight years ago a Canadian modeller, Alan Breeze, designed and had produced by Letraset, sheets of markings specifically for use by aircraft and AFV modellers. The success of Mr Breeze's initiative was such that within a three year period over 45 sheets of different markings came on to the market, and although they appeared to fade out and became hard to obtain, they are now back in full production and stocked by most mail order specialist shops. A major advantage of this type of transfer is that there is no carrier film, so once the marking has been applied to the model and rubbed down with a soft pencil or ball-point pen, there is no unsightly surround to

mar the adjacent paintwork. This advantage really comes into its own in applying very small markings such as serial numbers which are too fine to be trimmed closely in the water-slide type. But a disadvantage is that once the marking is positioned and rubbed-down it cannot be moved, therefore 100 per cent accuracy is essential when locating markings on the model. If a mistake is made, the only solution is to apply adhesive tape over the marking and remove it completely; after this operation it cannot be used again, thus making relatively simple errors a costly business. It is also necessary to ensure that the marking is held perfectly still whilst it is being rubbed-down for even the slightest movement will make the part attached to the model detach itself from the part that has still to be rubbed. This is not as disastrous as incorrect placing, for with care the two parts can be lined up again and the resulting crack will be barely visible. The surface on which the marking is to be applied must be free of any blemishes including plastic shavings or raised paint, as when the marking is rubbed such blemishes will show through. Each symbol must be cut from the sheet and held with tweezers in the exact position it is required, the rubbing is then carried out gently starting from the centre and working outwards. A ball-point pen or paintbrush handle is the best tool, and rubbing strokes should be even and in one direction. As the marking detaches itself from the carrier sheet, it will appear to lighten in colour and it soon becomes evident when it is completely free of its carrier sheet. Before applying such markings experiment first on an old model or scrap plastic by using the various company trade marks and patent numbers, etc, that border the edges of the sheet, by doing this there is no wastage of valuable markings but useful experience is gained. Some of the very small numbers and letters require a lot of practice to ensure that they are all lined-up and equally spaced, and some modellers advocate that it is best to rub this type of marking on to a water-slide sheet then use the resultant composed serial as a water-slide transfer. My view is that this entirely defeats the object of the dry transfer and is admitting defeat at not being able to apply them correctly. To help in the correct alignment of small markings, which is the area where most

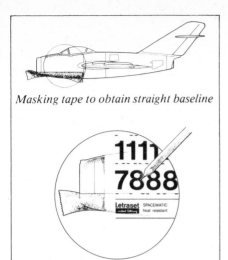

Masking tape to obtain straight baseline

Line up dots on Letraset sheet on masking tape base then gently rub down letters and figures with pencil or biro

problems appear to occur, all that is required is a very fine pencil line drawn on the model with a 3B pencil which is used as a base line, when the markings are applied this line can be removed by a gum eraser or artist's putty rubber. An alternative is to mark the base line with a strip of masking tape which is simply peeled off once the rub-down markings are applied.

Dry markings are, in most cases, much thinner than the water-slide variety and therefore produce a much more authentic 'painted on' look; they are not affected by age and once applied will not peel off. On new sheets the markings come off very easily but the longer a sheet is kept in storage the harder it is to remove the symbols, the answer to this particular problem is to carry out a pre-releasing exercise. To do this gently rub the surface of the carrier film over the marking before it is applied to the model, but do not carry out this initial rubbing too hard otherwise there is a danger of removing the symbol and transferring it to the backing sheet. A few light strokes with the selected rubbing tool will be enough to loosen the symbol and it is then applied in the normal way. It is safe to say that rub-down transfers have a greater following among more experienced modellers, but as the technique

becomes more universally accepted, and sheets are produced in greater quantity, thus bringing their price nearer that of the more conventional water-slide type, they will grow in popularity. In fact one Italian manufacturer introduced this type of decal sheet in his kits during 1975 so he may well become the first pioneer in this field.

The quality of all sheets of markings, whether of the water-slide or rub-down variety, has now reached a stage that will be difficult to surpass. The many hundreds of subjects that are now available — from simple black codes to multi-coloured unit insignia — are beginning to create a situation for the modeller where the choice of subject depends a great deal on the aesthetic appeal of the markings available. This in turn often leads him to produce several models of the same type which creates more business for the kit manufacturer, who is thus possibly influenced into considering models that can be finished in a variety of schemes. The end result is that everyone is happy. A far cry from the day when, if the modeller wanted to finish his model in a scheme different to that supplied on the decals in the kit, he had no choice other than to resort to hand-painting.

The variety of decals that are now available has led to a decline in the art of hand-painting of markings; although this is not a skill that every modeller has or can cultivate, it is not as difficult as at first it may seem. The necessity to hand-paint on small scale models is now more or less non-existent, on larger scale models however, there is still a lot of scope for those who wish to try this method as the choice of alternative markings, especially in 1:32 and 1:24 scales, is fairly limited. In many respects this is particularly fortunate as with models of such size hand-painting does not present the problems that are encountered in smaller scales.

The three 'Ps', Planning, Practice and Patience, that are so essential in all aspects of modelling, are just as applicable when it comes to hand-painting alternative markings. If a study is made of national insignias and styles of code letters, it will be quickly appreciated that in most cases these are fairly symmetrical which means that masking tape and film can be used to achieve accuracy and straight lines. The first step, after select-

Cutting roundels from Frisk tape for spraying with airbrush

First mask: spray
centre white

Second mask: cover
centre, spray exposed
area blue

Third mask: centre
hole sprayed red

End result: a perfect
painted roundel

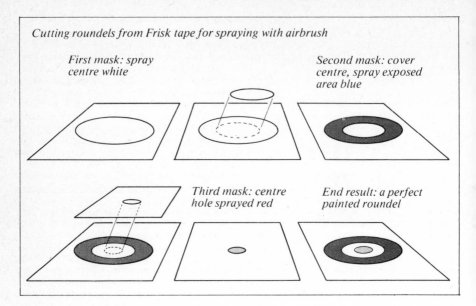

ing a suitable set of markings, is to obtain as much reference material as possible, as all national insignia and code letters are painted to conform to set standards laid down by the air force concerned. Such books as those published by Patrick Stephens Ltd in the Airfix Guide series, the Harleyford books on markings, and many others, all contain comprehensive details of such markings and their correct proportions which can easily be transferred to the scale in which one is working.

To paint a three-colour RAF roundel start by cutting a template from Frisk masking film which is the exact diameter of the roundel, place this in position on the model and spray paint the area left exposed through the template, matt white. While the paint is drying cut out a disc whose diameter is the same as the total area of white that will be exposed, or in other words, the inner diameter of the blue, and when the paint is dry, place this disc over the exact centre of the still white disc. Now paint the circle of white that is exposed blue and remove the centre masking disc. You will now have a roundel that has the correct proportion of blue but with the whole centre white. Finally cut-out a circle the exact diameter of the red, place this in position and apply the red paint.

This may sound complicated but once it is transferred from the written word to

a practical exercise it will be realised just how simple it is. The essential points to watch for are accuracy in cutting the templates and discs, and precise placing of these on the model and in relation to each other, the latter is not difficult if the centre point of the roundel is marked as a small dot on the initial white disc, and this is used as a datum point for the location of the others.

United States stars and bars are painted in exactly the same way, starting with a template through which is painted a white disc with longitudinal arms. The star and white areas of the bars are also cut in template form and placed over the white to mask it, then the exposed area is painted blue. The red bars that appear on the white longitudinal arms can be painted in the same way or alternatively marked with red Letraset stripes. This technique can be applied to any marking if the sequence of discs and templates is worked out beforehand.

Large fuselage or underwing codes can also be painted by using templates cut from Frisk film but in many cases masking tape can be used equally as successfully especially in painting letters with straight edges. Unless you have a particularly steady hand, serials and other very small markings should be avoided and the correct size Letraset or Blick markings used, but it is possible to paint these providing the paint used is kept thin and a good quality brush with a fine point is used. There really is nothing that can be written to advise on this type of painting as it is something that you can either do or you can't, and only experimentation and practice will indicate the extent of your limitations. Once having found these, always work within them and never, never be tempted to try something that you know you cannot do on a model that you have spent hours working on, for it is very easy to overstep the mark and spoil all the work that has gone before.

One subject that has so far not been discussed and which may appear odd to introduce in a chapter that is primarily concerned with painting, is the rigging of biplanes. However, this part of modelling very much reflects the authenticity of the completed model and is considered to be in its rightful place in a chapter covering authentic finishes.

There is a magic about biplanes that makes them attractive to most modellers, but the quantity of kits produced would suggest that such modellers are not the younger ones to whom kit manufacturers look for the majority of their sales. There is no doubt that assembling a biplane from a kit can present the young and inexperienced with many problems, especially when it comes to painting, alignment of the various struts, and rigging. The latter is essential if the model is to capture the air of the original and it is sad to see many well-built models which may be forming part of a collection marred by the fact that the bi-

planes look incomplete simply because the builder has not added the rigging. Some so-called experienced modellers who readily decry others' work because in their opinion the colour tone is wrong, or the wheels oversize, will argue that on a 1:72 scale model of a biplane such as the Tiger Moth or Sopwith Camel, it is not possible to reproduce rigging to scale and if it were such rigging would be invisible therefore it is best to leave it off, and are really only admitting their own inability to even try to add this essential ingredient. In some respects their argument is correct inasmuch as scale rigging on small models would to all intents and purposes be invisible, but in my opinion this is one area where a deviation from scale can only enhance the finished product. Naturally the use of correct material will disguise the over-scale effect which is exaggerated when rigging is added using completely unsuitable material such as ordinary domestic cotton. However, those who have used such material should be commended for at least trying to obtain authenticity.

There are many ways of rigging a biplane and every modeller eventually finds the one that suits him best, usually after much experimentation, and thereafter sticks rigidly to it. Unfortunately there are no short cuts and the following methods are three of those that have proved successful after a period of trial and error, highlighted by success and marred by despondency. Those who aspire to concentrate on biplanes must be prepared to cultivate rigging skills by

This Blériot Monoplane by Paul Roeder from the Impact 1:48 scale kit would look very incomplete if the modeller had not taken endless pains to add all the rigging (photo Kunze).

constant practice during which they will also experience various levels of elation.

The method of using cotton tied to struts is one that must be deprecated since this does not capture the delicacy of rigging which, if transferred to the model, is over half way towards winning the battle.

If instead of cotton, thin nylon fishing line is used, several of the problems with ordinary domestic cotton will immediately be overcome. Such fishing line is obtainable in various grades or strengths and the finest available should be looked for when starting out. The size is, of course, dictated by the scale of the model, but even on 1:32 scale biplanes it is easy to overestimate the size of rigging material used and end up with a clumsy looking model.

The biggest problem in the use of nylon fishing line is fixing it to the model so that it stays taught. The best method is to drill a small hole with a dental or watchmaker's drill at the base of the strut right through the wing surface, pass a length of nylon through this, then with a toothpick apply a quick drying epoxy glue such as 'Five minute Devcon', into the hole and around the nylon. When the cement has set hard, pass the other end of the nylon through another hole drilled at its locating point and once again apply epoxy glue, making sure that the nylon is held tight whilst the glue sets. The necessity of using rapid drying cement becomes obvious as it is time consuming to sit for long periods simply holding nylon taut, furthermore, however careful you are, if the nylon is constantly moving whilst you are holding it, the glue will not stick it firmly enough, slow drying glues therefore accentuate such movement and cause considerable headaches. The epoxy glue must be applied sparingly and to the outer extremities of the drilled holes, these will be in the top surfaces of the top wings and the bottom surfaces of the lower wings. The evidence of the holes in the lower surfaces of the top wings and the top surfaces of the bottom wings — which will already have been painted — is hidden by filling them with a touch of Polyfilla added with a cocktail stick and touched in with the correct colour paint once it has set. Ordinary body putty or Green Stuff can be used but this does not usually dry as smoothly as Polyfilla and attention from wet and dry or sandpaper in such a con-

The heat-stretched sprue rigging on this Albatross D1 is overscale but makes the model look more authentic than it would have if it had been omitted altogether. The model is made from parts from the Revell D11 and E 111 kits. Model by Paul Roeder.

fined space is impossible.

Once the glue has set the excess nylon protruding from the wing surfaces should be cut off flush with a very sharp modelling knife and, as these areas have not yet been painted, any slight blemishes can be removed by careful sanding. This method of rigging must be done with very great care as it is easy to end up with unsightly 'blobs' on the wing surfaces where the material has been cemented in position, and sagging rigging if the glue has not been allowed to set hard before the ends of the nylon were released.

The most successful alternative, at least as far as I am concerned, is the use of stretched sprue or very fine wire. Sprue costs nothing as it comes in every plastic kit, and with practice can be stretched into very fine filaments. Clear or silver/grey sprue is best for rigging on 1:72 scale models but on larger scales it is better to heat stretch flat strips of plastic card as the cross-section is then more in keeping with actual rigging wires which do have an aerofoil section. The method to employ is to stretch several lengths of sprue or plastic card to as uniform a cross-section as possible then place them aside for future use. Now take a pair of dividers and measure the distance between two attachment points, fix a length of sprue on to a flat surface with Sellotape strips, and measure off a length with the dividers which are already set at the distance needed for this particular piece. Using a sharp modelling knife cut the sprue to the exact dimension indicated by the dividers, then holding it with a pair of tweezers, add the minutest spot of polystyrene cement at each end. Remember that this adhesive is designed to melt plastic so it is vital that only the smallest possible amount is used. Carefully insert the length into position making sure that any paint that is present at the attachment points has first been cleaned off. An alternative to applying cement to the ends of the cut sprue, is the use of liquid cement applied with a small brush at the attachment points, but the warning made earlier applies equally to this form of adhesive.

White glue such as Reeves PVA Adhesive — obtainable from art supply shops — does not have the same properties as polystyrene cement and can be used as an alternative. Apart from the fact that it does not melt plastic, another advantage is that it dries transparent, but one disadvantage is that it takes longer to set and it is therefore easy to disturb rigging that is already in place when adding additional strips.

Thin hard wire, not fuse wire, is perhaps the ideal way of representing rigging. But this is hard to obtain and requires a higher level of skill if it is to look right on the completed model. Suitable wire can be obtained at some radio component shops where it is sold for winding resistance coils, another source of supply is the local car breaker's yard, where it might be possible to obtain an ignition coil which will supply enough wire for years of biplane modelling. The method of application is similar to the one used for sprue, but the wire must be straightened first. To do this cut off a length which is approximately the size needed, then roll this on a smooth metal surface or a sheet of glass, with a flat piece of wood. This should be about four inches wide and half an inch thick and is rolled over the wire with the flat of the hand making sure that at no time does the wire creep out around the edges. PVA glue will hold the wire in position, but if a wire with sufficient spring tension in it is selected, it will stay in position without any form of adhesive.

Another method that is inexpensive and effective, but probably requires the most practice, is the use of stretched *glue*. Any rubber-based adhesive such as Uhu, Bostick or Humbrol Universal is suitable. Squeeze a drop of the selected glue on to a clean piece of card or paper and use a pointed cocktail stick to pick up a small portion of it. Make sure that there are no straggling ends, then carefully place the point of the cocktail stick at the first fixing point and very gently move it towards the other attachment point. A very fine filament of glue will stretch between the struts and can be cut with a sharp knife at the point where it is attached. As this type of adhesive 'goes off' very quickly, a fresh amount is needed for each piece of rigging. This method produces extremely fine rigging with the advantage that is is very easy to replace should it become broken. It is difficult to stretch glue over very long distances so it is best to use this method only on small-scale biplanes. One other advantage of this method which is hard

Another fine model from Paul Roeder, this 1:72 scale Bristol F2B from the Airfix kit captures the feeling of the original almost perfectly. Standards such as this are not beyond any modeller who is prepared to practice and persevere (photo Kunze).

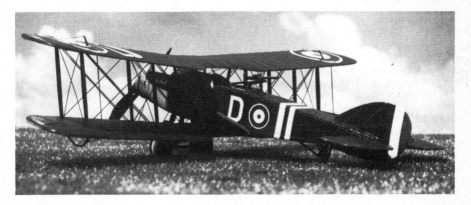

to produce with the others, is the use of double rigging wires. If a close look is taken at some biplanes it will be seen that some of the interplane rigging is in fact comprised of two wires running parallel to each other from the same attachment point. By using a cocktail stick with the end cut to a flat and a 'V' cut in this flat, it is possible to pick up two sections of glue and stretch them at the same time between the selected points. This is aiming for a very high level and should not be attempted until the basic method has been mastered.

With any type of rigging always start with the wires that are near the centre of the wings and work outwards, this stops damage occurring to wires already attached since you will always be working away from them.

Rigging diagrams are not often included with kits but box art usually gives a more or less accurate guide to their positioning, and of course if a reference source is being used this is almost certain to show all the rigging that is applied to the particular aircraft being modelled. The complete rigging of a 1:72 scale biplane is next to impossible, unless you are a real expert, but even the addition of just the basic elements will improve the model. Obviously the methods outlined can be used on other aircraft to represent aerials, control wires, undercarriage bracing, etc, it is also possible to combine the methods on one model, selecting each one to suit the part that is being rigged.

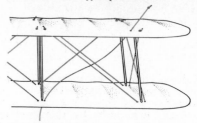

Drill holes adjacent to struts, draw nylon or other suitable thread through, knot end and seal with epoxy. When firmly set trim off exposed ends

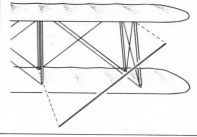

Wire or stretched sprue cut to exact size and held between struts with a touch of epoxy glue or liquid polystyrene cement

As experience is gained and the habit of looking at aeroplanes at every opportunity to seek ideas for adding additional detail is cultivated, the feeling of the actual aeroplane will be transferred to the model, and this itself will go a long way towards capturing a truly authentic appearance.

seven

Conversions

Although the number of aircraft kits is constantly increasing there are certain types that are highly unlikely ever to be produced in kit form, but their omission from a collection will leave serious gaps in continuity, especially if the theme of the collection is historical. It therefore often becomes necessary for the serious modeller to look towards existing kits with a view to converting them to either different marks of the aircraft concerned, or using parts which can be modified to produce an entirely different type of aeroplane.

Generally speaking conversions can be split into two categories; those which can be done from the basic kit using parts that are scratch-built from wood or plastic card, and those that use parts from a variety of kits in addition to additional scratch-built components. Naturally the first is the least expensive and to a certain extent easier than the second, but it does not enable every type of model that one wants to be collected. The second can be expensive if you set out to buy three or four kits just to obtain small pieces, but there are two ways of looking at this: one is that relatively speaking even the cost of three kits is not that expensive if an otherwise inobtainable model is to result, and the other is that the parts that remain when those that are required for the conversion have been taken, will be useful additions to the spares box which is an essential part of the avid converter's equipment.

The current tendency to include parts in basic kits that enable the modeller to produce two or even three versions of the model depicted, is one that automatically gives a start in building up a collection of spare parts. Quite often such parts will be limited to a variety of underwing and fuselage stores, but it is surprising just how useful these will become as with thought they can be turned to a variety of uses far removed from their original intention. Kits such as

the Matchbox Wellington Mk X include alternative parts — in this case a different nose for the Mk XIV — and these should also be kept for future adaptation.

There are now a variety of conversion kits available which take a lot of the hard work out of building, the use of which often results in the replacement by them of kit components, so here again there is another source of useful ready moulded components.

Gradually the parts collected will accumulate to such a degree that it is well worthwhile storing them in a special box, or boxes, categorised as to their use. A good way to do this is to purchase from a chain store, hardware shop or motor accessory shop, a small cabinet with several perspex drawers. The components collected can then be placed in their own drawer, for example one can be earmarked for canopies, another for drop tanks, another for wheels and so on. This immediately puts an end to what can be a long rummage through a discarded kit box into which all spare parts have been confined, looking for a part you know you have but can't quite remember exactly where it is.

Most major conversions are limited to 1:72 scale mainly because this is the most popular scale for large collections, but also because there are more kits produced in this scale than any other. Another factor that must also be considered is the cost. Few modellers will think twice before buying a 25p kit with the intention of cutting it up, but it is another story when it comes to a large scale kit that might cost several pounds. For this reason the examples described have been confined to inexpensive kits, where major work has been necessary, but more expensive ones have been used to illustrate just what can be done if you feel so inclined and tackle the problems in a logical way.

The addition of parts omitted from a kit, such as flap guide rails, cockpit detail and the like, is not converting but merely improving the basic kit. But if, for example, long span wings, a modified fuselage and four-bladed propeller are added to a Airfix Bf 109G to make it into a high altitude version of this famous German fighter, then it is correct to say that the kit has been converted from one mark to another. It is as well to make this seemingly obvious point clear right from the start as on many occasions when I have been invited to judge modelling competitions basic kits, with a few refinements added, have been included in incorrect categories simply because the builder thought that he was carrying out conversion work.

Every modeller who has some experience of converting kits has his own way of researching the basic subject and deciding which kits are likely to produce the parts he will need. One pitfall in this respect is to consider the models available first and what it might be possible to convert them to. In cases where one aircraft has been developed from another, such as the Nimrod from the Comet, or various marks of aircraft differ in major or minor components, such as the Canberra, Spitfire, P-47 and P-51, Lancaster Mk I and Mk II, this method is obvious and will work. But my own method is to study as much material as I can find on an aircraft I want to make then break down the major parts into sections that I might be able to obtain from kits. Only then do I take the various kit manufacturers' catalogues or products and compare my thoughts with reality. It is surprising just how effective this method can be and it was one that I used when I constructed a model of a Bristol Brigand for the 1973 *Airfix Magazine Annual*. After studying drawings and photographs of the Brigand I broke the components needed into fuselage, mainplanes, engines, tail unit and cockpit. As the aircraft came from the Bristol stable the first step was to look at kits that were available of this manufacturer's aircraft. The Beaufighter was looked at and quickly discarded as, apart from the radial engines, which had possible potential, the rest of the components came nowhere near what I needed. Similarly the Blenheim and Beaufort also fell by the wayside, then I came across the Airfix Bristol Freighter, and it became immediately evident that this model would provide the material needed.

The outboard wing panels, although far too large, had the same basic outline shape of the Brigand's, and the engines were almost exactly right. I therefore earmarked these parts and continued looking for others from different kits. This search proved fruitless so I decided to use as much of the Freighter as I possibly could. In the end the Brigand's fuselage was carved from balsa from which a plastic card shell was moulded. The complete wings were made from the Freighter's by first cutting cardboard templates of the Brigand's then using these to mark out the shape on the Freighter's, the tailplanes were also made from the Freighter's and the same kit provided the wheels. Fins and rudders were cut from plastic card and the cockpit was moulded using the already described male and female mould method. The final result was a model of an important RAF aircraft that it seems unlikely will ever be produced in kit form (other than as a vac-formed model), for the outlay of only one kit.

In the example quoted the balsa wood fuselage was used as a mould simply because the model was intended to be entered in an IPMS competition and this society deprecates the use of wood in the proportions I had used it. This is a somewhat short-sighted policy as the judges should really be concerned with the skill of the modeller in producing a realistic model rather than the materials he chooses to use. However, it is one of their rules and must be adhered to until such time as it is rescinded if you are competition-minded. I make this point because in a lot of my conversion I use balsa or other wood as I consider it a much better and easier to work with material than anything else.

If you decide to make conversions the major part of your hobby, long term planning will pay dividends as it is often possible to select several models that can use components from the kits you have to buy. An example of this is the use of a Halifax and Lancaster to produce two alternative models of these famous bombers. The radial engines from the Halifax can be adapted to fit the Lancaster to produce the Mk II version and the rest of the Halifax kit modified to make the Mk I or Mk II Series I or IA versions with in-line engines and new rudders. The Merlin engines left over from the Lancaster kit will come in useful if you want to make the Miles M20 described later, or a Mk IIF Beaufighter.

The examples that now follow will give an idea as to just what can be achieved and many of the techniques can be adapted to any type of conversion in any scale. By careful selection of the subject, adequate research, a knowledge of available kits, and patience in overcoming problems, a whole new aspect of modelling aircraft will open its doors to you, and you may well find that you will soon become one of the 'converted'.

Hawker Siddeley Nimrod
1:144 scale

The Nimrod is the first land-based four-jet maritime reconnaissance aircraft to enter service anywhere in the world and can trace its origins back to the de Havilland Comet airliner. The first two prototypes were in fact modified from Comet airframes and flew within two months of each other, the Spey-engined version taking to the air on May 23 1967 and the Avon-powered version on July 31 the same year. Packed with highly sophisticated radar aids, the Nimrod represents the very latest in anti-submarine warfare and entered service

with the Royal Air Force on October 1 1969 with Strike Command which absorbed Coastal Command in name if not in spirit and tradition.

As Airfix have a Comet IV in their Skyking range of airliners the basic material is available to produce a small-scale model of this very important aeroplane, so this conversion falls into the first category mentioned earlier in this chapter whereby a kit of one aircraft is used in conjunction with scratch-built components to produce an entirely different model than can be made from the original kit parts.

Comparison of the Nimrod with the Comet shows that the major change is to the fuselage where an additional 'bubble', housing the weapons bay and other equipment, has been added to the original pressure cabin.

The first step is to cement strips of plastic card behind the windows that are not required, these being clearly shown on the drawings. The length of the kit fuselage also has to be reduced by 24 mm so a section of this length is cut out of the fuselage, the first cut being 5 mm aft of the door on the starboard side (part 4). Before cementing the shortened nose to the other two halves make sure that the

An RAF Nimrod of No 206 Squadron, RAF Kinloss, observing a Russian guided missile destroyer in the Orkneys area (MoD).

plastic window blanking strips are secure and that weight is inserted in the extreme nose. Cement the two doors (parts 1 and 3) in position, then cement together the four parts that form the fuselage shell, ensuring that the nose lines up correctly with the rear section. If the cuts made when the 24 mm section was removed were executed with care, there should be no problems. But if the saw was not kept vertical then the nose will tilt up or down depending on which way you allowed the saw to move. If this has happened the only remedy is to add a circle of plastic card strip around the inside circumference of the fuselage parts, then fill any resulting gap with body putty.

While the fuselage is setting cement the two parts of the wings (15 and 16) together but leave off the jet pipes (parts 19, 20, 21, and 22). The wings must be extended in span, so to give a bigger area for the adhesive file the cross-section of the tips flat, then cement plastic card to each one. When this has dried hard it can be shaped as shown on the plan. Before going too far with the wings place them in position in their cut-out on the fuse-

lage underside and hold them in place with strips of Sellotape at the front and rear, but *do not* cement them in place at this stage.

Now select a soft piece of balsa wood and trim this until it is the same width as the fuselage and 18 cm long, place it on the underside of the fuselage and with a pencil mark the curvature of the bottom line of the fuselage from the nose to 35 mm aft of the wing root. Remove the surplus wood above the marked line until the block fits snugly along the fuselage. To obtain a good fit it will be necessary to slightly hollow out the top surface of the block so that it follows the fuselage cross-section. Once the block has been roughly carved to shape and fits around the wing sections, the wings can be removed and work carried out on them. In addition to the lengthened span it is also necessary to widen the jet engine intakes, add fuel vent pipes at the tips, wing fences, and the long-range fuel tanks. The intakes are enlarged by using a small file to remove plastic around the intake lips; this is a delicate operation which must be done carefully if the

The mighty Nimrod as converted by the author from the Airfix 1:144 scale Comet kit. The work, which is detailed in the text, is very extensive but the resulting model is worth all the trouble. The aerials are from stretched sprue as are the fuel vent pipes seen at the wingtips (photo by John Carter).

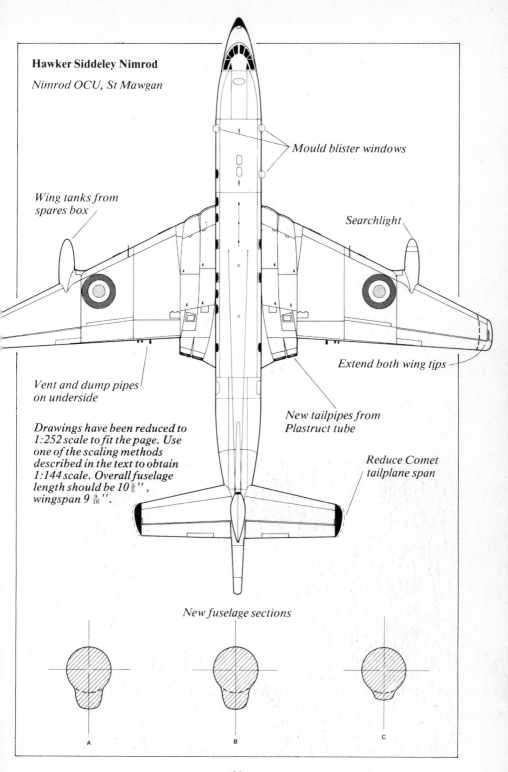

Hawker Siddeley Nimrod

Nimrod OCU, St Mawgan

Mould blister windows

Wing tanks from
spares box

Searchlight

Extend both wing tips

Vent and dump pipes
on underside

New tailpipes from
Plastruct tube

Drawings have been reduced to
1:252 scale to fit the page. Use
one of the scaling methods
described in the text to obtain
1:144 scale. Overall fuselage
length should be 10⅝",
wingspan 9 9⁄16".

Reduce Comet
tailplane span

New fuselage sections

A   B   C

symmetry of the intakes is to be retained, and constant checking against the drawings is a must. Once satisfied that the intakes are correct, holes are drilled between the inner and outer ones on each wing, and also outboard of the outer engines. The outer holes are then filled with clear sprue which is filed to the leading edge contours and polished to represent the aircraft's landing lights. The fuel tanks and other parts can be added after the wings are fitted to the fuselage but their assembly will be described at this stage. Vent pipes are nothing more than stretched sprue cemented to the extended tips and sanded at their leading edges to blend into the wing surfaces. The wing fences are cut from 10 thou plastic card and held in place with liquid cement. To obtain the correct shape of these where they fit the wings, cut a slot into a piece of cartridge paper and slide this over the wings until it is in the position the fences are to occupy. Hold the paper as vertical as possible and mark the curvature of the wing aerofoil on it with a hard pencil, slide the paper off the wing and cut the curved bottom surface with a sharp knife. Use the cartridge paper as a template to transfer the shape to the plastic card then draw the rest of the wing fence before cutting it out. The result should be a perfect fit that will not require any filling.

The tanks are made from similar components taken from the spares box, those on the model shown coming from an Airfix Harrier. If you have not yet accumulated enough spares and do not wish to purchase a Harrier just to obtain tanks, they can be carved from 8 mm dowelling. It is necessary to modify the tanks so that they fit the Comet's wings and the inboard fairings are made from plastic card. Any gaps are filled with body putty which is also used to ensure a smooth fairing into the wing surfaces. The tanks are completed by adding vent pipes and small bumpers from sprue. The starboard tank has the front section removed and replaced by a transparent cone to cover the searchlight. This part is made by making sure that the front section is removed accurately with a vertical cut, it is then firmly cemented with Devcon or Araldite to a cocktail stick and allowed to dry.

Once this part is secure on the cocktail stick, reduce its diameter to allow for the

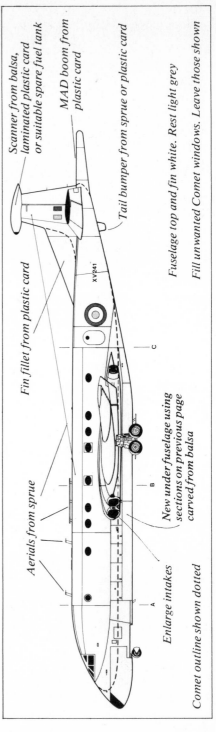

100

A Comet IVB cockpit interior (photo by Ian Wallace). *Compare this with the earlier shot of a Bulldog instrument panel.*

thickness of the clear sheet by even sanding with wet and dry used wet. Now drill a hole in a spare piece of fairly thick balsa sheet through which the nose cone will pass. Pin a sheet of clear acetate over this hole and heat it under the grill until it is soft, then plunge the cone through this and you will have moulded a clear cover that is trimmed to size whilst the cone is still inserted, the clear cover is then cemented in position with PVA glue. To simulate the searchlight wrap a piece of silver paper from a sweet wrapping or cigarette packet around a short piece of sprue, and push this into the tank before the clear cone is cemented in position.

New jet pipes are made by either wrapping 10 thou plastic card around a

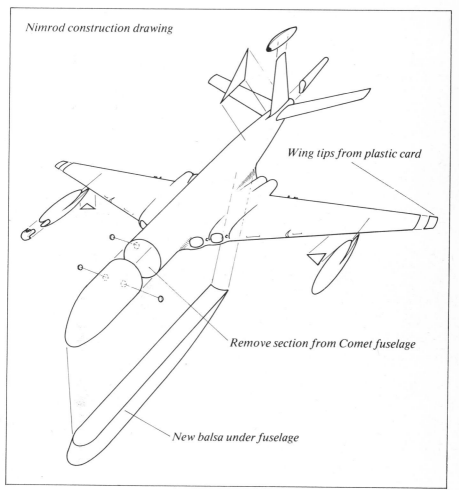

Nimrod construction drawing

Wing tips from plastic card

Remove section from Comet fuselage

New balsa under fuselage

dowel to form a hollow tube which is then cut to the lengths needed, or cutting these from 4 mm diameter Plastruct.

The wings are cemented into position on the fuselage then the balsa block is also cemented into place using either polystyrene cement or preferably an epoxy glue. It is essential that the block is allowed to set really hard before it is carved and sanded to the shape of the lower fuselage contours. Pay particular attention to getting the cross-sectional shape correct, especially at the nose and where it is faired into the rear fuselage. Body putty is used to fair it into the fuselage but apply this carefully otherwise the distinctive double bubble effect will be lost. The MAD (Magnetic Anomoly Detector) boom at the rear is made from two laminations of 20 thou plastic card with the front end cut in a 'V' to mate into the rear of the original tail cone.

To complete the fuselage add the tail bumper from plastic card, fill the windows with body putty, except those that are still required, and add the blister windows on the port and starboard sides. The latter are probably the trickiest part of the fuselage work and after a fruitless search through the spares box I resorted to moulding them from clear sheet. I did this by pinning a sheet of acetate to a soft balsa block, softened it under the grill, then pushed the tip of a biro cap into the

block through the acetate. It took only a few moments to produce a dozen blisters which yielded three perfect examples. Two of these are fitted over the first two windows from the nose on the port side, and the other over the first window on the starboard side.

The leading edge of the fin was sanded flat and a dorsal fin cut from 20 thou plastic card was cemented into position, final shaping being carried out after this had set. The radome fitted to the top of the fin was one half of another discarded drop tank with the bottom being filled with scrap plastic card and body putty. A sprue peg was inserted through the fin just aft of the leading edge and 7 mm below the radome, to give locating points for the two aerials, the other ends of which were cemented to similar pegs inserted in the top of the fuselage. Other aerials were added from stretched sprue and plastic card offcuts and the model was completed by the addition of the Comet's undercarriage, the nose oleo requiring a new locating hole in the balsa underbelly.

The model was painted in dove grey and white and the roundels came from the same Harrier kit that had provided the wing fuel tanks. The fuselage and underwing serials came from a Letraset sheet.

The resulting model is an attractive addition to any collection of military air-

The distinctive shape of the Nimrod is visible in this picture from which it is easy to see its close resemblance to the Comet airliner from which it was developed (photo by R. L. Ward).

Top *A P2V-5 Neptune WX514 L-R of 210 Squadron photographed at Linton-on-Ouse. This aircraft has the original flat canopy and large wing tanks but the nose turret has been replaced by a clear canopy as provided in the Hasegawa kit* (photo by R. L. Ward). **Above** *This photograph of WX506 of 236 Squadron clearly shows the modifications needed to the nose and canopy. The large wing tanks and revised tail are also very evident* (photo by R. L. Ward).

craft and the work involved is not too difficult if it is tackled carefully. The out and out beginner might run into one or two problems but should be capable of overcoming these. So the Nimrod is an ideal starting point for those who have tried one or two minor conversions and want to take on a greater challenge without running the risk of ruining an expensive kit.

Lockheed P2V-5 Neptune
1:72 scale

Whilst the Nimrod represents the very latest Maritime Reconnaissance aircraft of the RAF, the Neptune is the same type of aircraft but from an earlier era. Although it is still in service with the United States Navy and serveral other air forces throughout the world, it has long since passed from the RAF's inventory.

The Hasegawa kit of the P2V-7 is a much later version than that used by the

RAF and to convert it back into the -5 version is a challenging task, for although at first glance the work might appear minimal, this is not in fact so.

In the immediate post-war years Coastal Command operated Sunderlands, Lancasters and Lend-Lease Liberators and Fortresses. In an air force that was drastically reduced in size from its war-time strength, these proved adequate until the borrowed aircraft were recalled and the demands of NATO increased. In the early 1950s the planned Lancaster replacement, the Avro Shackleton, had not reached operational status so a modern (for the period) stop-gap had to be found. This proved to be the Lockheed P2V Neptune which had first flown in May 1945 as the XP2V-1 and had first made its presence felt in September 1946 when, in the hands of Commander Thomas D. Davies of the US Navy, had established a record for long distance non-stop duration flying of 55 hours 17 minutes during

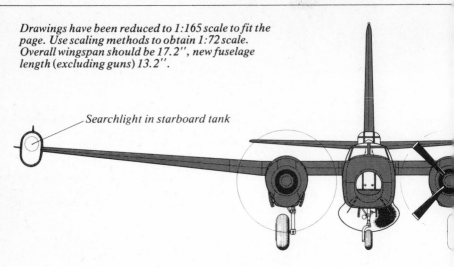

Drawings have been reduced to 1:165 scale to fit the page. Use scaling methods to obtain 1:72 scale. Overall wingspan should be 17.2", new fuselage length (excluding guns) 13.2".

Searchlight in starboard tank

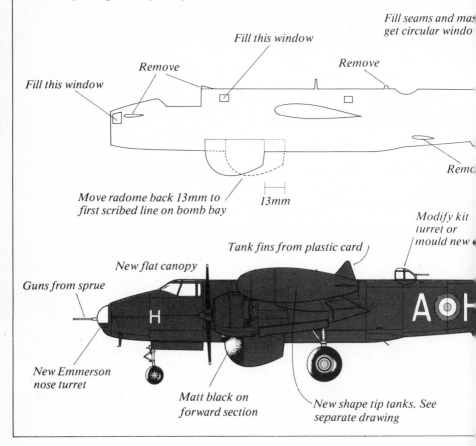

Outline of Hasegawa kit fuselage showing necessary modifications

Fill this window

Remove

Fill seams and mas▮
get circular windo▮

Remove

Fill this window

Remo▮

Move radome back 13mm to
first scribed line on bomb bay

13mm

Remc▮

Modify kit
turret or
mould new

Tank fins from plastic card

New flat canopy

Guns from sprue

New Emmerson
nose turret

Matt black on
forward section

New shape tip tanks. See
separate drawing

104

Lockheed P2V-5 Neptune

Aircraft drawn is WX504
A-H of 217 Squadron 1953

Fill holes for jet engines on both wings not fitted to P2V-5 version

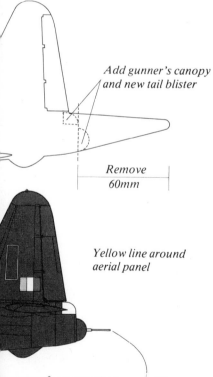

Add gunner's canopy and new tail blister

Remove 60mm

Yellow line around aerial panel

ear guns from stretched sprue. These were ometimes removed on actual aircraft

Sea blue gloss overall
White codes and serial

which it covered 11,326 miles. This achievement brought an immediate order worth over 16 million dollars from the US Navy and started the Neptune on an illustrious career which is still continuing today, over 30 years since it first saw the light of day.

In the spring of 1951 it was announced that the RAF was to receive 52 aircraft which were to be the P2V-5 version. The intention was for Coastal Command to use these until such time as the Shackleton was available in sufficient numbers. The first two aircraft arrived at St Eval on January 13 1952 having been flown to England by RAF crews who had been receiving training on the type in America. For the following five years the Neptune served the RAF well, and although during its service it was modified to later standards by the removal of the nose turret and the fitting of the extended MAD tail, it is the early version that is the subject of this conversion.

The cockpit area is assembled exactly as the kit instructions and placed on one side until the major modifications to the fuselage are completed, a lot of this work having to be carried out before the two halves are cemented together. Start by cementing all the windows in place but omitting the astrodome (part 84) and the turret blanking disc (part 82). The under fuselage radome is now removed by cutting each half from the respective fuselage halves using the moulded lines immediately in front and at the rear of the radome as guides. The horizontal cuts which finally remove the moulding from the fuselage are made along the line of the bomb bay just below the ridge which is moulded to the fuselage sides. Now measure 13 mm from where the rear end of the radome was located, which you will find lines up exactly with the second row of moulded rivets on the bomb bay doors. Cut along the rivet lines on both fuselage halves and also the top of the bomb bay line to remove a 13 mm section, this section is then replaced behind the nose gear door and behind this the radome is relocated. These operations have, in fact, moved the radome back 13 mm and at the same time shortened the weapons bay. If the work is carried out with a fine razor saw and sharp knife, it will be found that the parts fit easily into their new locations and a minimum of filling will be needed.

The next step is to remove the two

blisters aft of the nose windows and those located on the lower half of the fuselage behind the weapons bay. The large blister situated under the rear square windows on the underside of the fuselage also has to be removed, and this will leave a big hole that must be backed with plastic card. Measure 60 mm from the end of the tail MAD fairing and cut this off at this point with a vertical saw cut.

The square windows on both sides at the nose should now be covered with filler as should the small square window immediately behind the cockpit on the port side. Filler is also applied around the joins of the square windows in the aft fuselage below the leading edge of the fin, but do not cover these completely.

The two fuselage halves should now be cemented together, with the interior, including the dorsal turret (parts 87 and 59), in place. Filler is now used to fill the gap where the large underside blister at the tail was removed, and when this has set hard, it is shaped to follow the line of the lower fuselage. It is now very much a question of patient work with wet and dry to smooth all the filler as this must be blended smoothly into the fuselage, especially where it has been used to cover windows.

Once the work outlined on the fuselage has been completed, a plastic card blanking plate is cut to fit the hole at the rear end where the MAD fairing was removed and a suitable rounded cone fitted in its place. On my model I found that a blister turret from an Airfix B-29 filled the bill ideally although once it was in position body putty was needed to increase its diameter to match the fuselage cross-section. A balsa block or plastic card laminations will do just as well if your spares box has not yet reached the proportions where it is likely to yield a ready moulded part.

The nose ball turret presented some problems but these were eventually solved by reshaping a nose turret from an Airfix Dornier 217. This was too narrow at the bottom, but once the flattened windows had been rounded off the top section fitted perfectly and body putty came to the rescue in building up the shape of the bottom half.

The rear gunner's cockpit was built up from clear plastic cut from a kit stand and cemented into place below the rudder. The final major operation on the

Neptune P2V-5

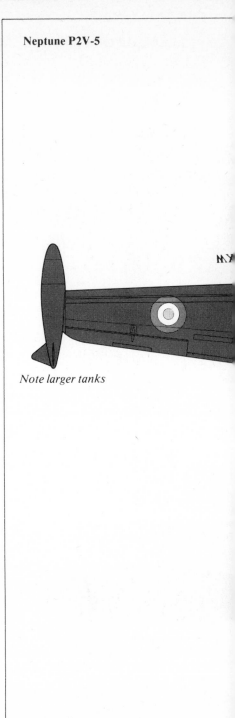

Note larger tanks

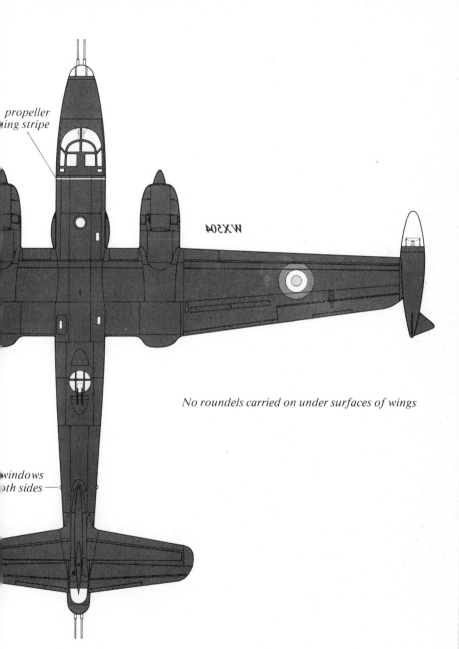

propeller
ing stripe

WX204

No roundels carried on under surfaces of wings

windows
th sides

Serials in white are painted on wing under surfaces reading forward on starboard
wing, rearward on port

fuselage was the replacement of the kit's main canopy, and here there is no alternative to moulding a new one. The canopy provided is far too bulbous for the P2V-5 and cannot be modified, so carve a new low profile canopy from a balsa block and mould it from thin acetate sheet.

Before cementing the wing halves together cement strips of plastic card over the holes into which the jet engines fit as these are not used on this particular model. Now assemble the wings and engines as per the kit instructions, filling the aforementioned holes with body putty and leaving off the wingtip tanks. The latter are entirely incorrect for the -5, and once again correct ones must be scratch-built. I did this by carving one balsa tank then moulded four halves on a Mattel vac-form tool. The balsa master was cemented together again to form one component and I then cut off the nose which was used to mould the searchlight cover for the starboard tank. Again the

Mattel was used but all these parts can be produced equally as well by the male and female moulding technique already mentioned several times elsewhere. Fins for the tanks were made from 20 thou plastic card and cemented in position just prior to painting. The undercarriage and all other components were added following the kit instructions, then the whole model was given a coat of matt white which, as well as well as giving an ideal undercoat, also served to show up any areas that still needed attention from wet and dry.

Before applying any paint cut two discs 3 mm in diameter from masking tape and place these exactly central over the rear fuselage square windows. These are removed after all painting has been completed and will produce the circular windows that were in this position on the -5.

The model was sprayed with Humbrol Sea Blue Gloss (HB9) to which was added a touch of black, and exhaust

The extensively re-worked Hasegawa Neptune detailed in the text. The canopy on this model is the later 'blown' type whereas it should be the 'flat' type illustrated in the drawings (photo by John Carter).

Another view of the Neptune in RAF service. The nose and tail have been considerably altered and new tip tanks fitted. The underneath radome has been moved back 13mm. Exhaust stains were a prominent feature of the Neptune however clean the rest of the airframe might have been.

stains were applied around the engine exhausts with a mix of light grey and white. All markings came from Letraset sheet M11 apart from the code letters which were 'borrowed' from various other sheets. The propeller warning stripe around the fuselage came from the kit markings as did the yellow aerial lining on the fin. Nose and tail guns were added from stretched sprue which also provided the various aerials that were to be seen sprouting from different places on this aircraft.

The mould and plastic moulding from it for the Neptune wing tanks. The mould is carved in balsa then used on a vac-form machine.

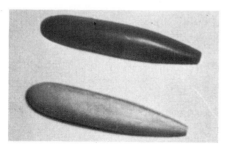

The plastic moulded half of the Neptune wing tank as it comes off the vac-form tool. The dimples are the area where the holes for extracting the air from the moulding chamber are drilled on the moulding platform.

During their later years of service the RAF's -5s were modified to a later standard by the fitting of the MAD tail, and the removal of the nose turret which was replaced by the transparent cone as supplied in the kit.

If you wish to make this version modify the radome position as detailed, remove the large forward blister under the tail but do not fill the front windows. This version has the old larger wing tanks, also the circular rear windows and the flatter cockpit canopy, so the work needed is still considerable although the problems of the nose and rear gun positions are removed.

North American FJ-4 Fury
1:72 scale

For many years naval aircraft were often modified versions of successful or planned land-based aircraft, because the economies involved in producing special navalised designs for small production runs were not viable. But as the carrier grew in both size and importance, the desirability of designing custom-built aircraft to operate from them became apparent.

Immediately after World War 2 the eyes of naval aviators turned to jet-propelled aircraft and it was not long before land-based aircraft were sprouting arrestor hooks and undergoing sea trials. However, the necessity of specific designs based on naval requirements soon saw an end to the pre-jet age of improvisation, and in England the Vickers Attacker and Hawker Sea Hawk heralded the dawn of a new era of jet-engined aircraft designed for carrier operations.

In the United States of America similar development was also taking place but there was a noticeable exception where a planned naval aircraft turned out to become one of the USAF's greatest fighters, the F-86 Sabre. It is not often appreciated that this well-known machine was developed from a design that was carried out to meet a US Navy requirement of 1945.

The original design of the Sabre, known as the XP-86, stemmed from the North American NA134 which was a straight-winged naval fighter ordered by the US Navy on January 1 1945. The NA140 evolved from this and appeared with swept wings to finally materialise as the FH86 Sabre. Meanwhile the NA134 continued in straight-wing form and became the XFJ-1 which eventually became the FJ-1 Fury. This aircraft entered service with the US Navy in 1948 and Commander Pete Aurand made the first operational landings aboard a carrier at sea when he put his FJ-1 Fury on the flight deck of the USS *Boxer* on March 10 1948.

This rotund but pleasing fighter, of which only 30 were built, deserves a

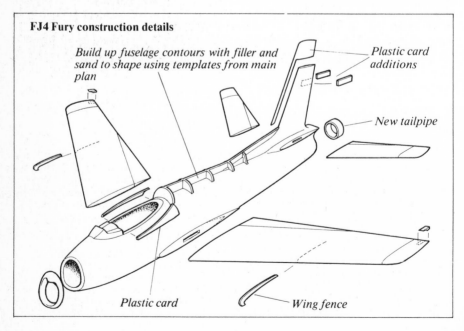

FJ4 Fury construction details

Build up fuselage contours with filler and sand to shape using templates from main plan

Plastic card additions

New tailpipe

Plastic card

Wing fence

A Navy FJ-4 high over the Rockies. The modified shape of the fuselage is very evident in this photograph as are the under fuselage dive brakes, refuelling probe and underwing stores (photo courtesy North American Aviation).

An FJ-4 of a Marine/Navy training unit. The extended nose wheel, taller fin/rudder, modified cockpit and flight refuelling probe can all be clearly seen (Aviation Photo News).

place in US Naval aviation history and a very good 1:72 scale model is available of it in the Rareplanes range of vac-formed kits. From the basic design the swept wing FJ-2 and FJ-3 were developed, and although these have a remarkably similar shape to the F-86, they are in fact entirely different. An interesting fact about the FJ-3 is that it was powered by a licence-built version of the British Armstrong-Siddeley Sapphire engine designated J65-W-2. The FJ-3 proved to be more successful than either the FJ-1 or FJ-2 and equipped 12 naval squadrons.

The conversion of the Hasegawa/Frog

F86F to an FJ-3 is not a difficult one and proves an ideal primer for those wanting to add this to a collection alongside the FJ-1, before advancing to the much more complex FJ-4 version.

Brief details of the FJ-3 conversion are as follows, but these are by no means definitive and should be carried out in conjunction with research from Profile 42 and Ray Wagner's monograph, *The North American Sabre,* published by Macdonald's.

Start by detailing the cockpit as required and add some weight to the nose before cementing the fuselage halves together. Fill the gun ports and

North American FJ-4 Fury 1:72 scale

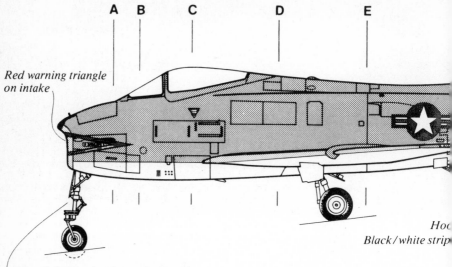

A   B   C   D   E

*Red warning triangle
on intake*

*Hoo
Black / white strip*

Extended nose oleo from plastic rod

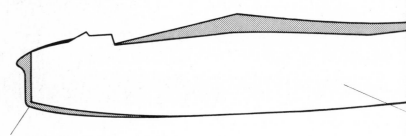

Build up fuselage with plastic card laminations

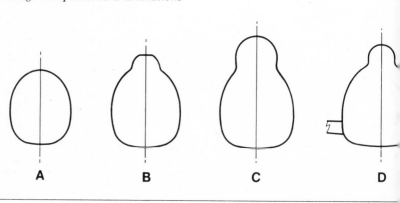

A   B   C   D

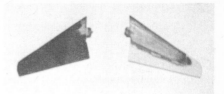

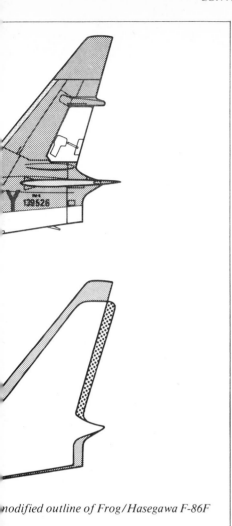

Y 139526

modified outline of Frog/Hasegawa F-86F

E   F

Above *The FJ-4 tailplanes. The one on the right shows the parts added in plastic card (light colour), while the one on the left has been completed and painted with an undercoat to show up any blemishes which might need further attention.* **Below** *Modifications to the Hasegawa F-86F to convert it to the FJ-4 Fury. The top decking has been added from plastic card, the nose reshaped and the fin and rudder extended and changed in outline.* **Bottom** *The wings of the F-86F modified to the shape of the wider chord ones used on the FJ-4 Fury. Plastic card extensions have been added to the trailing edges and surface detail removed by sanding.*

clean up the tail area by adding a new tail pipe from 10 thou plastic card rolled into a tube. After sanding all the filler smooth cut out new gun ports for the four 20 mm cannons in the nose, then enlarge the nose intake by building up the top line with filler and plastic card strips. The FJ-3 had no dihedral on the tailplanes so the tongues on those in the kit must be removed and the tailplanes cemented in place so that they are horizontal when viewed from the front. Wing fences are added to the wings from 10 thou plastic card, and the nose wheel oleo is lengthened to 16 mm by replacing the kit one with a new part made from Slaters rod or stretched sprue. The arrestor

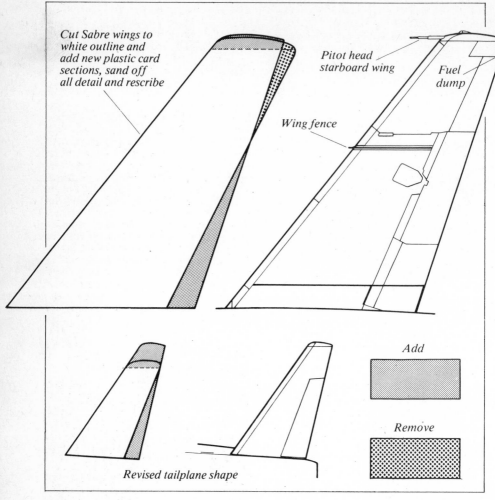

Cut Sabre wings to white outline and add new plastic card sections, sand off all detail and rescribe

Pitot head starboard wing

Fuel dump

Wing fence

Add

Remove

Revised tailplane shape

hook and aerials are added from sprue and the various equipment containers that appear as bulges around the tail area are fabricated from odd scraps of plastic. Since this is not the major conversion that we shall be concerned with, details of colour schemes have been omitted as these are plentiful in the sources already mentioned. The resulting model will look sufficiently different to the original F-86 to bring comment from the knowledgeable, as well as paving the way for the FJ-4 version which is a major undertaking.

When production of the various FJ-3 versions ended in August 1953 over 20 Navy and Marine squadrons were operating a variety of different versions

of the Fury, and some of these were soon to be replaced by the definitive version, the FJ-4, on which design work had started in February 1953.

This aircraft was entirely different to those carrying the same name, having a completely redesigned airframe, thinner wings of greater span and area, a modified and repositioned undercarriage, 50 per cent greater fuel capacity, and a performance that was about equal to its then contemporary, but land-based fighter, the Hawker Hunter. The FJ-4B had a strengthened wing and could be fully-equipped for the low level attack role as well as LABS bombing, it also had facilities for in-flight refuelling which extended its combat radius by 50 per cent. This equipment was used when Furies of Marine squadrons VMA-212 and 214 completed the first trans-Pacific crossing by single-seat naval aircraft in October 1958.

A total of 222 FJ-4 and FJ-4B Furies were manufactured and these served into the early 1960s when they were relegated to second-line status and experimental work. The Hasegawa/Frog F-86 is again the basic kit but for this conversion it simply provides the various components which must be modified in many ways.

Major work is needed on the fuselage as the FJ-4 differs in every respect to the components supplied in the kit.

The first step is to trace the complete outline of the FJ-4's fuselage, including the cockpit canopy, from the plan on to a sheet of 20 thou plastic card. Cut out this shape then place the kit fuselage halves on it and draw around these, which immediately reveals the extent of the work involved. The shape left outside the kit fuselage line is cut out and it will be found that the top portion will mate

along the kit fuselage top decking to form a vertical keel. Cement the two fuselage halves together and insert the dive brakes, then add the plastic card top keel to this. A half-circular bulkhead from plastic card is cut out and cemented at the rear of the cockpit opening and the front of the new keel, which is cut at its rear end to follow the line of the existing fin. Similar section bulkheads are then cemented along the length of the keel; and whilst these are setting a layer of plastic card is added on the underside of the fuselage to increase its depth even more. The top of the nose intake forward of the windscreen is also increased in size by the addition of plastic card laminations.

Plastic card is also needed to alter the line of the cockpit bottom edge, this being done by cutting two triangular shaped pieces and cementing them in place from the front of the windscreen rear line to the keel behind the cockpit canopy position. Wait until all the plastic card additions are dry, then fill all gaps

The FJ-4 Fury modified from the Frog/Hasegawa F-86F. The new shape of the fuselage, wider wing chord and redesigned tail unit are all clearly visible (photo by John Carter).

with Green Stuff. When this has set hard the fuselage is shaped by sanding with wet and dry, used wet, constantly checking the cross sections for symmetry on both sides. This is a long hard slog and constant filling will be needed in small areas from which the Green Stuff falls away, or is removed too vigorously. Cockpit details can be added after the main fuselage work has been carried out as the floor provided in the kit can be tilted sideways to enable it to be inserted. The seat which comes in the kit is best discarded and replaced by a new one built from scraps of plastic card and based on the design in the Airfix F-86D.

While the initial plastic card additions to the fuselage are drying, attention can be turned to the wings and tailplanes. These should first be sanded smooth to remove all traces of panel lines and control surfaces. They are now placed over the plan with their leading edges lined up with those on the drawing, it will now be seen that the root chord is far too narrow and the line of the join is incorrect. Scribe the correct join line and cut out triangular shaped pieces from 30 thou

Below *The FJ-3 Fury which is a much simpler modification to the F-86F kit but forms a useful stepping stone before proceeding to the FJ-4.* **Bottom** *A Rareplanes kit of the FJ-1 Fury which was the forerunner of the FJ-4 featured in the conversion. This kit and the conversions detailed would enable the whole Fury family to be collected* (photo courtesy Rareplanes).

Top *The prototype FJ-4 on an early test flight.* **Above** *An FJ-2 Fury just after roll out. The stencil detail on this picture shows how many instructions are painted on the airframe of a modern jet aeroplane* (photos courtesy North American Aviation).

plastic card to insert at the trailing edges. The trailing edges of the kit wings are filed flat to give the plastic card insertions a good key, and the additional parts are cemented in place. Once these have set hard it is back to the wet and dry for another session of hard work which reduces the plastic card to a correct aerofoil section. After the initial shape has been obtained, filler is used in liberal amounts to achieve a nicely faired surface that blends with the remaining kit parts. During the work on the wings the undercarriage locating holes are filled as are *all* the control surfaces. The tailplanes are modified in exactly the same way with plastic card additions producing the increased span and root chord.

A noticeable feature of the FJ-4 was

its extremely tall fin and rudder, needless to say this part is again fashioned from plastic card, the existing fin having a new leading edge and top added to it using this material. The fairing fitted two-thirds up the fin is made from laminations of plastic card cemented either side of the fin and filled with Green Stuff.

Fuel dump fairings and wing fences are added to the wings from 10 thou plastic card and the same material, combined with stretched sprue operating jack fairings, is used for the new under fuselage dive brakes.

Fix all the components to the fuselage making sure that the tailplanes are horizontal and have no dihedral, and use filler to close up any gaps that occur

117

between the wing joins and fuselage. Once the wings have set measure 25 mm from the fuselage centre-line to each wing undercarriage location point and drill new holes to accept the oleos. The moulded fork on the kit nose wheel oleo leg is cut off and its top drilled to accept a new leg which is made from stretched sprue or plastic rod, this leg having a total length of 16 mm from the centre of the wheel to the point where it enters the fuselage.

All control surfaces and panel lines are scribed into position using a scriber and steel rule then lightly sanded to remove any burrs. The flight refuelling probe was detachable and may be fitted under the port wing if so desired, this can be made from stretched sprue but a better alternative is one from a Frog BAC Lightning kit suitably reduced in length and fixed to a new plastic card pylon.

The arrestor hook is recessed into the underside of the fuselage and is made from flat strips of plastic card.

The main undercarriage legs provided in the kit are the wrong shape for the FJ-4 so once again sprue has to come to the rescue, wheels from the kit, with the central brake discs filed off, can be used or alternatives which should be 10 mm in diameter found in the spares box. The kit nose wheel is used exactly as it comes.

Apart from underwing tanks or missiles, all that remains — apart from painting — is the provision of the cockpit canopy. There is really no way in which the one from the F-86 kit can be used, so it is necessary to carve a mould from wood and produce a new canopy from acetate sheet. If the initial work in adding the plastic card components to the fuselage was done accurately, the canopy should fit perfectly, if it was not it will have to be rectified as to try and build up any unevenness between the opposite sides of the revised canopy bottom line, will not be successful. So careful work and constant checking in the early stages will prevent disappoint and frustration when it comes to the last lap.

The choice of finishes for the Fury is a wide one, most of them were finished in the customary gull grey and white, and adorned with colourful markings that seem to be a prerogative of the US Navy and Marines. Providing research is carried out with existing decals in mind, it is not too hard to find a scheme that can be completed using bits and pieces from ESCI, Microscale and Modeldecal sheets.

Miles M20
1:72 scale

In June 1940 there were grave doubts concerning the supply of equipment to the Royal Air Force to combat the expected onslaught of the Luftwaffe prior to the anticipated invasion of the British Isles by the German army.

While Spitfire and Hurricane production had top priority and these aircraft were being delivered to the squadrons at a rate that had been hard to perceive only a few weeks before, the might of the enemy was not underestimated and everyone realised that a tough task faced the nation as a whole. During this time aircraft such as the Tiger Moth were being fitted with bomb racks to harass enemy troops and shipping, and there was even a plan to turn the Miles Master advanced trainer into the fighter configuration. It was during this period that the Miles Aircraft Company of Reading, who were already supplying Magister and Master trainers, put forward the idea of a heavily armed utility fighter constructed of wood that had the performance of its more complicated contemporaries, but could be produced much more quickly and from more readily available material.

This idea had great appeal to Lord Beaverbrook who at that time was the Minister of Aircraft Production, and he gave immediate authority to Miles to proceed with their design.

Nine weeks later, on September 14 1940, the prototype Miles M20, AX834 was flown, thus proving the theory of quick production. The performance of the aircraft also vindicated the company's other claims as the diminutive fighter, powered by a Rolls-Royce Merlin XX, proved to be faster than the Hurricane and only marginally slower than the Spitfire.

The aircraft was designed by F. G. Miles who sacrificed everything in the way of refinements in his quest for speed and easy production. Constructed of wood with ply and fabric covering, the M20 had a fixed spatted undercarriage, no hydraulics, and used many standard components from the Master trainer. It was armed with eight .303 Browning machine-guns fitted into the wings and

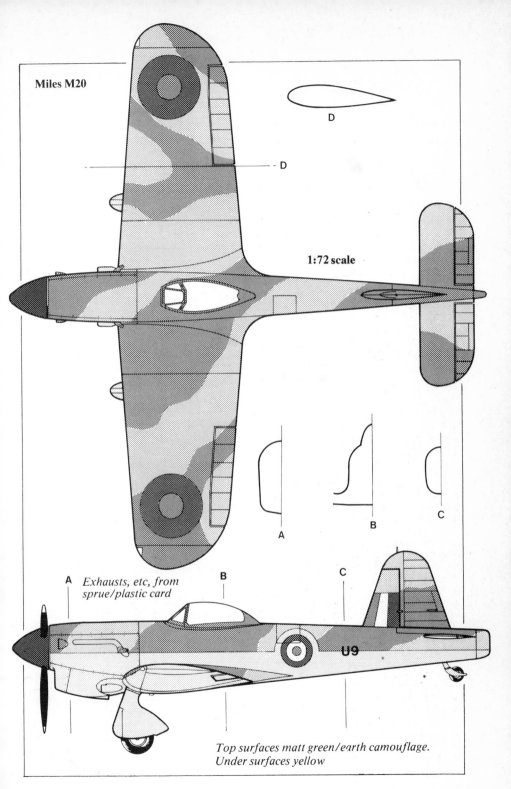

Miles M20

D

1:72 scale

A

B

C

A *Exhausts, etc, from
sprue/plastic card*

B

C

U9

*Top surfaces matt green/earth camouflage.
Under surfaces yellow*

The 1:72 scale Miles M20 built as described in the text. The fuselage is from a Lancaster engine nacelle and Me 110, while the wings are from the Frog kit of the Gannet. Model by Tony Woollett (photo by John Carter).

firing outside the arc of the three-bladed Rotol propeller, and could carry more ammunition for these than either the Hurricane or Spitfire. It also boasted a greater range, quick interchangeability of its Merlin power egg, and had one of the first all-round vision 'bubble' canopies to be fitted to a fighter aircraft. Although it was as long as a Spitfire its span was 2 feet 3 inches less, which gave it more readily executed manoeuvres in the rolling plane, a fact that had already been recognised by German aircraft designers, and was to lead to the various clipped-wing versions of the Spitfire.

As production of the Hurricane and Spitfire managed to keep apace of demand it never became necessary to proceed past the prototype stage with the M20, but a second prototype with catapult spools and a redesigned under-carriage was produced as a private venture for shipboard use, this one being completed in April 1941.

Although neither version of the M20 was put into quantity production or used operationally, it is an extremely interesting aeroplane and one well worth model-ling.

The Miles M20 is an ideal conversion subject as it is one of those aircraft that is never likely to feature in the ranges of any of the injection-moulded kit man-ufacturers; it is also ideal as it enables a worthwhile exercise in the cannibalism of several kits to take place.

Obviously there are many ways in which a model of this aircraft can be produced and to some it will prove to be an ideal scratch-building project, but for the purpose of illustrating how seemingly the most unlikely parts can be utilised it fits the bill perfectly.

As the original was based on the Mer-lin power-egg used on the Lancaster and Beaufighter II, it is to this part that our attention is first directed. The ideal source of the engine and cowling is the Airfix kit of the Lancaster. If you have become an avid converter it is very likely that this kit will already have been turned into a Manchester or Mk II Lancaster so there is a ready supply of engines. If this stage hasn't been reached a Lancaster can be purchased primarily with the M20 in mind but with a view to carry out the conversion mentioned at a later date.

One of the Lancaster's outer engines is cemented together then the rear part of the cowling removed 27 mm from the front, the exhaust stacks are then filed off but the two scoops either side of the cowling left in place.

The rear half of the fuselage is made from either the Monogram or Airfix kits of the Bf 110, the components being cemented together then cut off aft of the cockpit opening, leaving a length, from the tail cone to the cut, of 102 mm. Make sure that both the cuts on the engine nacelle and fuselage are vertical then cement the two parts together. When this sub-assembly is dry measure 32 mm from the front and mark the position of the windscreen, from this measure a distance of 26 mm which marks the rear extremity of the cockpit opening. Now cut out the cockpit area and add internal detail bearing in mind that this was greatly simplified when compared with more elaborate contemporaries.

Body putty is used to fill any gaps between the two components and the whole fuselage is then sanded smooth. After this add the exhausts from stretched sprue keeping in mind that the forward part was recessed flush into the fuselage.

The tailplane and fin/rudder are cut from 30 thou plastic card and sanded to aerofoil section before having the elevator and rudder hinge lines scribed on them. These parts can now be cemented in position and faired into the general fuselage shape with body putty.

Manufacture of the wings can be tackled in several ways. The shape is such that they do not present too great a problem for a first attempt at scratchbuilding, as described in the next chapter, or they can be shaped from balsa wood. But on the model illustrated they were in fact produced from the wings of a Frog Fairy Gannet.

The wing shape is marked on to the Gannet's wing panels which are then cut out using a sharp knife. Cut slightly oversize then reduce to the final shape by sanding with a fairly coarse grade of wet and dry paper. Use the same grade paper to reduce the trailing edge to acceptable proportions, then finish with a lighter grade until a completely smooth surface results. Ailerons are either cut out or scribed into the surface and the gun ports are drilled into the leading edges. Ammunition and gun access panels are scribed on to the top surfaces before the port and starboard halves are butt jointed at the correct dihedral angle. Once the wings have set, use them to mark their position on the fuselage then with a razor saw and modelling knife cut

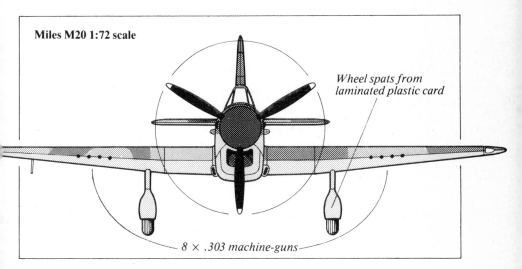

Miles M20 1:72 scale

Wheel spats from laminated plastic card

8 × .303 machine-guns

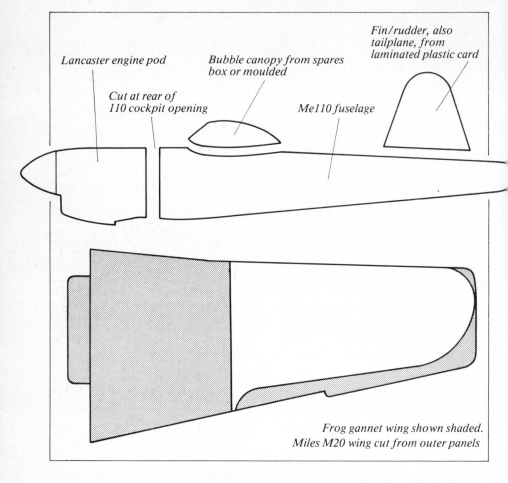

Lancaster engine pod

Cut at rear of
110 cockpit opening

Bubble canopy from spares
box or moulded

Me110 fuselage

Fin/rudder, also
tailplane, from
laminated plastic card

Frog gannet wing shown shaded.
Miles M20 wing cut from outer panels

out a recess in this component to accept them. Fit the wings in place making sure that they are aligned correctly with the tail, then make wing root fairings from 10 thou plastic card which are cemented between the roots and fuselage. Allow the model to dry for at least 12 hours, then fill any gaps where the wings were fitted with body putty and use the same material to merge the wing root farings into both the wings and fuselage.

The undercarriage spats are made from laminations of plastic card with a 9 mm wheel from the spares box sandwiched between them, the drawings show the Mk II or shipboard version, whereas the photographs are of the Mk I, the main differences being the wheel spats and catapult spools, so decide which type of spats are to be made

before committing your design to plastic card.

The tail wheel is from the Bf 110 kit and the canopy can be either moulded or taken from a Tempest kit, the latter is not strictly accurate but is close enough not to be too obtrusive. The propeller and spinner are from the Lancaster kit.

Finish is standard RAF trainer camouflage of the 1940/41 period, Dark Earth and Green on the top surfaces, and yellow on all undersurfaces. The first M20 had a solid demarcation line halfway down its fuselage for a short period but was then repainted so that the fuselage camouflaged extended to a wavy line along the top of the radiator duct and extending on the level of the trailing edge.

Markings from the spares box can be

used but the fin flash which covered all of the lower section of the fin will probably have to be hand-painted. The M20 Mk II carried the number U 0228 aft of the fuselage roundel on both sides, this being the experimental number allotted to the Miles factory by the Air Ministry.

The description of this conversion has been kept deliberately short as it will enable the reader to develop his own techniques without feeling too inhibited by instructions that might be translated too literally. But with those that are given, plus the drawings, it should not be beyond the ability of even the fairly newcomer to the hobby to produce a good replica of an interesting aircraft that would no doubt have given an excellent account of itself if it had been called upon to do so.

Bristol Beaufighter Mk IIF
1:32 scale

On the night of November 19 1940 a No 604 Squadron Beaufighter shot down a Ju 88 thus recording the first of many victories that were to be achieved in the following years of the war by this pugnacious looking fighter.

But it was not solely as a night fighter that the Beaufighter was to contribute to the war effort, for it eventually equipped 52 operational squadrons, acquitting itself well in every role it was called upon to undertake.

The Beaufighter was the first twin-engined night fighter that possessed sufficient performance to turn to advantage the early airborne interception radar equipment first used in its predecessor the Blenheim IF, and in so doing laid the foundations from which the RAF's highly efficient night fighter force evolved.

Designed as a private venture, the prototype was based on the Beaufort torpedo bomber and first flew on July 17 1939, by which time the Air Ministry had undertaken adoption of the aircraft for which they issued Specification F17/39.

The first major production version was the IF and this was issued to the RAF's Fighter Interception Unit at Tangmere on August 12 1940 for operational trials. The following month Nos 25, 29, 219 and 604 Squadrons each received one aircraft and on the night of September 17-18 , 29 Squadron put their

example to use, becoming the first squadron to carry out an operational patrol with the aircraft.

By early spring 1941 over 200 aircraft had been delivered and the Luftwaffe's night bomber force was beginning to suffer at the hands of their new antagoniser. Prior to this 80 Beaufighters had been modified for use in the Middle East as

The plastic card filler used to fill the gap left after the Hercules engine nacelle has been cut from the Beaufighter wings. The new moulded Merlin engines are fitted over the inserted section (photo by John Carter).

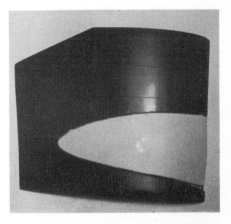

Balsa moulds for the Merlin engines for the 1:32 scale Beaufighter conversion (photo by John Carter).

long-range day fighters and they were soon in operation with Nos 252 and 272 Squadrons.

The Beaufighter went from success to success gradually replacing not only obsolescent types within Fighter Command but also the Blenheim F IVFs used by Coastal Command.

These first versions were all powered by the Bristol Hercules radial engine which was also used by the Stirling and Halifax heavy bombers whose demands for the engine prompted the design team to consider an alternative power supply for the Beaufighter. As a result of this the Rolls-Royce Merlin XX was selected and the prototype Beaufighter, known as the Mk IIF, fitted with these power units made its debut on March 22 1941.

Over 400 of this type were built and used mainly in the night fighter role on home defence duties. Replacement of the huge radial cowled Hercules with the slim-line Merlins caused one or two problems as the reduced area forward of the centre of gravity adversely affected the directional stability. One modification that came about during investigation into this loss of stability, was the intro-duction of 12° dihederal to the tailplane which was subsequently retrospectively fitted to all versions.

A Mk IIF Beaufighter (T3032) was also fitted with an extended dorsal fin which was later used on the Mk X which reverted to the Hercules engines.

During its lifetime the aircraft was subjected to many experiments, ranging from the fitting of twin fins and rudders to the use of Griffon engines, and a proposed slim-line fuselage which in fact never materialised. One armament experiment involved the fitting of a Boulton Paul four-gun turret behind the cockpit, but this reduced performance to an unacceptable level and further development was abandoned.

The Merlin XXs gave the Mk IIF a slightly better performance than the original Hercules-engined versions, but when supplies of the latter became assured they continued to be used, so it was only this mark of Beaufighter that saw service using the in-line liquid cooled Rolls-Royce power unit.

When the war ended the Beaufighter continued to serve with the RAF, mainly in the Far East, and the last squadron to use them as front-line equipment was No

Moulded halves for the 1:32 scale Merlin engines. The top is as it came from the mould and the bottom has been cut to fit the wing section (photo by John Carter).

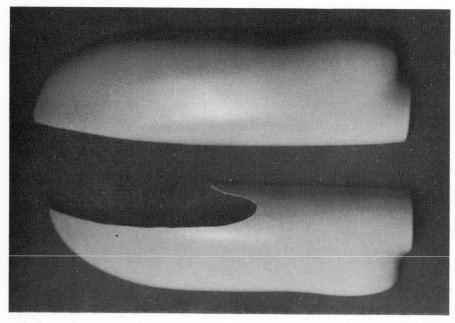

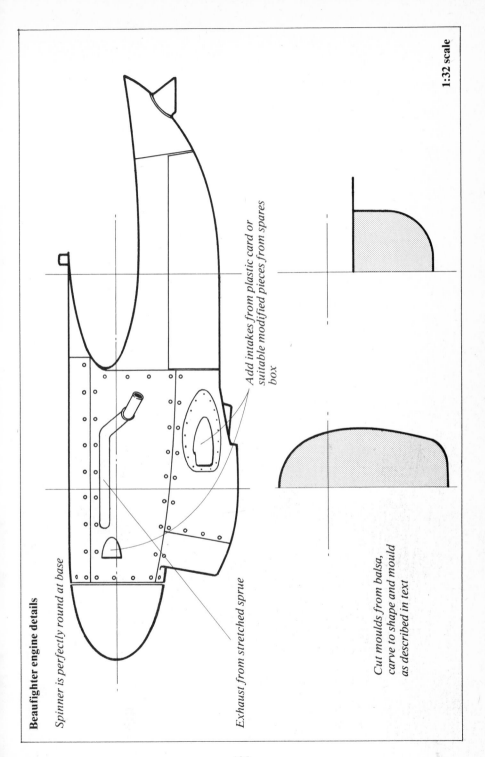

Beaufighter engine details

Spinner is perfectly round at base

Exhaust from stretched sprue

Add intakes from plastic card or suitable modified pieces from spares box

Cut moulds from balsa, carve to shape and mould as described in text

1:32 scale

125

45 who did not retire their aircraft until February 1950 when another Bristol design — the Brigand — replaced them. The service life of this heavy twin did not end then as some were converted for use as target tugs and meteorological reconnaissance aircraft, and soldiered on until May 12 1960 when a TT10, RD761, made the last operational flight by a Beaufighter from Selatar.

Although most conversions are confined to 1:72 scale models, mainly because the costs involved are low, there is no reason why some of the larger scale kits that are now available in quantity should not be changed in similar ways to their smaller bretheren. Since the initial purchase price of a large scale model is likely to be several times the amount one would spend on an equivalent 1:72 or smaller scale kit, some thought has to be given before such a model is subjected to drastic changes. It is important therefore not to try anything too dramatic as a first attempt and also to be sure that the necessary expertise and experience has been gained with less expensive kits.

The Revell 1:32 scale Beaufighter is the Mk IF but to change it to the Merlin-powered IIF is not difficult providing you are prepared to carry out a fair amount of hard but varied work.

Although basically accurate in outline the kit does have one major shortcoming which is with the cockpit canopy. The one supplied in the kit is of a very early type that was fitted to only a few of the first Beaufighters to enter service, so to be strictly accurate this must be replaced by a moulded one on which the panel lines are correct for the later canopy. Should you have a vac-form tool the best way to tackle this is to remove all the frame lines from the kit canopy, then use the smooth transparency as a master mould to form a new one. The erroneous lines are on the windscreen being in the form of 'quarter lights' behind the main screen, and on the port side where the lower canopy frame should be removed. Some Mk IIFs, including R2270, were in fact fitted with the canopy as supplied in the kit for a period of time, so if you chose one of these this work is not necessary.

Still in the cockpit area the kit falls down in providing a complete rear bulkhead behind the pilot (part 13) whereas on the actual aircraft this did not exist. To rectify this remove the top half of this

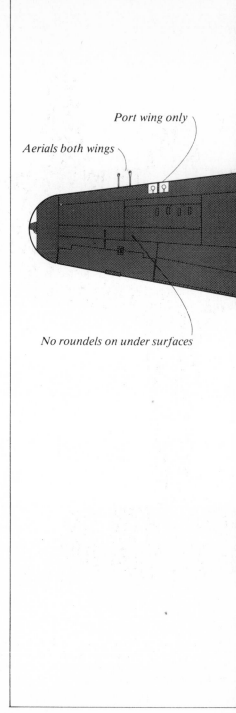

Port wing only

Aerials both wings

No roundels on under surfaces

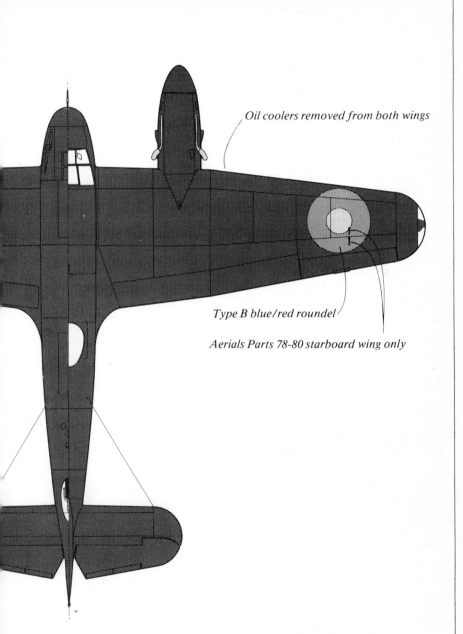

Oil coolers removed from both wings

Type B blue/red roundel

Aerials Parts 78-80 starboard wing only

Drawings have been reduced to 1:90 scale to fit the page. Use scaling methods to obtain 1:72 or 1:32 scales as required. Overall wingspan should be 9⅝'' in the former, 21¾'' in the latter; fuselage length should be 6 9/16'' or 14¾' respectively, excluding nose probe.

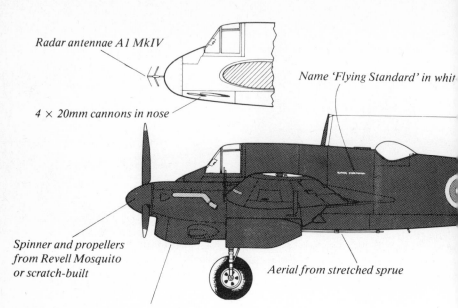

Radar antennae Al MkIV

Name 'Flying Standard' in whit

4 × 20mm cannons in nose

Spinner and propellers
from Revell Mosquito
or scratch-built

Aerial from stretched sprue

Merlin engines with flush exhaust. See separate drawing

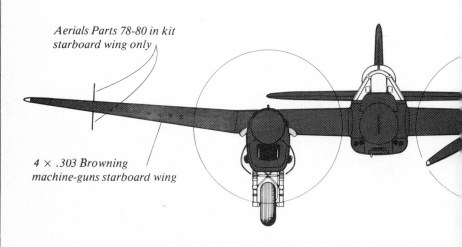

Aerials Parts 78-80 in kit
starboard wing only

4 × .303 Browning
machine-guns starboard wing

Night black overall (RDM
Serials dark red

Bristol Beaufighter Mk 11F

3426

roundel with yellow surround

The port wing of the Beaufighter showing the area inboard of the landing light where the oil cooler intakes have been removed and gaps filled.

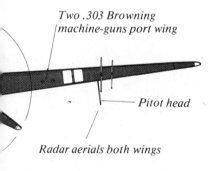

Two .303 Browning
machine-guns port wing

Pitot head

Radar aerials both wings

Port Merlin engine fitted to the centre section and exhausts added. The gap between wings and fuselage has been filled with Green Stuff.

part on a line with the cockpit side consols. However, if this is done the interior immediately behind the pilot is revealed and since this is devoid of any detail the model will look totally inaccurate. To overcome this the interior can be added by inserting strips of plastic card to represent the stringers which form the fuselage, and fabricating other equipment from bits and pieces. An excellent set of drawing including a cutaway one showing all the interior, was published in the May and July 1974 magazine *Scale Models* and a copy of this or just the drawings from the MAP Plans service is invaluable when carrying out this conversion. Alternatively the complete nose section of a Beaufighter is on view at the RAF Museum Hendon and is well worth a comprehensive study. Examination of the mentioned drawings, or the exhibit, will also quickly indicate that the navigator's compartment as supplied in the kit is nothing more than a figment of the designer's imagination and should be completely replaced by a new scratch-built interior with the seat facing towards the rear (although it does swivel), a new floor, and new instrumentation.

Space does not allow a fully detailed description of these changes so if you are enthusiastic enough to attempt this conversion, then you should by now know enough about the joys of carrying out research into such items, and formulating your own methods in rectifying the errors mentioned.

Obviously the major task is the provision of the Merlin engines which ideally should be carved from balsa then moulded from plastic card as described in the chapter on scratch-building. It is best to carry out this work first for if you do not complete it successfully the conversion is impossible until such time as a 1:32 scale Lancaster is produced from which the engines can be cannibalised! Trace the outline of the Merlin on to a block of balsa and carve it as you would

do when building a solid scale model, the width is then marked on to the top of the block equally about the centre-line, and the plan view marked and shaped. Once the basic shape has been achieved, split the mould down the middle and make the female portion from ¼ inch thick balsa. Use 30 thou plastic card to produce four halves plus a couple of spares, then place the new engine parts safely to one side and turn to the wings.

The moulded portions of the Hercules engines incorporated in parts 35 and 36 are removed with a sharp modelling knife following accurately the cowling shape. Clean up the area where the cuts were made then hold a flexible piece of card under the wing and trace the cut out portions on to this. The shape drawn is cut out with scissors and used as a template to make two identical shapes from 20 thou plastic card. Test fit these shapes and once you are happy that they are accurate, but not until then, cement two pieces of 20 thou plastic card inside the wing halves thus blocking off the hole that was made when the cowlings were removed. Once this underlayer has set, the two shaped plastic card inserts are cemented into the holes from the top, thus restoring the flat surface of the top of the wing. The bottom halves of the

Plan view of the completed MkII Beaufighter. The all-back (soot) finish is badly weathered with Rub 'n' Buff. The new engines and radar aerials can be clearly seen in this shot.

Top *Three-quarter head-on view of the completed Beaufighter conversion which gives a good indication of the different appearance given to the model by the sleek in-line Merlins instead of the huge radial Hercules engines.* **Above** *The spinners and propellers for the Merlin engines came from a Revell Mosquito, but could be moulded and scratch-built from plastic card if spares from the latter kit are not available.*

cowlings are treated in the same way but do not cut templates to fill the holes as part of these will form the wheel well. On the bottom section (part 38), it is enough to simply cover the holes on the inside with 20 thou plastic card. When the new moulded engines are fitted, the level of the wings outboard of the new nacelles can be built up using scraps of plastic card or filler.

The Merlin engines were much thinner in cross-section than the Hercules so this work is necessary as there is no way in which a short cut can be taken by only fitting new front sections to the existing engine cowling mouldings.

When all trace of the original cowlings has been removed, cement parts 35, 36 and 38 together then take one half of the new mouldings and mark the cuts that

The exhaust stacks for the Merlins are made from hollow plastic tubing heated and shaped as shown.

have to be made to fit this to the revised wing section. This operation is very much a case of trial and error, hence the spare mouldings, and it is best to proceed with caution, removing small areas at a time. The top line of the Merlin cowling ends on the line of the main spar which is moulded into the Revell wing surfaces. When the wing sections have been successfully removed from the moulded engines, they are assembled by inserting a round bulkhead at the front, to ensure perfect symmetry as well as to provide a solid base for the location of the propeller, and parts 37 which are reduced in width until they fit into the Merlin nacelles. It is essential that these parts are used as they form a really solid base for the undercarriage location, the points of which will remain if the width is reduced equally either side. Cut out the front of the cowlings for the radiator intakes then block these off with plastic card bulkheads which can be scored to simulate the radiator honeycomb sections. At this stage it is also as well to fit the exhaust pipes which on a few of the early Mk IIFs were completely shrouded but later took the form of a pipe recessed into the cowling and only protruding at the rear end.

Cement the halves of the Merlin engines together then assemble them to the wings, making sure that their centre-lines are level with each other and the top and bottom sections of the nacelles locate in the correct positions on the wings. As already stated, the top fairing

ends on a line level with the main spar, while the underneath ends at exactly the same point, just forward of the flaps, as did the Hercules. When this sub-assembly has dried mark out the undercarriage doors and remove them for relocation in the open position, then add the various intakes and 'blisters' from parts taken from the spares box.

Spinners can be either moulded in the same way as the engines were, then fitted with propeller blades made from 30 thou plastic card sanded to shape, or the complete propeller and spinner assemblies used from a Revell Mosquito, if finance allows the purchase of this kit just for these parts.

The outer wing panels (parts 31/32 and 33/34) have oil cooler intakes moulded into their leading edges and these must be removed as they were not needed on the Merlin-engined version. Revell have conveniently marked panel lines around these intakes so use these as a guide to cut out two almost square sections from each wing. Line the undersides of each half with 20 thou plastic card, cement the wing sections together, then build up the level of the plastic card lined squares with filler.

The model is now assembled as per kit instructions but dihedral can be added to the tailplane if you have chosen a model that had this. Should you wish to include this feature then remove the locating lugs on parts 39/40 and 43/44 then sand the tailplane root to an angle of 12°. This can be achieved quite simply by making a template from cardboard on which the correct angle has been marked and constantly checking the tailplanes against this as the sanding work proceeds.

The model will now require a considerable amount of filler where all the new moulded parts have been fitted and the oil coolers removed, followed by a lot of sanding to smooth this filler into the airframe. This work must be carried out conscientiously otherwise the whole model will be spoiled.

Fit radar aerials and the undercarriage then paint a matt white or light grey undercoat overall, this will show up any imperfections where further work is needed as well as sealing the filler and making sure that the final paint texture applied to these areas does not contrast with the normal moulded parts.

Most Mk IIFs were finished black overall when used in the night fighter role but an interesting variation would be the prototype, R2058, which was painted in standard Dark Green/Dark Earth camouflage with yellow under surfaces. Dependent on the finish chosen, the roundels in the kit can be used but codes will need to be obtained from other sources or even hand-painted, which on a model of this size is not that difficult.

The Beaufighter is a challenging subject on which to end this chapter and makes an interesting model to add to 1:32 scale collections; it is particularly impressive when displayed alongside the original Beaufighter kit when the changes that have been made become very evident.

eight

Scratch-building

The opportunities that now exist as far as available materials for scratch-building are concerned are better than they have ever been, it seems ironical therefore that so few modellers try this method of producing aircraft for their collections. Those who have tried solid modelling, as outlined in chapter three, are already well on the way to taking the next logical step, those who haven't still need not be deterred for there is an immense amount of satisfaction to be gained from creating a model from basic materials instead of building and improving a commercial kit.

Less than 30 years ago 'solid' modelling, as it was then called, had reached a peak of popularity, with wood, as the most readily available material, being the chosen medium of all but the very few. Today, with the advent of plastic, there is the opportunity to produce components that can be moulded into complex shapes, thus producing models to a standard that could only be dreamed about by the early solid model enthusiasts.

What then is required of the modeller who wishes to try his hand at scratch-building? The most important attribute must be a complete dedication to the hobby, closely followed by patience and the will to spend a little more time than is required in building a normal plastic kit.

At the outset it is important to set yourself a high standard and not be prepared to accept anything that does not come up to the requirements of this. Before starting a model make sure that you thoroughly research it and that the drawings you propose to work from are the most accurate available. In some cases there will be a variety of drawings from which to take your pick, but comparison of these with photographs will usually enable you to pin-point any inaccuracies, which must be put right before the actual task of modelling begins. If you belong to a modelling society or club, take every opportunity that pres-

ents itself to discuss and show your work, during its various stages, with other members. By doing this you will find that many comments are helpful and can lead to improvements in the model as well as your own standards. Do not be over-sensitive to criticism as in most cases it will not have been made with any intent to belittle your efforts, and from it can grow an understanding of the way other modellers work which in turn can be helpful to you.

Above all view your own work critically as it is so easy to see what you want to see rather than things as they appear to others, so remember to take off those 'rose coloured spectacles' when examining your own efforts.

Finally, before actually starting work on the model, indulge in a little mental exercise during which you take the construction through each step. By doing this you will make yourself aware of any problems that are likely to occur before they actually do so. During this mental trip into the unknown, try to picture the shape of each part and how you propose to make it, how it will fit to other components, and above all what you hope the finished model will look like. This will give a 'feel' for the subject and throughout its construction a second sight at each stage of whether or not you are achieving your goal.

Experience in working with wood is a good grounding to building with plastic card, which in scratch-building, becomes the basic material. It has many advantages over wood which makes it an ideal choice for this type of modelling. Among these advantages are the facts that it is easily cut with a modelling knife; it softens when heated and can thus be moulded to practically any shape, while when the heat source is removed, it retains the shape to which it has been moulded; in its natural form it has a smooth surface; it is readily available at most model shops in thicknesses ranging from 5 to 60 thou, in sheets which are usually 13 × 9 inches; and construction is easily and quickly accomplished using normal polystyrene tube cement for the thicker sheets, and liquid cement for the thinner ones.

These six points result in almost the perfect modelling material, which is superior in practically every respect to wood, when it is used in the correct way. The tools required are no different to those which have already been discussed in previous chapters, and most scratch-builders find that a modelling knife with a selection of blades, a set of files, sandpaper, wet and dry and flour paper, a six and 24 inch metal rule, tweezers, a razor plane, and a selection of probes (obtained if possible from our old friend the dentist), are adequate for their needs.

Other tools have their uses but once again we come back to the old question of personal choice and depth of pocket, both of which are the prerogative of the individual modeller.

Whether or not you are a complete beginner to scratch-building, it should be obvious that the choice of a first subject should be as simple as possible. But at the same time it must retain an element of interest, which will provide you with the will to complete it. After all, if you are a dedicated modeller of jet fighters, you will soon loose interest in trying to scratch-build a pre-war biplane, so the choice of a subject of this type for such a modeller is almost certainly doomed right from the start. So select a simple model that you are keen to build for from your enthusiasm and dedication will

This model of the Blohm and Voss Ha 139 flying boat is made from an Airframe vac-form kit. When this kit was released in 1972 it was one of the largest vac-form models available (photo courtesy Airframe).

grow the ability to overcome each problem as it occurs. Such a subject should preferably avoid complex shapes such as those found on the Phantom and Harrier, similarly biplanes can also present certain problems so should be avoided until some experience has been gained.

Aircraft with basically simply outlines that are ideal as a first attempt at scratch-building are the MiG 15, Miles Magister, DH Chipmunk, Fokker D VIII and the Comper Swift which is fully detailed at the end of this chapter. These are only a guide as there are many other subjects which are equally as suitable for the beginner to cut his teeth on. An hour or two spent mulling over the pages of aviation books or magazines is certain to produce an aircraft within the range of your interests that has the qualities of simplicity common to the examples quoted.

One of the major advantages of scratch-building is that you are not tied to a particular scale, unless of course the model chosen is to form part of a constant scale collection, so the choice of size is the first decision that has to be taken. This of course brings us to the first hurdle which is the acquisition of a suitable general arrangement (GA) drawing.

It is possible that a plan to the scale you want is readily available from commercial sources, but on the other hand, you may find that the only drawing you are able to locate is too small or too large. If this happens you must enlarge or reduce it to the size you want either by using the grid method described in chapter three, or by taking the drawing to a photocopying agency who have the equipment to reproduce it exactly to the size you specify. Once you have a useable plan, research is completed, and any available photographs are readily to hand, work on the actual construction can begin, and a good starting point is the fuselage.

Basically there are three types of construction methods suitable for making the fuselage, these are: moulding, built-up box type, or a combination of both, the one selected depending very much on the model being constructed.

To mould a fuselage it is first necessary to produce an accurate master from balsa or obechi. This is done in exactly the same way as that described earlier for wooden models, except that it is essential to use two blocks of wood joined along the centre-line. Having joined the blocks, mark the outline of the aircraft on one side by placing the block under the plan and pin-pricking the shape on to the wood, the pricks are then joined with a line drawn with a ball-point pen and the shape cut out. The plan view is transferred in the same way and this is also then cut to shape. The shaped block is carved to the correct cross-sections using templates, the final shaping being accomplished with a fine grade glass-paper or flour paper. It is very important that both sides of the fuselage are identical since if they are not, the fault will become very apparent when the moulded plastic card halves are produced.

As accuracy is vital it is well worth going over the main points to remember when carving. Use a razor blade plane for the initial shaping, and set the blade so that it does not take too coarse a cut; try to take small cuts rather than big ones as it is always easy to remove more material, but not so easy to put some back; cut with the grain of the wood whenever possible and make frequent checks with the templates to ensure that the correct shape is being formed. If the fuselage has a circular section at each end, such as in the MiG 15, metal washers of the correct diameter fixed to each end of the block will ensure that both orifices are perfect in section. When you have neared the end of shaping achieve the final result with glass-paper and finish off with fine flour paper.

Once you are satisfied that the fuselage is the correct shape, split the block down the centre-line and you will have two identical fuselage halves, which are the male moulds.

To produce the female mould, lay one of the completed fuselage halves on to a flat sheet of balsa wood which should be about ¼ inch thick, and draw around its outline with a soft pencil or ball pen. Cut out this shape using a very sharp knife and making sure that the marked line is followed accurately. If this is done correctly the end result will be a shape in the sheet balsa through which the fuselage half will pass, the amount of clearance to aim for being approximately 1/32 inch all round. This point is extremely important as on it will depend the success or otherwise of the final moulding.

The final operation before moulding

can start is the addition of a handle to the inside of the two male moulds. This need only be a wooden block large enough to hold comfortably which can be screwed or glued to the flat inside surfaces of the split fuselage halves.

Moulding plastic card is a vital part of scratch-building, and now that you have made the male and female components it is time to attempt this. Several practice runs may be necessary but once you have learned the basic techniques it should be possible to produce an accurate moulding every time you try.

Generally speaking most scratch-builders find that 30 thou thick plastic card is ideal for aircraft of between 1:72 and 1:36 scales, while for smaller components that do not require any particu-

lar strength 20 or even 10 thou will prove adequate.

Using the female mould as a guide, cut a piece of plastic card sheet to the same size then clip it with bulldog clips to the balsa wood. This type of clip, which can be obtained from any stationery shop, is ideal for the purpose as it is strong and not likely to be affected by the heat source. But remember that they will get hot so avoid touching them when the mould is first removed from the heat source.

Once the plastic card sheet is attached to the female mould, hold it up to a strong light and trace out the shape to be moulded. This operation is a vital one as it will enable you to see exactly where the male mould has to be inserted once

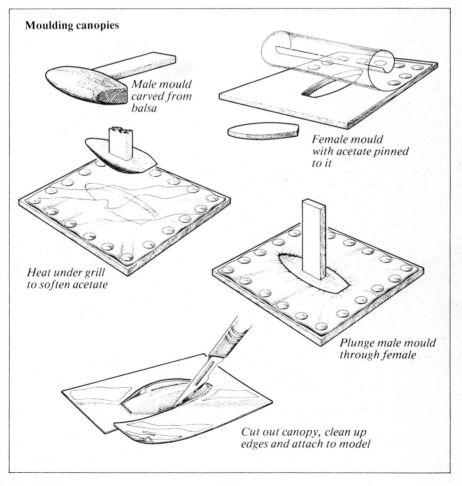

Moulding canopies

Male mould carved from balsa

Female mould with acetate pinned to it

Heat under grill to soften acetate

Plunge male mould through female

Cut out canopy, clean up edges and attach to model

the plastic card has been heated to a moulding state.

Prepare some supports for the female mould, which need only be two strips of hardwood deep enough to allow the male mould to pass through but not touch the surface on to which the female mould is to be placed. In other words the strips must be deeper than the proposed depth of half the fuselage. It is important to make sure that these support strips are strong enough to withstand some pressure otherwise the mould might crack at a vital moment.

The heat source in which the plastic card will be placed must be capable of producing equal heat over the whole mould, and an ideal source is the normal grill that can be found on most domestic gas or electric cookers. Switch on the grill and allow it to get hot then place the mould with the plastic card attached underneath it. As the heat begins to affect the plastic card, the first thing that will be noticed is that the card starts to curl up towards the heat, it will then flop back, start to smoke at the same time becoming very malleable. When it reaches this point remove it from the grill, place it on the prepared supports, plastic card uppermost, then firmly press the male mould through the previously marked hole. Push it through until the top of the male mould is just below the level of the hole in the female mould, allow the plastic card to cool off then remove the male mould. If the plastic card was the correct temperature and the male mould was pushed through accurately and firmly, the end result will be a perfectly shaped fuselage half in the plastic card.

First attempts might not work out exactly as you hoped but once you have tried a few times you will soon find the correct method after which faulty mouldings should become a rarity.

Some of the faults that can occur and their reasons are: male mould refuses to pass completely through female mould; cause — plastic card not heated sufficiently. Strain marks on edges of finished mould; cause — female mould has insufficient clearance around the edges. Finished moulding too thin; cause — either plastic card moulded whilst it was too hot, or female mould clearance not sufficient. Male mould passes right through plastic card; cause — plastic card far too hot or too thin a gauge has been used for component being produced.

When the mould has been satisfactorily produced, cut out the shape using a sharp knife and bring it down to the final dimensions with wet and dry paper.

Mould the other fuselage half in exactly the same way but remember this time to turn the female mould over and use the second fuselage half, it is very easy to become absorbed in the work and end up with two port or starboard fuselage halves! This moulding process enables practically any shape to be produced but clearly some, especially those with double bubble contours, will require careful working out as it is not possible to use this technique when two curves undercut on to each other. Although in the example quoted the fuselage block was cut down a vertical centre line, there is nothing to prevent you making the cut along a horizontal line, thus moulding a top and bottom section instead of port and starboard halves. In some cases such as the Venom and Vampire it might be better to follow this procedure.

If 30 thou plastic card has been used it will be possible to join the two halves together with ordinary tube cement, but before doing this add interior detail and bulkheads and make sure that some provision has been made for wing and tail unit locations.

The built-up box section fuselage is fully detailed in the practical example of the Comper Swift, so there is little point in repeating the process here, as it is basically similar for any fuselage of this type.

The combined type is clearly ideal where the fuselage has a box section as its base and a curved top decking, all that is necessary in such cases is to make a mould for the curved top decking and build up the rest of the fuselage in a box section.

Every modeller will quickly find his own methods of working and tailor these to suit his particular requirements, but generally it will be found more convenient to produce all the components first before assembling them rather than completing the fuselage before going on to the wings and tail unit.

Turning to the wings, again there are three basic methods all of which will produce the same end result, but depending on the subject chosen each has cer-

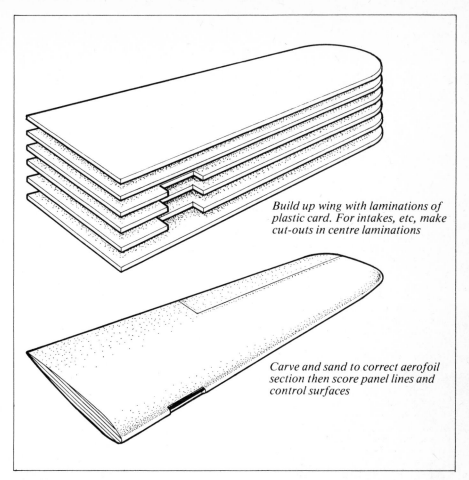

Build up wing with laminations of plastic card. For intakes, etc, make cut-outs in centre laminations

Carve and sand to correct aerofoil section then score panel lines and control surfaces

tain advantages over the other.

The first method is to make the wings from solid laminated sheets of plastic card. This is ideal for wings that have radiators incorporated in their leading edges such as those to be seen on the Westland Whirlwind and DH Mosquito. Start by tracing the wing outline on to plastic card then cut this out and use it as a template to draw the wing on as many laminations as required to achieve the correct thickness at the wing's thickest point. If leading edge radiators are included, remove the area required from the inner three or four laminations, which when sandwiched between the top and bottom ones will leave a convincing radiator intake. Wheel wells can be made in the same way by cutting their shape into the bottom two or three laminations. Once the preliminary work has been

done, cement all the laminations together and either clamp them tightly or, if no clamps are available, place them under a heavy weight. Leave the laminated sections in this state for at least three or four days to allow the glue to set really hard, then remove the clamps or weight and start the hardest part, which is filing, sanding and cutting them to the correct aerofoil section and taper along their length. When you have done this, panel lines, ailerons and flaps can be scored into the surface with a scriber and steel rule.

Moulded wings follow the same procedure as that used for fuselages and again it is emphasised that accurate carving is essential. Wings that have their internal ribs very prominently shown on their surfaces, can be produced very effectively by the moulding process. To do this lightly mark the positions of the ribs on the male mould, then attach thread across the chord in the positions required, remembering to use thinner thread for the under surfaces where the ribbing is usually less pronounced.

When the two halves of each wing have been moulded they should be cut out from the plastic card and cemented together using the male mould inside as a core to give them additional strength.

Although nothing is easy as far as scratch-building is concerned, the third method of making wings is probably the simplest and the best for the beginner to use if his chosen subject allows it. This method is to use plastic card folded over a wooden wing which, if the results are to be successful, must first be accurately shaped. Start by tracing the true shape of the wing on to a sheet of 10 thou plastic card, this will eventually become the bottom surface of the wing, so enough plastic card must be left at the leading edge as this will be folded over the wooden former.

If the wing is of the ribbed variety, score in the rib positions with a ball pen across the bottom and what will be the top of the wing, by placing the plastic card on a perfectly smooth surface and using a steel rule as a guide for the ball pen. Gently score along the line of the leading edge using a ball point pen but make sure that you do not press too hard as in this thickness of plastic card it is very easy to cut right through. Now slightly chamfer the trailing edges and wing tips and you are ready to undertake the final shaping.

The carved wooden wing should be slightly undersize and completely accurate along its whole length as far as the aerofoil section is concerned. Coat the undersurface of the wooden wing with an impact adhesive such as Versifix, which

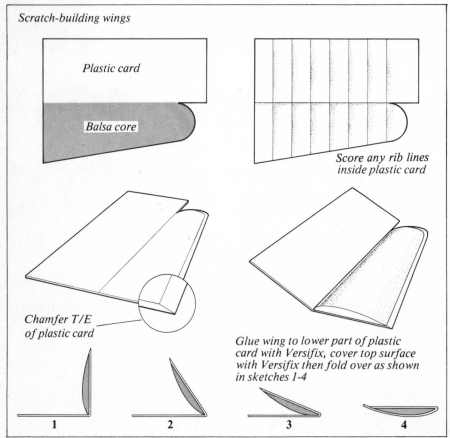

Scratch-building wings

Plastic card

Balsa core

Score any rib lines
inside plastic card

Chamfer T/E
of plastic card

Glue wing to lower part of plastic
card with Versifix, cover top surface
with Versifix then fold over as shown
in sketches 1-4

1   2   3   4

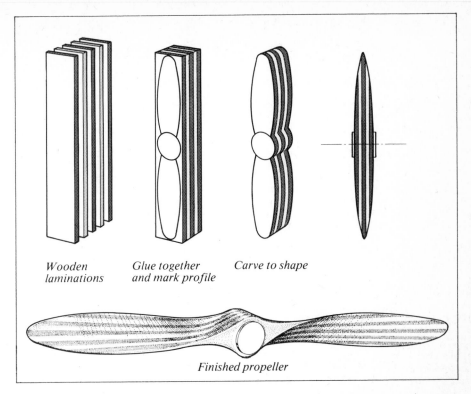

Wooden
laminations

Glue together
and mark profile

Carve to shape

Finished propeller

is made by Rexel, and place it in position on the plastic card which should also have had a layer of the adhesive spread over it a few seconds before. Now coat the top surface of the wing core and the surface of the plastic card which is to be folded over it and leave the assembly for a few seconds before you start trying to bend over the plastic card top surface. This operation is the most crucial of the whole exercise and must be carried out carefully as described. Hold the wing in both hands with the leading edge pressed vertically on to a hard flat surface, and the bottom of the wing facing you. Now move the wing away from you pivoting on the leading edge so that the plastic card makes contact with the wooden core as you roll the top surface on to it. Continue to press down until the trailing edges of the top and bottom surfaces meet, then with a brush, run liquid cement along the join between the top and bottom leading edges. Leave this to dry and when it has done so, join the top and bottom surfaces of the wing tips in the same way. In some cases, especially where double curvatures are involved, it

will be found impossible to shape the wing tips in this way, and the only satis-factory solution is to cut off the tip and replace it with a new one made from laminated plastic card. Tidy up the wing by smoothing the trailing edges and tips with wet and dry, then score in the panel and control surface lines. In some cases it is advisable to completely cut out the ailerons and flaps, then cement them back into position as this results in a much more authentic appearance. In this type of wing construction the wooden core, as it does in the moulded wing, gives a solid base into which can be fitted undercarriage legs, guns and underwing stores.

Unless the model you are making is a very big one, or a small one to a large scale, when the fin/rudder and tailplanes can be made in the same way as the wings, it is best to make these compo-nents from one piece of thick plastic card or laminations. If ribbing is required on these components it can be simulated with thin strips of plastic card or stretched sprue attached to the surfaces with liquid cement, since in most cases such ribbing is not so pronounced on tail units as it is on wings.

One important component that can make or mar a scratch-built model is the propeller, this is especially important where the aircraft concerned is of the type that used a wooden laminated airscrew. A propeller is, in essence, nothing more elaborate than a twisted aerofoil section, and if this is kept in the forefront of the mind, a lot of the mystery in carving it is dispensed with.

For vintage aircraft with wooden propellers there is no finer way of reproducing these than using wooden veneers as sold for use in marquetry, as these will enable exquisite results that really enhance the finished model to be obtained.

Select two veneers of differing rich brown colours, bearing in mind that final varnishing will tend to slightly deepen the chosen colours, then cut out an equal number of each to a size that will cover the diameter and width of the propeller blade. Use a good quality wood glue to join the veneers together, alternating the colours as you go along. When the glue has set mark the centre point and glue metal washers, the diameter of the propeller boss, to the front and back of the veneers at this point. These washers will ensure that a perfectly round central boss results when the carving operation is completed. Mark the front elevation on the veneers and carve them to this shape, then do the same with the side elevation. Study the aerofoil section required and once you have a mental picture of this firmly impressed in your mind, carve the front and rear of each blade until it is the shape you require it. Finish the propeller with flour paper and finally remove the washers before giving the completed propeller two coats of clear varnish, lightly sanding with flour paper after the first.

Metal propellers can be made in a similar way using laminated plastic card and painted the correct colour, but in the case of multi-bladed propellers, it is easier to make each blade separately by shaping it from plastic card of the correct thickness then twisting it to the correct pitch angle before setting it into a previously manufactured boss or spinner.

Commercial kits will provide many components for the scratch-builder, such as wheels, bombs, propellers, canopies and so on, but you will find that as you become absorbed into this style of modelling you will prefer to make as many

Some of the parts which go to make up the Rareplanes YB-17 vac-form kit. This kit also includes a spare fuselage which can be used with parts from the Revell B-17E to make the RAF's Fortress 1.

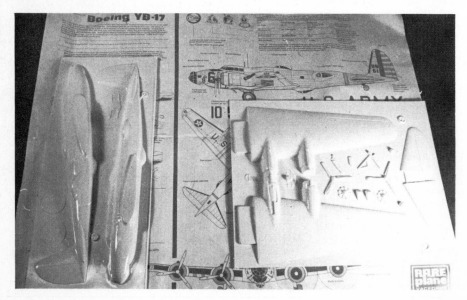

Rareplanes 1:72 scale vac-formed De Havilland Dragon Rapide. This kit is unusual in that the fuselage mouldings are made of thick, clear acetate which requires the use of liquid acetone solvent as an adhesive. The obvious advantage of this innovation is that there are no windows to fit and the modeller simply paints the internal fuselage after masking off the window areas (photo courtesy Rareplanes).

components as you possibly can, and the sources of material for such parts can be discovered in the most unlikely places.

Examples of such items that will be sufficient to set your thoughts along the right tracks are large and small plastic curtain rings, that make ideal tyres for 1914-18 and pre-war biplanes; press-studs which have a remarkable similarity to wheel hubs used on aircraft during the war years; foil from cigarette packets, which makes superb wing walks and radiator grilles; plastic tubing for shock absorbers, guns, pitot heads, complete cowlings, or even the knurled tops from tooth paste tubes, which can be used for Lewis gun magazines. All around you there are hundreds of items waiting to be discovered, and with a little thought you might be the one to come up with an item that no one has used before.

The fitting together of the major components depends a great deal on the way these have been produced and the size of the model. It is very difficult to generalise as every scratch-builder has his own favourite way of accomplishing this. Moulded or wings made by the folding method are very much lighter than

the laminated variety and can often be simply butt jointed with tube cement to their correct location points. In some cases locating dowels made from thick sprue or plastic rod will be of tremendous help, and on models where the wing has a fairing over the root to fuselage join this can be made from 10 thou plastic card. Assembly of sub-components is very much a matter of experimentation and personal preference and after a while you will decide on the method that suits you best.

Undercarriage legs and wing struts can be cut from 60 thou plastic card and one advantage of using this method is that the resulting struts will be very strong. Plastic card also has the useful property of breaking evenly down a scored line, which enables useful lengths to be accurately produced without the necessity of tedious cutting down a steel rule. Naturally, on larger models interplane struts can be made by using a balsa core around which 10 thou plastic card is folded as was done for the wing, these turn out most effectively and are useful when they are not required to carry any stress.

Emphasis on the art of improvisation cannot be stressed strongly enough and the way any particular model is approached rests very much in the hands of the modeller concerned, for unlike the man who is content to assemble standard kit components, the scratch-builder has the tremendous advantage of making every part in the way he wants to.

Many of the points that have not been

Rareplanes 1:72 scale Lockheed Super Constellation. This kit can be made into several versions, such as the EC-121M early-warning radar ship shown. In such large sizes, vac-forms need to be extremely accurate in shape, smoothly and sharply moulded, and finely detailed to make the resulting model convincing (photo courtesy Rareplanes).

covered in depth are dealt with in the practical example of the Comper Swift, and these can be adapted to suit any project. Some modellers will argue that the scratch-builder is making a rod for his own back, or even turning the clock back to the days before the plastic kit, when it was necessary to make every part of a model from odds and ends. Once you have tried scratch-building it is unlikely that you will subscribe to this school of thought, for when the model you have selected is complete, you will know that it is the only one that exists, and is not just a greatly improved version of a commercial kit that any modeller can assemble, albeit with varying degrees of success.

Vac-form kits are often considered to be an ideal stepping stone towards scratch-building, so it is worth taking a look at this type of kit as it does present certain challenges that are lacking in the normal injection-type moulded kit.

From very small beginnings several years ago, the vac-formed kit has now mushroomed into an important part of the hobby and there are several companies engaged in producing this type of model.

This type of kit is usually confined to a subject that it is unlikely the bigger manufacturers will produce, although in some cases kits that have been released

in this form are now also available as injection-moulded items.

The basic kit consists of parts formed on one or two sheets of fairly thick plastic card and these parts have to be cut out and worked on before they can be assembled in their intended final form.

All such kits are produced by the manufacturer first making wooden masters then forming the plastic card sheeting over these either by extracting the air as the plastic softens in the same way as described in chapter two for the Mattel or home made vac-form tool, or by making the masters hollow shells and forcing the softened plastic card into the shape by forcing air in under pressure.

Whichever method is used the final quality of the kit is very dependent on the accuracy of the master moulds and the detail that has been included on it. In England Rareplanes of Earlswood, Surrey, are the true pioneers of this type of kit and their products have now reached a standard that matches some of the commercially produced injection-moulded kits. This company includes a tremendous amount of extremely fine surface detail and in the hands of a competent modeller the resulting model is hard to tell from a normal plastic kit.

Contrail Models is another English company which started in a small way and would no doubt be the first to agree that some of their early offerings, although fulfilling a need, were rather crude. Their standards have now improved and their range includes some of the popular flying boats and 'between the wars' aircraft that have a magic of their own which so far has not rubbed off on some of the injection-moulded kit manufacturers.

Much the same can be said about the Canadian company, Airframe, whose extensive range extends from World War 1 subjects to unusual aircraft of World War 2, and even post-war experimental jets. In America Horizon

1:72 scale Westland Pterodactyl from an Airframe vac-form kit. This is one of the easiest vac-forms kits to make and is a good starting point for anyone who has yet to try this type of modelling (photo courtesy Airframe).

On some occasions vac-form kits are produced before the conventional injection-moulded ones. This Provost T 1 from the Airframe range was released in 1973, but sales are likely to be affected now that Matchbox have the same aircraft in their injection-moulded range. Model by Tony Woollett.

models have produced component parts as well as one or two complete kits, whilst in Germany the firm Airmodel continue to produce both conversion parts and complete kits at a remarkable rate.

So the area of choice for those wishing to try a vac-form kit is wide open. As a primer before scratch-building, the assembly of a vac-form kit provides practice in working with plastic card, and does to a certain degree instill some confidence to those who prefer to cross each bridge as it comes. Those who are bold enough and wish to plunge straight in at the deep end, will no doubt regard making a vac-form kit as purely an extension of assembling components already made for them. If you feel this way then by all means go ahead and start making your own moulds, but if you are more conservative and want to try every aspect of modelling, then a good quality vac-form kit will provide you with hours of enjoyable work and a model of which you can be proud.

The comments that were made at the start of this chapter in relation to acquiring a 'feel' for the selected model apply equally to vac-form modelling. So it is important to choose a subject in which you are interested, research it thoroughly first and form a mental picture of how you want the model to look.

Providing you have some of the basic skills that are necessary in any form of modelling the present day vac-form kit should hold no problems for you, but if you are a complete beginner to this style of model making it is wise to select a simple one on which to start. The first impression you are likely to form is that this type of kit is expensive for what you get, which is true, but must be viewed in the correct perspective. The production runs of this type of kit are very much smaller than those for injection moulded kits so the initial production costs are spread over less quantity, since the manufacturer is looking to recover his overheads as well as make a small profit on maybe a quantity of 1,000 as opposed to the several million that might be produced from an injection-moulded tool. But one must keep in mind that the kit being purchased is, because of the limited production, something of a rarity and therefore a collector's item. It also presents a much greater challenge than the normal plastic kit, and the amount of hobby time needed to turn it into a classic model is therefore greater, thus giving pleasure to the modeller for a longer period of time. So if you have a mathematical or accountant type mind and evaluate the cost of your modelling in proportion to the time spent doing it, the vac-form kit represents very good value for money!

The first step in construction is to remove the moulded parts from the plastic sheet, and it is best to do this with a sharp modelling knife and removing only those parts you are going to use during each stage of construction.

Once the components are removed pin a sheet of medium grade wet and dry paper to a flat board and, keeping the plastic card part level, rub its edges down until they are perfectly flat, making sure that plenty of water is used on the wet and dry paper during this process. All kits are moulded so that there is

a certain amount of excess plastic present when the moulds are cut from the basic sheet, but remember to constantly check the part you are working on against the plan as the wet and dry removes the plastic at a useful rate and it is easy to end up by removing too much plastic. Providing each component is kept perfectly level whilst this sanding operation is being carried out, the edges will end up with flat surfaces which will mate together leaving a barely perceptible join line.

Should you be careless when sanding the fuselage halves and end up with one or both undersize, the fault can be remedied, providing you have not made too serious a mistake, by cementing the halves to correct thickness plastic sheets, then cutting these to the fuselage outlines and removing the solid sheet from cockpit and intake areas. By exerting more pressure from your fingers on

The Bucker Bu 133 Jungmeister from By-Planes. This kit, the first from this manufacturer, sets new standards in vac-forms with the inclusion of cast metal accessories, moulded wheels, decals and surface detail comparable to that of many injection-moulded kits. It is also one of the few 1:48 scale vac-form kits available (model and photo by John Carter).

the trailing edges of wings and tailplanes, these components can be reduced to a truly lifelike thickness during the sanding operation. Very small components such as struts and undercarriage legs can be attached to double-sided Sellotape to help with the handling problem but if you do this, do not use any water in the operation or this will quickly cause the part to become detached from the tape.

When the edges of the fuselage halves are nearing completion constant checks must be made on their compatibility with each other and great care taken not to sand too much plastic away. Once a smooth flat edge has been produced on both halves they should be mated together to ensure that they are equal about the centre-line and the fit is exact along this line. Openings for the cockpit, air scoops, radiators and any other similar attachment can now be removed by scoring the area that has to be removed with a sharp modelling knife, removing the unwanted plastic and finish the shaping with a file. Interior detail is added at this stage to suit the whim of the individual concerned, and this should be painted in the correct colours at this

stage as should the inside shells of the fuselage. If the plastic concerned is thick enough the two halves can be simply butt jointed together with tube cement, but if it is fairly thin plastic it is wise to cement a locating strip around the edges. This strip should protrude over the edge of the half into which it is cemented thus forming a 'step' on to which the other half can be located and cemented in position. In such cases it is best to hold the two halves together with masking tape then run liquid cement all round the join with a fine brush. Don't forget to remove the tape when the fuselage has set fairly solid and insert cement into the areas where the tape was located. If this is not done the plastic that was under the tape will separate from its adjacent component and leave an unacceptable gap.

The fuselage assembly should be put safely on one side to set hard before any further attempt at working on it is made, in the meantime work can continue on other components. Wing sections are treated in exactly the same way as the fuselage with special attention being given to the finish of the trailing edges. It is often helpful to insert plastic card

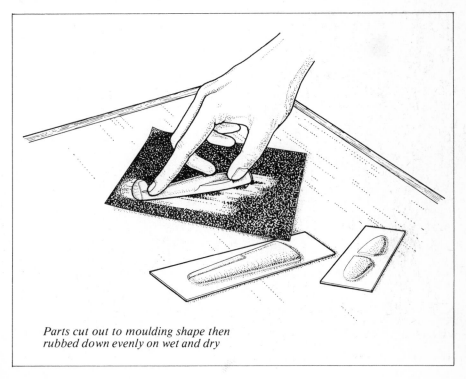

Parts cut out to moulding shape then rubbed down evenly on wet and dry

spars inside the wing halves before joining them together which is best accomplished with liquid cement in the same way as the fuselage was treated. It is particularly important to make sure that the wing roots are shaped accurately and fit the fuselage with their chord parallel to the aircraft's centre-line.

Before fitting the wing halves together it is advisable to insert small blocks of plastic card at the points where undercarriage legs or underwing stores are to be fitted as these will give very positive location and fixing points for such components. Wheel wells and leading edge radiators must also be provided for before the wing halves are joined and careful thought must be given to how these important parts of the model are going to be included, remember that a wheel well is not just a shaped hole in the wing undersurface, but is lined around its edges and has equipment included in it. This can all be reproduced with pieces of plastic card cut and trimmed to the correct sizes.

In many vac-form kits, especially those of radial-engined aircraft, engines are included but many builders prefer to use equivalent components from injection moulded kits. Cowlings are moulded with a solid front which should be removed with a sharp knife or reamed out with a pair of divider points, cutting well inside the final cowling line. Finish such components with a fine round file or better still, sandpaper wrapped around a pencil or wooden dowel.

In cases where interplane struts or undercarriage legs are included, these will invariably be hollow on one side. If you wish to use these, rather than replace them with kit components or new ones shaped from thicker plastic card, fill the hollow sides with body putty before removing them from the master sheet, leave this to dry hard, then remove the components and carry out final shaping with sand paper or wet and dry.

During the sanding process carried out on all components some of the original smooth surface will be removed, but this can be restored before final assembly of the components by lightly brushing every part with liquid cement. Do this very carefully and make sure that you are not too enthusiastic with the application of the cement or you will damage the surface you are trying to improve.

When the cement has dried hard the model will have a smooth finish which will provide a good base for the final paintwork. Sub-assemblies must have the surface detail added by scribing panel marks and control surfaces. The latter can be removed and replaced in realistic positions if you so desire. If you do this the wing or tailplane will be hollow where the elevators or ailerons have been removed, so any small gaps that appear after these components are cemented back at the desired angles, must be filled with strips of plastic card. On many of the newer vac-form kits, in particular Rareplanes, surface detail is included and will need very little attention. Some of them, however, have no detail or that which is included has been done far too heavily. In the former instance it can be marked as already described, in the latter, it is best to fill all detail with body putty then re-mark the detail once this has been sanded smooth. Internal wing or fuselage ribbing can be simulated by scoring the insides of the components with a biro as described for scratch-building, or alternatively represented by stretched sprue added to the external surfaces with liquid cement.

The main components should be cemented to the fuselage with the aid of supporting braces made from plastic card or cocktail sticks and inserted into the wings and fuselage. A quick drying liquid cement must be used as this enables the parts to set in their correct positions very quickly and helps prevent changes in dihedral and general alignment.

Cockpit canopies provided in vac-form kits must be carefully removed from the moulded sheet and the edges sanded or filed flat, in most cases this component is moulded from thin acetate sheet and should be fixed to the completed model with a glue that dries clear such as Uhu, Evostick or PVA White Glue.

The completed model is painted in exactly the same way as any other model but does need to be handled rather carefully as it will be more prone to damage than a injection-moulded kit.

Modelling from this type of kit is much more demanding than that required with the conventional plastic model; but the end results are extremely satisfying and the range now available is certain to provide at least one subject that will prove attractive to even the most critical enthusiast.

Comper Swift
1:36 scale
by Tony Woollett

Light aircraft enthusiasts usually refer to the 1930s as 'The Golden Years'. This was a period of record-breaking flights, the First Endeavours, and many with only a casual interest in this side of aviation history, usually associate it with the de Havilland Moths, Percival Gulls, and the like. But one aircraft that was very much to the forefront was the dimunitive Comper Swift, one example of which, with C. A. Butler at the controls, left Lympne on October 31 1932 and flew to Australia in nine days, two hours and 20 minutes. This aircraft which was serialed G-ABRE, was fitted with extra fuel tanks which gave it an endurance of 11 hours, this amount of fuel represented 42 gallons and gave the Swift an all-up weight of 1,146 lb,, nearly twice its empty weight.

The Swift was designed by Nicholas Comper who received his technical training at the de Havilland company school before joining the RAF when he was a lecturer at Cranwell. Several of Comper's designs were built by the Cranwell Light Aeroplane Club, but the Swift, which was his seventh design, was manufactured by his own company which he left the RAF to form.

Comper's intention was to produce an aircraft that had the handling qualities of contemporary RAF fighters and be in advance of any other club or private aircraft. Since the aircraft could match the 400 hp Fairey Flycatcher and the 480 hp Bristol Bulldog in rate of climb, and exceeded the former's maximum level speed flight, Comper succeeded on all counts and this from a mere 75 hp engine!

In addition to being something of an aeronautical genius, Comper was also an avid practical joker, and his liking for this type of light relief ended in tragedy. On the evening of June 17 1939 Comper, who was then 42, left a public house in Hythe, Kent and threw a lighted firework on to the pavement. To a passer-by he shouted 'I am an IRA man'. Thinking that the firework was a bomb, the unfortunate passer-by pushed Comper to the ground and in the ensuing struggle the designer received serious head injuries from which he did not recover.

One of his obituaries claimed that Nicholas Comper had never designed a bad aeroplane; a fitting tribute to a talented man, which leads one to muse over what his talents might have produced for Britain's war effort.

Building a model of this successful and interesting aircraft, examples of which are still flying, is an ideal first attempt at complete scratch-building as it involves many of the techniques described in the main text of this chapter. If the following instructions are followed and care is taken, there is no reason why the end result should not be a pleasing example of an aircraft that featured so prominently in the Golden Years of British light aviation.

Construction is best started with the wings, as these are uncomplicated and when successfully made will spur you on to tackle the harder job of the fuselage. The wings are made by the one piece folding method, the first step being to mark their outline on a sheet of 10 thou plastic card, remembering to leave enough material to fold over to form the top surfaces. Cut out the shape with a sharp knife and chamfer the trailing edges of the bottom surface so that the top has a good area of contact when it is folded over. Score the top surface wing ribs slightly heavier than those on the bottom, using a ball-pen for this operation, and when this has been done accurately smear contact adhesive, such as Versifix, on the areas that are to be joined. Make sure that this adhesive does not seep on to the trailing edges, otherwise it will insulate them from the liquid cement that is used to seal the join. Once the top surface has been curved over and stuck to the bottom, take a fine brush and very sparingly apply liquid cement along the trailing edge. This *must* be done with care and the cement used sparingly otherwise unsightly blemishes will occur where the cement has softened too large an area of plastic card. Remember the material is only 10 thou thick. Allow the structure to dry for at least six hours then gently work your way around the wing tips, sealing down a small area at a time with liquid cement. There is no problem in this area if the work is not rushed, and solid wing tip inserts are not necessary, but if you feel

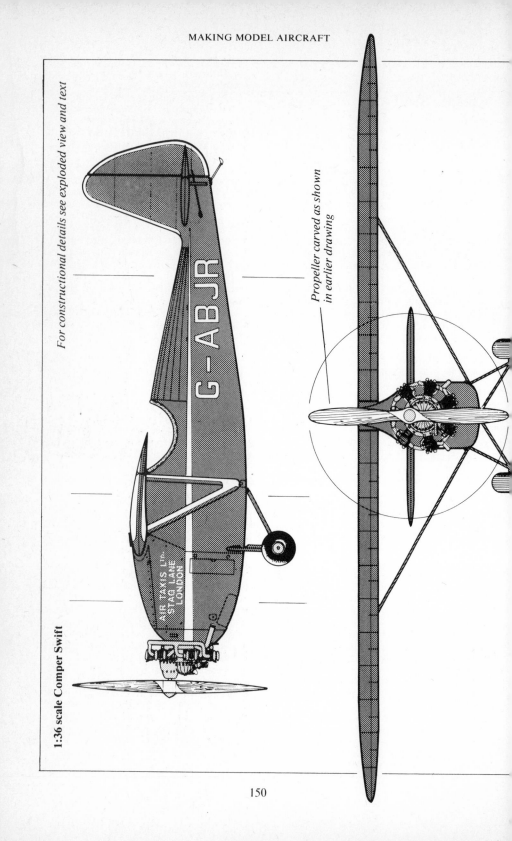

For constructional details see exploded view and text

Propeller carved as shown
in earlier drawing

1:36 scale Comper Swift

G-ABJR

AIR TAXIS LTD
STAG LANE
LONDON

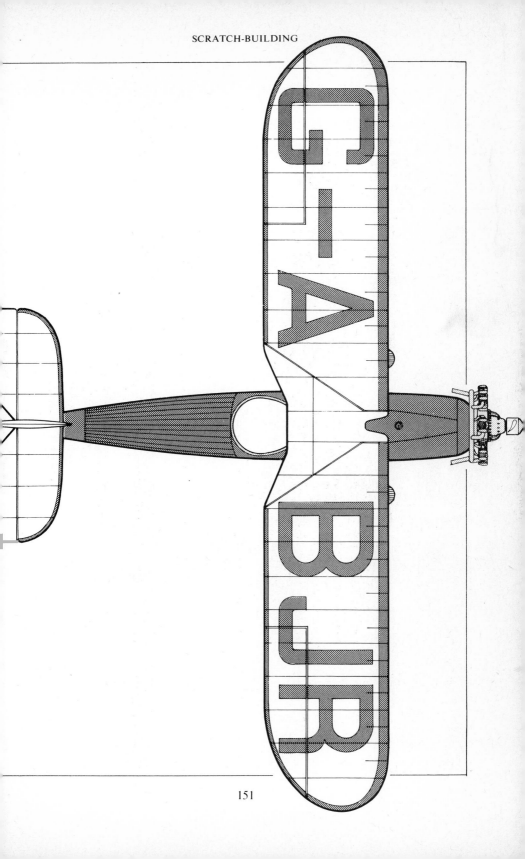

happier with them, by all means put them in.

All that remains to complete the wings is to carefully cut out the ailerons with a sharp knife and a straight edge, an ideal implement in place of the conventional steel rule, is the safe side of a six inch straight file. The teeth on the file tend to

Below *The balsa wood moulds used to form parts for the Comper Swift. The male and female parts for the top decking are top right, crankcase mould is bottom right, while that on the left is for the under cowling* (photo by John Carter). **Bottom** *The component parts of the Comper Swift before assembly. The wings are built over a balsa wood core and the ailerons have been separated. The base of the fuselage is made up in a box section and the top decking has been moulded. The fin/rudder and tailplane are cut from plastic card and the modified Airfix Boeing 747 wheels can be seen at the top of the photo* (photo by John Carter).

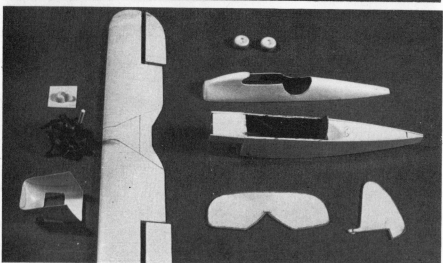

grip the wing surface when held in position and prevent any movement whilst the cutting is taking place. Finally score the wing folding hinges on top and bottom surfaces then place the completed structure on one side and turn to the rudder and tailplane.

These components are cut from 30 thou plastic card then filed to give knife-like trailing edges and rounded leading edges. Ribbing is added by applying very thin stretched sprue with liquid cement where shown on the drawings. These components should also be left for about six hours before any attempt is made to clean up the shape and thin down the ribbing with fine wet and dry. The fin and rudder as well as the elevators can, of course, be separated and re-cemented in any desired position.

During the time components are in the 'drying' stage, there are many other little jobs that can be done or at least started on. One of these is the production of the wheels. The Comper Swift had very small diameter wheels that had more than a passing resemblance to doughnuts, and to find the correct ones in even the most comprehensive spares box is a tall order. My eventual solution was the use of wheels from an Airfix kit of the Boeing 747 Jumbo Jet. These are the correct diameter but too thin so it is necessary to use four Jumbo wheels to obtain two for the Swift. Take a pair of Jumbo wheels and file one side of each of them flat, gradually reducing the thickness by about one third, then cement the two together with the flat sides mating and fill any gaps agound the circumference with filler. Sand the tyres smooth then paint them with a mix of flat black and sea grey medium to obtain that grey/black tint which tyres have. Wheel centres should be painted a dull metallic silver.

The fuselage is a combination of the box and moulded method fully detailed in the general section of this chapter, being made of a basic box which extends to the top longeron and forward to the front cowling, with a moulded top decking which includes the cockpit opening, completed with moulded bottom and front cowlings.

Start by cutting out two sides from 30 thou plastic card extending their length so that they are longer by about ⅛ inch at the front end which fits into the cowling. The bottom shape is also cut from the same thickness material but remember to reduce the width by 30 thou both sides to allow for the thickness of the sides which are butt jointed to it. Now cut out another shape similar to the bottom which will be fitted to the top thus completing the box. This part should extend further forward than the bottom to meet the join line of the front cowling.

Use the plan to cut internal longerons from 20 thou plastic card and add these, fixing with liquid cement, on to the fuselage sides in the area of the cockpit. Cut out the 'V' shaped holes through which the main undercarriage legs enter the fuselage then drill holes at the rear of the sides to accept the elevator control cables. Location of the bottom to each fuselage side is helped by cementing 20 thou strips of plastic card along the bottom of each fuselage side in a position whereby they will form a base against which the bottom component fits. The same additions are also made to the top of the sides to give location for the top decking base, but these must end just short of the cockpit otherwise they will interfere with the internal detail.

The fuselage sides are now gently bent between the fingers until they follow the contours of the plan view. and the bottom sheet is treated in a similar manner to follow the base line of the fuselage as seen in the side elevation. Once the correct shape has been achieved use tube cement to join one side to the bottom of the fuselage then cement the top in position after having first cut it off just short of the cockpit opening. The resulting three-sided box should now be fitted with two bulkheads, one just aft of the cockpit and the other at the nose, make sure these do not distort the fuselage shape which should be checked with a set square before they are finally cemented in position.

Before fixing the remaining side add cockpit detail which consists of a control stick, rudder pedals, bucket-type seat, throttle and a map holder which is located on the port side. Seat straps and control wires from the stick and rudder pedals can also be added from stretched sprue at this stage.

Colour detail for the cockpit interior is hard to pin down so either mid-grey or a grey-green could well be right. However, use a little artistic licence and do not paint these colours too dark a tone otherwise a gloomy interior will result. When satisfied with the interior detail, cement the other side in position but do not forget to paint its interior side first.

The top moulding for the fuselage is made as a one piece moulding, ignoring at this stage the cockpit opening and wing location. The male mould is carved from a suitably sized piece of balsa wood and must be slightly undersize to allow for the thickness of the plastic card that is to be used for the final shape. During the carving constantly check your work against the existing fuselage box to be sure of absolute accuracy. When satisfied that the shape is correct, cut out the female mould and proceed with the moulding as already described; it is a good idea to produce a couple of spares just in case any errors are made during the following work.

Ensure that the moulding is a good level fit along the top longeron then cut out the cockpit opening and wing location point just forward of the cockpit, using the already completed wing to check the fit as the cutting proceeds.

The instrument panel is now made, painted to represent varnished wood, and cemented into position, where it also serves as a bulkhead for the fuselage coaming. The cockpit is edged with a leather surround and this is simulated by slicing a suitable sized piece of plastic-coated electric wire, so that it forms a channel section. This is carefully trimmed to fit and then secured in place with matt varnish.

Position the completed moulding on the bottom half of the fuselage and with a sharp knife slice off the front at the point where it will meet the front cowling. Similarly slice off the rear of the decking at a point ⅜ inch in front of the tailplane leading edge position.

The shaped plastic card which was used for the top of the fuselage box and cut off level with the rear of the cockpit, is now cut so that the front portion can be butt jointed to the forward bulkhead where it is supported by an angle bracket of plastic card. The top fuselage moulding is then cemented into position on the box section and the assembly placed on one side to set.

Attention is now turned to the front and bottom cowlings, the moulds for which are again carved from balsa then moulded in 10 thou plastic card. Refer-

ence to the plan will indicate that there is a rectangular panel set inside the bottom cowling. This is best simulated by cutting away a rectangular hole in the cowling which is to be used, then from a second moulding, remove a panel slightly larger which is cemented inside the original. Once this has been accomplished, test fit the part to the fuselage and if it is OK cement it in position. The front cowling is now fitted after a suitable test run. These two cowlings will be very thin so cement must be used sparingly otherwise damage will result. Once the fuselage components have all set, panel lines are scored in place from the front cowling to the wing leading edge, and rivets are simulated by rotating a small rat tail file between the fingers so that minute raised rings are formed on the cowlings.

A plastic card block ⅜ inch long is now made from laminated sheets and cemented in position where the top coaming was cut off at the tail. When this has firmly set it is carved to the distinctive concave shape where the rear fuselage meets the leading edge of the tailplane. The stringers that are prominent on the top decking are reproduced by cementing strips of stretched sprue in the correct positions with liquid cement as was done on the tailplane and rudder.

The fuselage is now complete but there is one major task still to be accomplished and in many ways this is the hardest part of the model: the Pobjoy engine. This part is made by using one row of the 14-cylinder contained in the Life-Like (Impact) kit of the Fairey Flycatcher. As it comes in the kit the engine is too large in diameter so the first step is to reduce this by cutting off each cylinder head at the point where the finning diameter increases. File down each head on the underside reducing their length by about half then re-cement them back on to the cylinder barrels. The front crankcase, which houses the reduction gear, is moulded in two parts: the main crankcase, which is a circular domed shape, and the top part which is also circular but more pointed in outline. Once these parts are moulded, a semi-circular hole is cut out of the main crankcase and the top part is seated into this, the assembly is then backed by a square of 20 thou plastic card to which they are fitted with liquid cement, this being cut to shape after the glue has dried. The

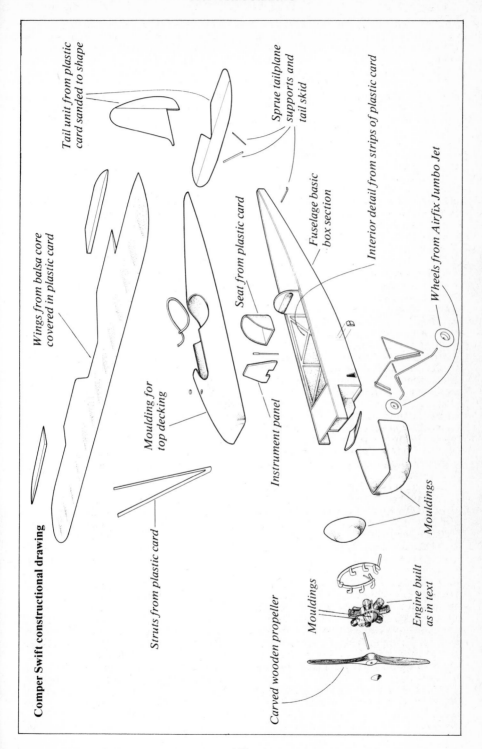

Comper Swift constructional drawing

Wings from balsa core covered in plastic card

Tail unit from plastic card sanded to shape

Sprue tailplane supports and tail skid

Interior detail from strips of plastic card

Seat from plastic card

Fuselage basic box section

Wheels from Airfix Jumbo Jet

Moulding for top decking

Instrument panel

Struts from plastic card

Mouldings

Mouldings

Carved wooden propeller

Mouldings

Engine built as in text

ribbing around the crankcase is produced by gently scoring with the point of a sharp modelling knife, then a hole is drilled through the nose of the top pointed part. Through this hole is inserted a piece of round sprue or plastic rod which forms a spindle for the propeller.

The circular row of securing bolts around the top of the crankcase are formed by cementing minute pieces of circular sprue into the relevant positions, then the whole crankcase assembly is cemented to the cylinder block. The finned component which protrudes from the crankcase between the bottom two cylinders is a cylinder taken from the Airfix RE 8 kit, and the pipe that runs from this to the rear of the engine is stretched sprue. At this stage it is best to paint the cylinders and crankcase, making sure that the latter has a slightly more shiny finish than the former. While the paint is drying, prepare seven inlet pipes and the exhaust collector ring which also has the same number of outlet pipes. The exhaust ring is made from sprue in the correct diameter bent to shape in the heat from a candle flame. This is probably one of the hardest tasks of the whole construction and requires much patience and perseverance as well as a good supply of sprue, as it is very unlikely that success will be achieved first time. When satisfied that the cylinder heads fit correctly to the collector ring and the exhaust pipes have been drilled out, assemble the complete engine and let it dry really hard before painting the exhausts a light rusty brown colour. The

engine is now completed apart from any wiring and other accessories you may wish to add from stretched sprue. It takes a long time to produce this engine but the result is well worth all the effort as it forms a vital focal point on the model.

The propeller is carved from laminations of veneer and the boss drilled to accept the spindle previously inserted into the crankcase moulding. The spinner is made from moulded plastic card but it is not necessary to carve a male mould as the point of a suitable sized component from a kit can be used; the spinner of a 1:72 scale Airfix Sunderland is ideal for this mould if one is available. Before fitting it to the propeller polish it with Rub 'n Buff or paint it silver to obtain a polished appearance. The propeller is held in place on ths spindle by windings of stretched sprue which forms a circular collar, these being held in place by a touch of liquid cement.

Undercarriage components are made from 1 mm diameter plastic rod, and consist of an inverted 'U' which passes through the 'V' shaped openings on the fuselage, two radius rods, and two axles. The axles are bent so that the wheels have a very slight 'toe-in' when viewed from the front. The streamlined fairings over the axles are formed from 50 thou plastic card bent over the axles and held with bulldog clips until the cement is set, there are then trimmed to shape. The final job before painting and assembly of all the components, is to make the 'V' shaped wing support struts from 30 thou sheet. These are simply cut out with a

The Comper Swift in the form modelled by Tony Woollett and described in full in the text. This is an early photo of a 75/80hp Popjoy-engined version as it appeared in 1932. The Comper Aircraft Company badge, complete with 'Swift', can be seen just forward of the leading edge strut (Flight).

The Comper Swift G-ABJR modelled completely from scratch in plastic card. The fuselage lettering is Letraset and the wing codes are hand-painted. Model by Tony Woollett (photo by John Carter).

sharp knife then sanded to aerofoil section.

Once all the components have dried and are set rigidly they are all painted in the colours of the scheme you have decided upon. A list of colours offered by the Comper Aircraft Company in their original sales brochure is appended at the end of this chapter.

The only problem likely to occur at this stage is the painting of the registration letters. If you do not feel capable of hand-painting these, 'Yeoman' transfers or Letraset of the right style and size can be used, these being ¼ inch for the fuselage and one inch for the wings.

Another fine example of scratch-building in plastic card, this time Tony Woollett's Miles Sparrow Hawk in 1:36 scale (photo by John Carter).

When all the components have been painted and lettered final assembly of the model is carried out. This is done by first cementing the wings into position on the fuselage, remembering to carefully scrape away any paint where the join is to take place. Allow these to set then add the support struts from the fuselage to the wing undersurfaces. Cement the tailplane and fin and rudder in position making sure that they are lined up vertically and horizontally to each other and the fuselage centre-line. Control wires which emerge from the fuselage are made from sprue and cemented to control horns on the rudder. The tailplane struts are now fitted, these having been cut from 20 thou plastic card and sanded to aerofoil section, during one of the periods of waiting for other parts to dry.

The undercarriage assembly is started by feeding the inverted 'U' shaped piece through the fuselage locating holes and cementing in place with liquid cement. The axles and radius rods are fitted using the same adhesive and the model is then propped up so that no weight is on the undercarriage until it has set.

Wheel centres are drilled out with a fine drill or dental burr and cemented in position making sure that they have the 'toe-in' mentioned earlier. The engine and propeller assembled is now fixed in place with liquid cement making sure that the top cylinder is absolutely vertical.

Swift in flight, the doughnut-shaped wheels being very evident (Flight).

The finishing touches include the addition of aileron control horns and wires from plastic card and sprue which is also used to fabricate the tail skid.

The Comper Swift is now complete and the true reward of your endeavours is the knowledge that almost every part has emanated from your skills and the basic raw materials that were available to you. It will be a model with its own character and unlike a kit will be the only one of its type, since however many are made from these instructions they are all bound to be different in some respect as each individual has found his own ways of tackling the problems discussed.

The following is the specification as it appeared in the Swift sales brochure which was released at the time the aircraft made its debut:

The Comper 'Swift', price, equipment and colour schemes.

Price £550 ex works.

The following equipment is included in the above price: *Instruments* — air speed indicator, oil pressure gauge, Altimeter, revolution counter, petrol gauge, Cross level, clock; *Accessories* — cockpit cover, picket screws, suitcase, notebook and pencil, engine cover, dipstick, map case, notebook container, full set of tools, tool tray, safety belt, owner's name plate, full set of log books.

Choice of colour schemes: No 1 — Fuselage, pillar box red; Fin, pillar box red with white leading edge and Gold beading; Rudder, pillar box red with white trailing edge and Gold beading; Mainplane, white with red leading edge and Gold beading; Tailplane, white with red leading edge and Gold beading; Strake line, white with Gold beading; Fuselage letters, white with Gold beading; Mainplane letters, pillar box red. No 2 — As No 1 only substitute dark blue for pillar box red. No 3 — As No 1 only substitute powder blue for pillar box red. Any one of the above colour schemes included in the list price to choice.

Comper Swift known colour schemes

G-ABUU — New in 1932, Royal Blue letters outlined in gold. Aircraft white; 1933, pale blue, white letters outlined in gold; 1960, cream aircraft with red letters; 1963, red aircraft, black letters outlined in gold; 1968, ivory aircraft, turquoise letters outlined in silver.

VT-ADO — As new, red fuselage, white letters, white wings, red letters; struts and undercarriage legs, front half white, rear red; 'The Scarlet Angel' in script on front cowling; '(G-ACTF in 1950 all silver with red trim).

G-ABUS — Pre-war in Shell colours. All red with green letters outlined in gold; post-war, all black with gold and latterly silver lettering; 'Black Magic' on cowling.

G-ABWE — New, white with red letters outlined in gold.

VH-ACG — All silver with polished cowling and Royal Blue letters.

appendix one

Magazines of interest to aircraft modellers

The following magazines are a few of those that are available and will prove invaluable to he serious enthusiast. Some of them are specifically for modellers while others have only a minor section devoted to modelling, and a few are devoted entirely to the study of full-size aircraft.

Airfix Magazine (Monthly). PSL Publications Ltd, Bar Hill, Cambridge, CB3 8EL, England.
Scale Models (Monthly). Model & Allied Publications Ltd, PO Box 35, Bridge Street, Hemel Hempstead, Herts, HP1 1EE, England.
Modell-Fan (Monthly). D-2800 Bremen 1, Postfach 919, West Germany.
Scale Modeller (Monthly). Challenge Publications, 7950 Deering Avenue, Canoga Park, California 91304, USA.
Aircraft Illustrated (Monthly). Ian Allan Ltd, Terminal House, Shepperton, TW17 8AS, England.
Flight International (Weekly). IPC Ltd, Dorset House, Stamford Street, London, SE1 9LU, England.
Air International (Monthly). Ducimus Books Ltd, DeWorde House, 283 Lonsdale Road, London, SW13 9QW, England.
Air Pictorial (Monthly). Coburg House, Sheet Street, Windsor, Berks, SL4 1EB. England.
Flugzeug Illustriert (Monthly). D-5142 Hückelhoven, Postfach 1209, West Germany.
Scale (Monthly). Göller Verlag, 7570 Baden-Baden, Postfach 240, Hauptstrasse 4, West Germany.
Air Classics (Monthly). Address as for *Scale Modeller*.
Aviation News (Fortnightly). 2 Sheepfold Lane, Amersham, Bucks, England.

appendix two

Mail order model shops

Although most medium and large towns have either model shops or shops that sell models in addition to other goods, there are some items that they do not stock. Many of these items have been mentioned in this book and they are usually obtainable by mail from one of the shops listed below who specialise in this type of trading. When writing to any of these establishments always include a stamped and self-addressed envelope for a reply.

BMW Models, 327-329 Haydons Road, Wimbledon, London SW19, England.
Modeltoys, 246 Kingston Road, Portsmouth, Hants, England.
Ernest Berwick Ltd, 11a Newland Street, Kettering, Northants, NN16 8JH, England.
Modelmark, 33 Plashet Grove, Upton Park, London E6, England.
Bridge Models, 1-2 Station Parade, Hoe Street Bridge, Walthamstow, London E17, England.
Jones Bros of Chiswick, 56 Turnham Green Terrace, Chiswick, London W4, England.

Polk's Hobby Stores, 314 Fifth Avenue (Cor 32nd St), New York 10001, USA.
VHF Supplies, Noble Corner, Great West Road, Hounslow, Middlesex, TW5 0PA, England.
Frank-Modellbau, Obere Vorstadt 21, 7470 Alstadt-Ebingen 1, West Germany.
Intermodell, 6551 Hargesheim 3a, West Germany.
Modell & Hobby, Werner Ehe, Sophienblatt 50 B, 2300 Kiel, West Germany.
Intermodell Hobby Shop, 1000 Berlin 12, 12 Sybelstrasse 40, West Germany.
The Squadron Shop, 23500 John R Hazel Park, Michigan 48030, USA.
Archers Hobby World, 1984 North Tustin, Orange, California 92665, USA.
Burnaby Hobbies, 5209 Rumble St, Burnaby BC, Canada V5J 2B7.

There are many other suppliers who advertise regularly in the magazines listed in Appendix 1, but the above have all supplied the author at some time or another and have given first-class service.